Jewelry
International

THE ORIGINAL ANNUAL OF THE WORLD'S FINEST JEWELRY®

BY CAROLINE CHILDERS

Jewelry International

THE ORIGINAL ANNUAL OF THE WORLD'S FINEST JEWELRY®

First published in the United States in 2009 by:
**CAROLINE CHILDERS AND
TOURBILLON INTERNATIONAL,
A Modern Luxury Media Company**

11 West 25th Street, 8th floor
New York, NY 10010
T: +1 (212) 627-7732 Fax: +1 (312) 274-8418

CHAIRMAN AND CEO Michael Kong

VICE CHAIRMAN Stephen Kong

COO Michael Lipson

PUBLISHER Caroline Childers

EDITOR IN CHIEF Elise Nussbaum

EDITOR Lynn Braz

ASSOCIATE EDITOR Claire Loeb

ART DIRECTOR Franca Vitali

DIRECTOR OF PRINT PROCUREMENT Sean Bertram

SENIOR VICE PRESIDENT OF FINANCE John Pietrolungo

DIRECTOR OF DISTRIBUTION Eric Holden

In association with **RIZZOLI** INTERNATIONAL PUBLICATIONS INC.

300 Park Avenue South, New York, NY 10010

ISBN: 978-0-8478-3229-3

COVER Spectacular yellow gold necklace featuring a floral design reminiscent of the most famous Renaissance master artists' paintings. The jewel is set with purplish pink pear-shaped sapphires used to form the flower petals, softly embedded into a background of cabochon-cut peridots highlighted by sparkling orange garnets and diamonds.
INSIDE FRONT FLAP Bayco necklace.
PREVIOUS PAGE Bulgari ring.
INSIDE BACK FLAP Bayco earrings.
NEXT PAGE Van Cleef & Arpels brooch.

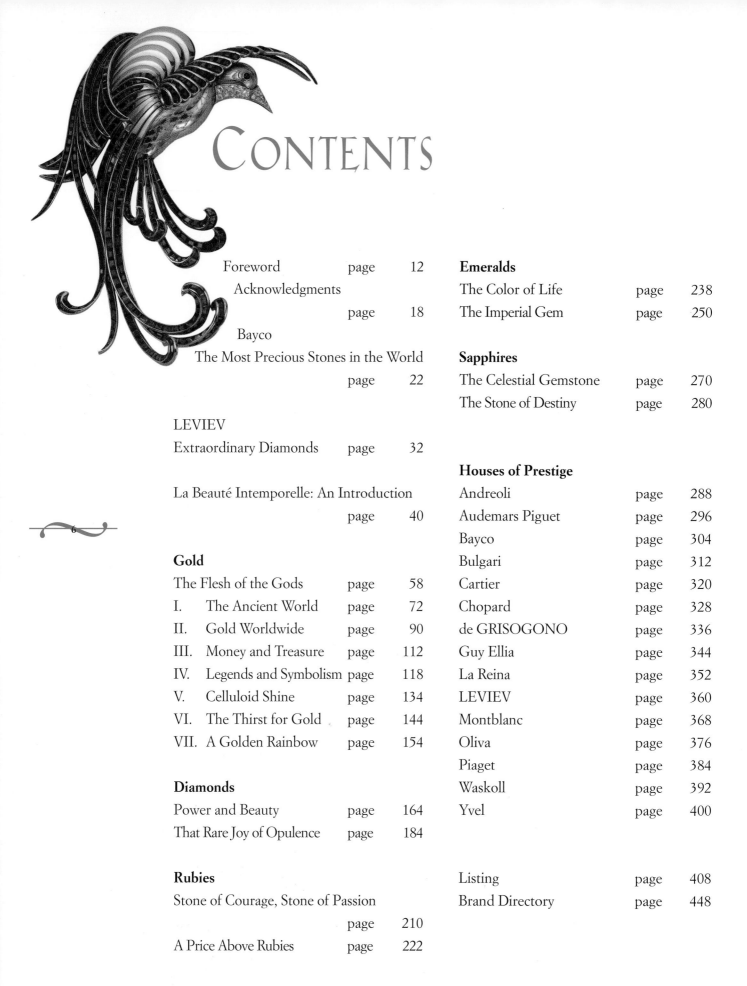

CONTENTS

BVLGARI

Celebrating 125 years

THE NEW PARENTESI COCKTAIL COLLECTION

BVLGARI

Celebrating 125 years

ELISIA DIAMOND COLLECTION

FOREWORD

In these uncertain times, some things still persist. Human history is cyclical; we seem to go through bubbles, booms and busts with periodic—though always unpredictable—regularity. The upheavals through which we live always appear to be the most world-changing, the most revolutionary. Throughout history, though, even in the most tumultuous of times, people have never stopped buying and treasuring their jewelry.

This impulse has many roots: fantasy, beauty, family heritage and investment. One day, the clouds will lift and the sun will shine again, turning our diamond rings back into shimmering morsels of starlight. Until then, we owe it to ourselves to remain loyal to our favorite pieces, to let our love of life and beauty prevail.

There is something ineffable about the hold that jewels have on us; their beauty is like a gift from the Earth—light and color that sing at us from among rocks and dirt. The history they hold is a gift as well. When we see a beautiful object, something inside us sings. Wearing an extraordinary jewel transports us to a different time and place. The warmth of gold was enjoyed by the ancient Egyptians; the lush emerald was a favorite of both Napoleon and Cleopatra.

For many pieces, getting rid of them is unthinkable—they have been in the family since before anyone can remember. They represent a family tradition, the impulse of every generation to pass on a valuable history to the children growing up and having children of their own.

When the stock market endures its drunken oscillations, some people put their faith—and their savings—into gold, sending the price as high as $1,000 an ounce. While gold can be stored under the mattress or in the backyard in the form of coins or bullion, there is another option. Coco Chanel once said she loved diamonds because they represented the greatest value in the smallest volume. This is still true today, with many people seeing all gemstones not just as an expression of love or accomplishment, but a sound investment. Unlike stock certificates, however, a ruby necklace is a stunning accessory for an elegant soirée.

In our second edition of *Jewelry International*, we explore the many charms of precious jewels: history, beauty, symbolism and the new aesthetic developments that the houses within our pages are constantly evolving. I am pleased to expand our focus to precious metals and colored stones as well as the eternal diamond. Thank you all for your support in these interesting times!

La Reina

de GRISOGONO
GENEVE

Created by nature,
designed by

YVEL

ACKNOWLEDGMENTS

We wish to express our profound appreciation and gratitude to everyone who helped make this book a reality: Jack Hadjibay, Caroline Hadjibay from Andreoli; Olivier Bacher, Nathalie Crausaz from Audemars Piguet; Giacomo Hadjibay, Moris Hadjibay, Marco Hadjibay from Bayco; Frédéric de Narp, Olivier Stip, Angela Cahill, Monica Sese, Blair Bartell from Cartier New York; Gerard Djaoui, Michel Aliaga, Véronique Sacuto from Cartier Paris; Caroline Gruosi-Scheufele, Annick Benoit-Godet from Chopard Switzerland; Susan Duffy, Marc Hruschka from Chopard New York; Fawaz Gruosi, Michèle Reichenbach, Laure Monney, Jasmine Favre, Julien Grandjean, Esra Aykac from de GRISOGONO Switzerland; Giovanni Mattera, Olivia Tornare from de GRISOGONO New York;  Guy Ellia, Hoda Roche, Fanny Duval from Guy Ellia; Samir Bhansali, Adi Jain from La Reina; Lev Leviev from LEVIEV London; Thierry Chaunu, Harriet Hunter, Lauren Curtin from LEVIEV New York; Jan-Patrick Schmitz, Kelly Hodrick, Rachel Konikiewicz from Montblanc; Nilly Gross, Motti Gross, Shalom Cook from Oliva; Philippe Léopold-Metzger, Béatrice Vuille-Willemetz, Annabelle Garcia, Sophie Aliot-Siret from Piaget Switzerland; Larry Boland from Piaget New York; Cyril Waskoll, Kirk Waskoll, Caroline Esterlin, Marilyne Houbani, Aurélie Girard from Waskoll; Isaac and Orna Levy, Livnat Antebi from Yvel. A hearty thank you to my partners, Michael and Stephen Kong, and of course my deepest gratitude goes to my writer and editor Elise Nussbaum, art director Franca Vitali, writer Lynn Braz, and associate editor Claire Loeb. We couldn't have done it without all of you!

Caroline Childers

WASKOLL
PARIS
*Jeweler of light
and colors*

Flamme collection
White gold, diamonds

www.waskoll.com

Mannequin : Sara Otto

PIAGET

BAYCO
THE MOST PRECIOUS STONES IN THE WORLD

"We are very fortunate to have grown up around
jewels," says Moris Hadjibay, co-CEO of Bayco Gem Corp.
"My eye was trained from the age of five." His father Amir
would gather Moris and his brother Giacomo together and sit
them down in front of a few precious stones (this was commonplace
throughout their childhood, having lived and played with gems their
whole lives). Amir would pick up two stones. "Now tell me," he would say,
"which is better?" This training has been crucial to the success of Bayco, which
is widely recognized to deal in the highest quality colored stones available.

FACING PAGE
28-carat carved emerald ring
surrounded by 12 rose-cut diamonds
weighing 5 carats, set in platinum.

THIS PAGE
Carved emerald parure: necklace consisting
of 26 carved emeralds weighing 94 carats and
75 rose-cut diamonds weighing 16 carats set in
platinum, earrings comprised of 8 carved
emeralds weighing 30 carats and 14 rose-cut
diamonds weighing 2 carats set in platinum, ring in
platinum set with 20-carat round carved emerald
encircled by 14 rose-cut diamonds weighing 7 carats.

A unique pink sapphire suite: necklace comprised of 11 cushion pink sapphires weighing 70 carats and 143 diamonds weighing 52 carats set in platinum and 18-karat yellow gold, bracelet consisting of 10 cushion pink sapphires weighing 33 carats and 90 diamonds weighing 20 carats set in platinum and 18-karat yellow gold, earrings made of 4 cushion pink sapphires weighing 22 carats and 34 diamonds weighing 14 carats mounted in platinum and 18-karat yellow gold.

13-carat cushion pink sapphire mounted in a diamond pavé platinum ring.

Some people go into the jewelry business for the money, but for the Hadjibays, the profit end of the equation seems almost like an afterthought. "We're like collectors," explains Giacomo. "We fall in love with the most beautiful stones, and leave everything else behind."

Indeed, the Hadjibay family often seems more like a family of passionate collectors than ordinary

jewelers. "We have to sell so we can buy," sighs Moris, almost wistfully. Once a piece leaves their inventory, the Hadjibays immediately start searching for another that will fill the new gap. "We will always try to find something better," declares Moris.

The brothers talk about gems they have known in very loving terms, describing in intimate detail the great loves, those that got away and gems that made serendipitous returns. "I tried for three years to buy a pink sapphire that was over 100 carats from Sri Lanka," remembers Giacomo, as one might recall an unsuccessful love affair. After a story about a 13-carat green sapphire or equally rare stone, Moris will say, "We haven't seen anything like it since." The Hadjibays never buy a stone that they don't instantly fall in love with, and if one of them falls for a stone, he can't *not* buy it. "In two seconds, we decide," says Moris. "In just two seconds, we know if we want it, and we know exactly what we want to offer." In the Hadjibays' eyes, the beauty of the stones trumps all. A ruby may have an impeccable Burmese pedigree, but it doesn't necessarily mean that a ruby from a different origin

27-carat cushion pink sapphire flanked by 2 shield-shaped diamonds weighing 2 carats mounted in platinum and 18-karat yellow gold.

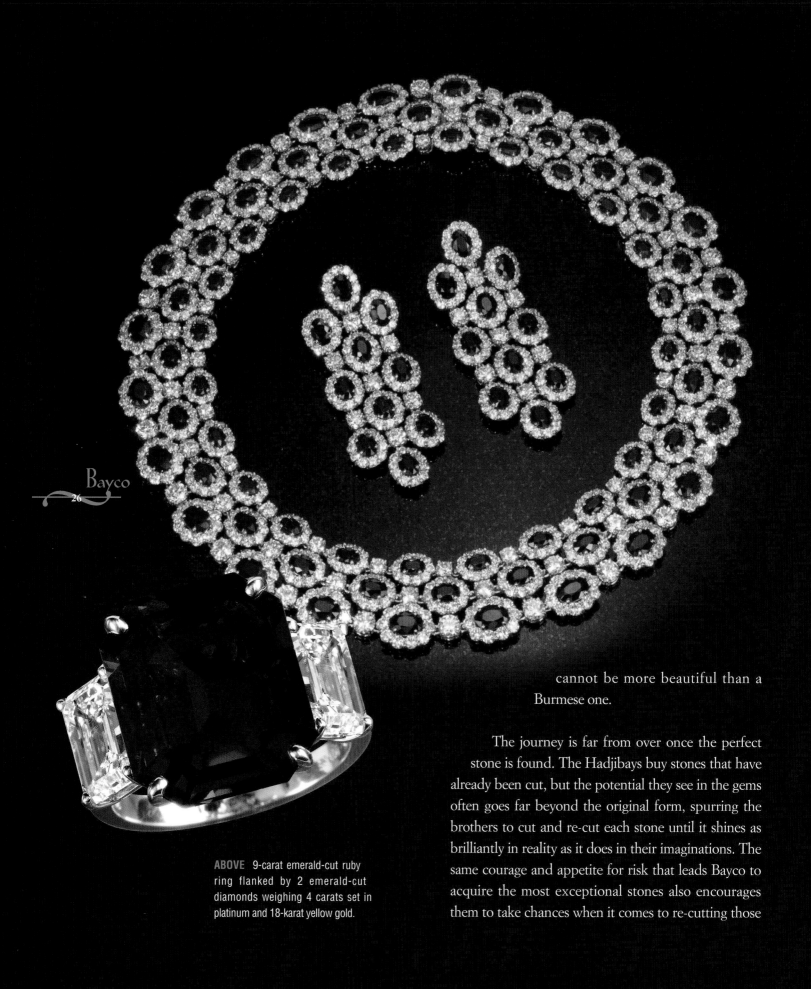

ABOVE 9-carat emerald-cut ruby ring flanked by 2 emerald-cut diamonds weighing 4 carats set in platinum and 18-karat yellow gold.

cannot be more beautiful than a Burmese one.

The journey is far from over once the perfect stone is found. The Hadjibays buy stones that have already been cut, but the potential they see in the gems often goes far beyond the original form, spurring the brothers to cut and re-cut each stone until it shines as brilliantly in reality as it does in their imaginations. The same courage and appetite for risk that leads Bayco to acquire the most exceptional stones also encourages them to take chances when it comes to re-cutting those

27

stones. Many dealers are scared to chance losing carats from a large gem, but the Hadjibays are willing to lose up to 20 percent—or even more—of a stone's weight in order to reveal its truest beauty.

Even more difficult than deciding how to re-cut a stone—one unique emerald took two years to find its true shape—is matching stones for a pair of earrings, a necklace, a bracelet, or all three. A single exceptional stone might become the centerpiece of a ring. If its mate is found, a pair of earrings is born. If, by some tremendous good fortune, more matching stones are found, all the gems might be reset into a necklace or a bracelet. The process is extremely time-consuming—all the stones must be from the same mine, or their color will not match with the exactitude that is one hallmark of Bayco jewels. One parure, featuring unusually large, perfectly bubble-gum pink sapphires, took almost three years just to find the right stones, going through several metamorphoses along the way. "The more stones we find," explains Giacomo, "the more the concept changes."

A sapphire suite: necklace made of 6 cushion sapphires weighing 43 carats and 152 diamonds weighing 42 carats set in platinum and 18-karat yellow gold, earrings with 2 cushion sapphires weighing 20 carats surrounded by 26 marquise diamonds weighing 10 carats mounted in platinum and 18-karat yellow gold, and ring with a 12-carat cushion sapphire bordered by 10 oval diamonds weighing 4 carats set in platinum and 18-karat yellow gold.

Historical significance is a powerful influence on Bayco's designs. The evolution of precious materials and their uses shows up time and again, as does references to certain mines and the purity of their stones. Large emeralds are carved for pendants or earrings in an allusion to the Mogul emperors who adored emeralds—and often personalized them. The carving adds just one more element of difficulty to an already difficult task. "Not only must the stone and the design be perfect," explains Moris, "but the engraving must be as well."

These references can be found in pieces with stones of every color, including diamonds. Emeralds hold a special place for the Hadjibays ("The most beautiful jewelry is with emeralds," rhapsodizes Moris) but they wax poetic about all colored stones. It is the challenge that interests them, the countless possibilities and difficulties that color brings with it. When it works, the effect is that of an artistic masterpiece. "A perfect Kashmir sapphire," says Giacomo, "is like a painting by Renoir."

CENTER 25-carat cushion sapphire ring enclosed in a cluster of pear-shape and round diamonds weighing 9 carats, set in platinum and 18-karat yellow gold.

RIGHT Necklace comprised of 75 carats of oval sapphires, of which the largest stone is 66 carats, and 22 carats of diamonds set in platinum. 14-carat sapphire earrings surrounded by 16 diamonds weighing 6 carats set in platinum and 18-karat yellow gold.

BOTTOM 4 oval sapphires weighing 19 carats set in platinum earrings with 44 diamonds weighing 11 carats.

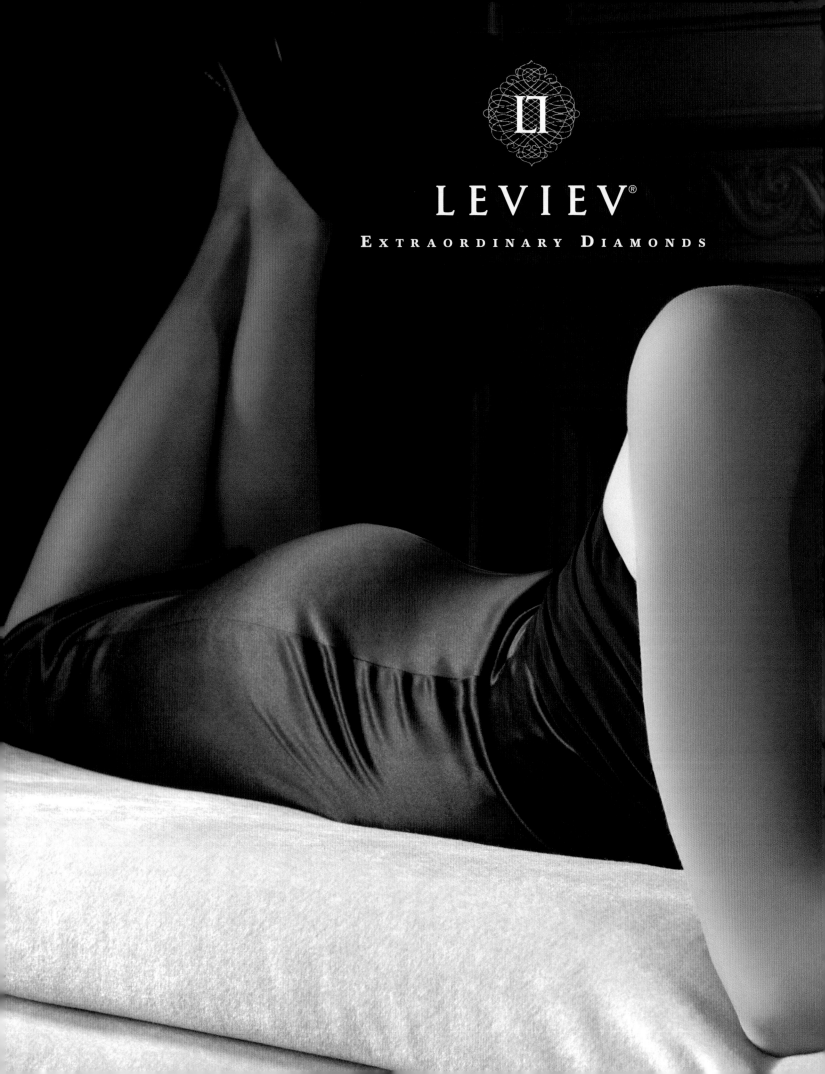

LEVIEV
EXTRAORDINARY
DIAMONDS

The tension between the modern and the traditional, the minimalist and the opulent, has always been a driving force in jewelry. In its relatively short time on the scene, LEVIEV has managed to harness these forces and keep them working in perfect harmony, in everything from its classic logo, to the design of its retail boutiques, to the exquisite diamond jewelry itself, and the expert, accommodating service,

Fancy vivid orange diamond ring: pear-shaped fancy vivid orange diamond weighing 5.01 carats mounted with 2 pear and 4 marquise-shaped diamonds totaling 5.37 carats, handcrafted in platinum.

Diamond necklace: pear-shaped diamond weighing 22.12 carats accented by 27 pear-shaped, 10 marquise and 6 oval-shaped diamonds weighing a total of 36.33 carats, hand-crafted in platinum.

Diamond earrings: 4 pear-shaped D flawless diamonds weighing each 8.01, 7.91, 2.53 and 2.51 carats, mounted with 2 round brilliant-cut D internally flawless diamonds, hand-crafted in platinum.

LL diamond bracelet: 36 oval-shaped diamonds totaling 14.80 carats mounted with 36 marquise-shaped diamonds totaling 11.90 carats, highlighted with 20 baguette-cut diamonds totaling 6.31 carats, hand-crafted in platinum.

Diamond ring: emerald-cut diamond weighing 56.29 carats flanked by 4 baguette-shaped diamonds weighing 5.23 carats, hand-crafted in platinum.

Boutiques in New York, London, Moscow and Dubai.

overshadows the jewelry. Pearl gray walls complement bronze fixtures and ivory-colored leather furniture, contributing to the aura of understated luxury that permeates LEVIEV. The stores dispense with counters and racks of jewelry, preferring instead to present the pieces in display cases among unobtrusive furniture, as if the shoppers were congregating in a private townhouse. There are no garish velvet curtains or Roman columns here, just leather, lacquer, marble, silk and cashmere. Materials that have always been used in the service of luxury receive a modern, minimalist interpretation.

This same careful attention to the mix of modern and traditional, to understatement and unmistakable luxury can also be seen in LEVIEV's retail stores, which are located in some of the most prestigious neighborhoods in the world. The sumptuous buildings on Old Bond Street in London, Madison Avenue in New York, and Kuznetsky Most in Moscow are all historical landmarks, with all the pomp—and restrictions that the status implies. In New York, for instance, though the brand completely redecorated the interior to match that of

CENTER Light pink and mixed color diamond necklace: square emerald-cut light pink diamond weighing 76.51 carats, highlighted by 32 mixed color diamonds totaling 9.63 carats, mounted with 10 marquis-shaped pink diamonds totaling 5.97 carats, 19 square emerald-cut, 18 oval and 10 marquis-shaped diamonds totaling 25.72 carats, hand-crafted in platinum and 18-karat pink gold.

LEVIEV
38

BOTTOM Fancy vivid blue diamond ring: radiant-cut fancy vivid blue internally flawless diamond weighing 2.08 carats, highlighted by 8 pear-shaped diamonds totaling 8.95 carats, accented by a diamond pavé band, and hand-crafted in platinum.

the London boutique, a plan to renovate the landmark façade was a non-starter.

The home of the boutique on Kuznetsky Most—Russian epicenter of luxury since the mid-eighteenth century—was built in 1820, a few years after Napoleon's armies had established camp in Moscow. Though the ground floor is modeled after LEVIEV's boutiques in New York and London, once through the doors of the upper floor, the twenty-first century melts away. The room is decorated with all the elegance and opulence of an eighteenth-century Russian aristocrat's parlor, complete with authentic seventeenth- and eighteenth-century Venetian mirrors and an extremely rare 1750 Baltic chandelier.

In the midst of this evocation of an opulent past shines diamond jewelry created using the most up-to-the-second technology, and LEVIEV's customer base is equally modern. "Our customers have a few common traits," explains Chaunu. "They are extremely smart and savvy, and they all demand the exceptional." They are primarily captains of industry, visionaries and entrepreneurs, with the taste to match. "We take pride in providing very unique service," says Chaunu. "We accommodate all their whims." This approach leads to an extremely faithful clientele.

Celebrities are drawn to LEVIEV like moths to the flame, often appearing in the spectacular pieces on the red carpet and at charity balls and photo shoots. Providing publicity and aid to charities is all part of LEVIEV's mission statement. In addition to the $50 million of his personal fortune that Lev Leviev gives to charity each year, LEVIEV stores in London, New York, Moscow and Dubai are strongly associated with charities local to the boutiques. The LEVIEV boutique in New York, for example, has collaborated on events with the Museum of the City of New York, the Whitney Museum and Denise Rich's Angel Ball. This intense relationship with the world of charity is a reflection of Lev Leviev's deeply felt religious obligation to return something to the world that has provided him with so much opportunity.

TOP "Chameleon" fancy grayish yellowish green diamond ring: cushion-shaped fancy grayish yellowish green diamond weighing 5.89 carats, mounted with 8 ovals totaling 1.68 carats, with white and pink pavé diamonds totaling 1.05 carats, hand-crafted in platinum.

RIGHT Fancy vivid orange and mixed color diamond ring: heart-shaped fancy vivid orange diamond weighing 1.98 carats, highlighted with 7 pear and 5 marquise-cut fancy intense yellow, fancy greenish yellow, fancy intense blue, pink, green and purple diamonds totaling 4.53 carats, hand-crafted in 18-karat pink gold.

LA BEAUTÉ INTEMPORELLE: AN INTRODUCTION

The Houses in these pages have always sought to give expression to the gifts the earth has to offer: gold, platinum, emeralds, rubies, sapphires and diamonds. Combining extraordinary artistic imagination with flawless specimens of diamonds and colored gems, today's jewelers are creating worlds of fun and fantasy that serve as an escape in troubled times. From inventing new colors of gold to utilizing age-old materials in brand-new ways, the future of jewelry has never been so intriguing. In examining the history of what humanity has always deemed its most precious matter, we must, of course, study the people who use it to create our adornments. They hold the key to our deepest wishes, our shadow selves.

PREVIOUS PAGE
ROW 1 Dita von Teese in LEVIEV, Naomi Campbell in de GRISOGONO, Julia Ormond in Piaget.

ROW 2 Teri Hatcher in Piaget, Eva Longoria in Piaget, Charlize Theron in de GRISOGONO, Demi Moore in Piaget.

ROW 3 Gwyneth Paltrow in Chopard, Salma Hayek in LEVIEV.

Always searching for the gems that best give expression to his designs, Jack Hadjibay of **Andreoli** has a fondness for colored gems— and the feeling is mutual. Cabochon-cut emeralds and sapphires provide instant—yet timeless—glamour and elegance to any pieces, and Andreoli mixes these classic cuts with elements both traditional (white diamonds) and untraditional (yellow and other colored diamonds). Multicolored sapphires are also the perfect paint with which to decorate titanium,

43

Andreoli's latest passion—and experiment. The vivid colors perfectly play up the tinted titanium setting, leaving imagination free of all constraints. Time-honored stalwarts of impressive colored gems blend seamlessly with newer high-tech materials.

Long a household name for its impeccably crafted watches, **Audemars Piguet** slips into the dazzling world of Haute Jewelry with a blaze of diamonds set in stunningly theatrical pieces.

Diamonds burst from the edges of an elaborately imagined cuff watch, and dance along the sides of a ribbon-inspired necklace. The joy of diamonds lies in the way they capture light, and let it go in all different directions. The nearly chaotic arrangement of the edges contrasts with the rigid geometric structure of the rest of the pieces, reminding us of the many personalities of this endlessly adaptable gem.

Jewelry by Bayco.

Some of the world's largest and most exquisite stones can be found at **Bayco**. Giacomo and Moris Hadjibay have made their life's work finding and using the largest stones with the richest color. Impossibly plump pink sapphires nestle up with flurries of white diamonds, and carved emeralds express the brothers' fascination with the rich history of precious gems. The finest, most luscious blue sapphires shine with unfathomable desire, a desire that the Hadjibay brothers express frequently. Sometimes waiting for years for a particular gem to pass through their hands, the

brother behind Bayco treasure each one, and take care to place each one in designs that truly sing.

Bulgari is one of the most daring designers around when it comes to the use of colored stones. Over the last 50 years, the House has mixed rubies, sapphires and emeralds, always to stunning effect. The early pieces in this vein explored the various combinations of red, blue and green, making a primary statement in these very primary colors and letting the value of the stones speak for itself. Over

Necklace and bracelet by Bulgari.

stones such as tourmaline and citrine to provide a palette that covers the spectrum. The old favorites are always in style, though, and rubies, emeralds and sapphires continue to rule the roost, sometimes matched with their more unusual cousins, like amethysts, coral and garnets. The allure of rich color is just too delectable to resist. The unadulterated appeal of pure gold has also been a major motif of the venerable brand, from its iconic Tubogas necklaces to bangles and rings.

the last few decades, however, the pieces have become more adventurous, using fancy-colored sapphires in pastel colors and even semi-precious

Bulgari necklace set with diamonds and Colombian emeralds.

Jewelry by Cartier.

One of the most emblematic motifs ever created in colored stones—the Tutti Frutti necklace—was engendered by Jacques Cartier's legendary voyage through India in 1919 and the extraordinary stones he saw there. **Cartier** has steadfastly held the standard for colored stones ever since, using them in pieces that represent the House itself, such as the Jeanne Toussaint panther perched upon a cabochon sapphire. Working in simple gold, Cartier also produced another classic, the iconic

Jewelry by Chopard.

Love collection, which comes in all colors of gold and screws onto your beloved's wrist, as well as using the metal in the brand's coveted timepieces.

As the undisputed favorite stone of Caroline Gruosi-Scheufele, diamonds have always been a forceful inspiration at **Chopard**. It was the Happy Diamonds collection, after all, with its freely floating gems in the belly of a clown, that launched Chopard's now-legendary jewelry division. With its news Haute Jewelry collection, Chopard delves ever

deeper into the mystique of this seemingly straightforward gem. Taking as its inspiration the ancient Greek belief that diamonds were stardust fallen from the sky, Chopard created a series of "heavenly" pieces that lend credence to that idea. The collection shows white diamonds in all their various incarnations, from a necklace that incorporates baguettes and emerald-cut stones to stunning geometric effect, to delicate ear pendants of heart-shaped diamonds that would be equally at home on the red carpet or paired with a simple sweater and jeans.

Gold is famous for being used in all sorts of colors: cool white, sunny yellow, charming rose, and... brown? **de GRISOGONO** has made huge strides in the acceptance of unusual colors of gold and the importance of experimentation and constantly striving to create something that no one has ever done before. Fawaz Gruosi, head of de GRISOGONO, has certainly surpassed all expectations with his use of what the brand calls Browny Brown gold. The deep, rich chestnut color adds a new level to jewelry design, bathing diamonds and other gems in a color of gold that had never been seen before. The warm gold undulates and curves like living material, lending an organic component to the jewelry design.

This adventurousness with gold also extends to the brand's use of other precious materials: diamonds, multicolored sapphires, rubies, emeralds and amethysts are often mixed in imaginative

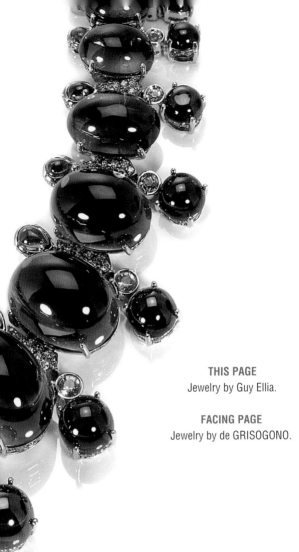

designs that let the colors play off each other. The depth of a blue sapphire might be paired with a bright ruby or a lush emerald, or even a semiprecious stone whose richness of color is undeniable. In some designs, stones of all colors and pedigrees mingle to create a shimmering, overwhelming, multifaceted burst of color.

Guy Ellia has been fearless in its quest for imaginative aesthetics, mixing different colors of stones to sublime effect. Diamonds of all hues, multi-colored sapphires, brown, rubies and even garnets and amethysts burst out in a riot of color. The first products from the admired brand were watches, and a horological influence works both ways in the jewelry and watch collections of the jeweler. The decades that Guy Ellia, founder of the eponymous brand, spent combing the globe in search of the world's most precious gems has paid off richly. His expert touch with a gemstone—especially his beloved diamond—has earned

the brand a worldwide reputation for quality and innovation.

Samir Bhansali, head designer of **La Reina**, is fearless when it comes to adapting precious materials to his innovative ends. In some pieces, Bhansali starts with the ancient rose cut for white diamonds before slicing them razor-thin in an unprecedented use of the gem. He then pairs them with yellow diamonds in gossamer butterfly wings. This is just one example of the way in which Bhansali draws inspiration from his Indian heritage, bringing it into today's jewelry culture. Age-old materials are reimagined through the most modern of techniques, including one that Bhansali has developed himself, to spectacular result.

The name of **Leviev** is rapidly becoming synonymous with the world's most extraordinary diamonds. One third of the world's diamond production is controlled by Lev Leviev, making for

Jewelry by LEVIEV.

an unequaled supply of absurdly large, strikingly colored diamonds. Many diamonds that would be exceptionally large for white stones have the added asset of bursting with vivid orange, soothing blue or blushing pink. These diamonds will settle for nothing less than an equally extraordinary setting, a promise on which Leviev delivers. And what suits a diamond like more diamonds? The precious stone abounds in Leviev's collections, always surrounded by its comrades. Traditional diamond designs bump up against the clean geometric lines to which the diamond lends itself. The double "L" logo of Leviev, when it shows up as a design element, is always outlined in diamonds, a subtle allusion to the brand itself and its reason for being.

LEFT Jewelry by Montblanc.

RIGHT AND BOTTOM Jewelry by Oliva.

The most striking design element in **Montblanc's** jewelry is the distinctive stylized six-pointed star of its logo, which evokes the brand's mountainous namesake seen from above. Now that star takes a new form, one that recalls its icy origins, as it appears in the "Montblanc diamond," a tour de force of diamond cutting. To celebrate the brand's 100th anniversary, it developed a brand-new diamond cut that mimics the star-shaped logo. The cut took a full eight years to develop, and reflects light from

43 facets. The cut gleams from every piece of Montblanc jewelry, whether it is the star of the show or a supporting player. Only diamonds of 1/2 a carat or larger can be cut into the Montblanc star, making it a valuable sign of the resources that go into Montblanc's burgeoning jewelry empire.

Oliva's whole reason for being is wrapped up in diamonds. The brand has a particular magic for arranging the precious stone in combinations

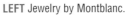

Jewelry by Piaget.

that elicit and even magnify its natural sparkle. In collections such as Reflections, Sweethearts and Shapes, diamonds cuddle up next to each other, each one illuminating its neighbor. Oliva understands that a large part of diamonds' appeal lies in the way they reflect any woman's fantasy, so its creations are endlessly versatile, offering customizable geometric shapes as well as the undulating, vigorous flair of the Flamenco collection.

Another House that got its start in exquisite timepieces, **Piaget** has grabbed new inspiration from the world's two capitals of art, fashion and culture: Paris and New York. Using 18-karat gold, diamonds, pink sapphires and rubies, Piaget perfectly captures both the solidity of architecture and the ephemeral glamour of Haute Couture, in a way that represents both the eternal qualities of precious gems and the cycles of high fashion. Diamonds stand in for both the solid braces that support the iconic structures, and the twinkling lights that play across their surfaces, taking a break to simulate sensuous corsets and their laces. Rubies and pink sapphires, meanwhile, act as stand-ins for playful trailing ribbons.

BOTTOM RIGHT
Jewelry by Waskoll.

TOP LEFT Jewelry by Yvel.

Sapphires of all colors pile up in grand heaps all over **Waskoll's** lines. The riot of colors—blue, green, yellow, orange, purple, pink—contrasts nicely with the fluid, yet highly structured, design that contains them. Waskoll's multicolored designs are a bit like looking at a cell under a microscope: the longer we look, the more clearly each element's function and relationship to the whole. When we pull away and take in the entire piece with one glance, the shimmering rainbow beauty pulls us in before we even register the lines of the piece. When we do, it adds a pleasing regularity, taming the wildness of the riot of color.

Orna and Isaac Levy of **Yvel** are known for their incredible creations in pearls, but the unsung element in all their creations is warm, lustrous gold. The links on their necklace chains are forged from 18-karat yellow gold, lending a warm glow to the piece as well as the wearer. Tiny diamonds are set in gold, creating unique embellishments that sinuously curve around the pearls' baroque contours. The use of this precious metal creates a warm or cool counterpart to the lunar glow exuded by the pearls.

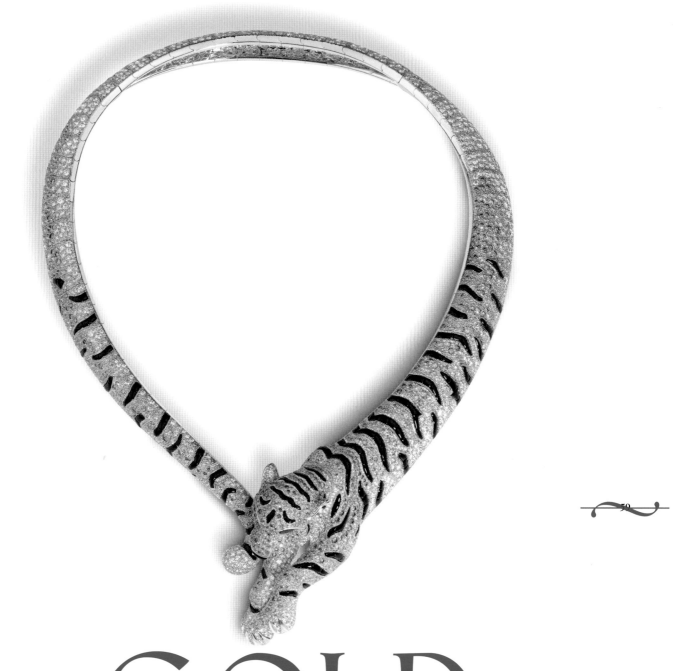

GOLD
THE FLESH OF THE GODS

Etruscan gold necklace from 5th-3rd century BC, found in Todi, Italy.

"All that glitters is not gold," warns the old adage,
a useful caution about the dangers of rushing to
judgment. But no one can deny the irresistible
allure of real glittering gold, the way it shines like
the life-giving sun, warmed by the heat of the body.

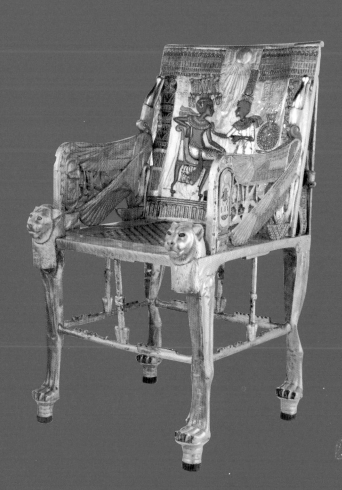

Every culture that has encountered gold has recognized it as precious, whether in a spiritual, atavistic way—the Aztecs called gold *teocuitatl*, "excrement of the gods"—or in recognition of its more profane, profitable uses—Spain's King Ferdinand ordered the Conquistadors, "Get gold; humanely if you can, but at all costs, get gold." In fact, the only culture that has not

revered gold is an imaginary
one: Thomas More's Utopia,
in which gold is despised and
disdained, used for the
lowliest of tasks.

To understand the universal
fascination with gold, let us imagine for a
minute that we are members of a Stone Age society.
(The oldest decorative gold objects of which
researchers are aware were found in Bulgaria and date
back to 4,000 B.C.) We come across a stream in which
the bottom sparkles a little more brightly than the play

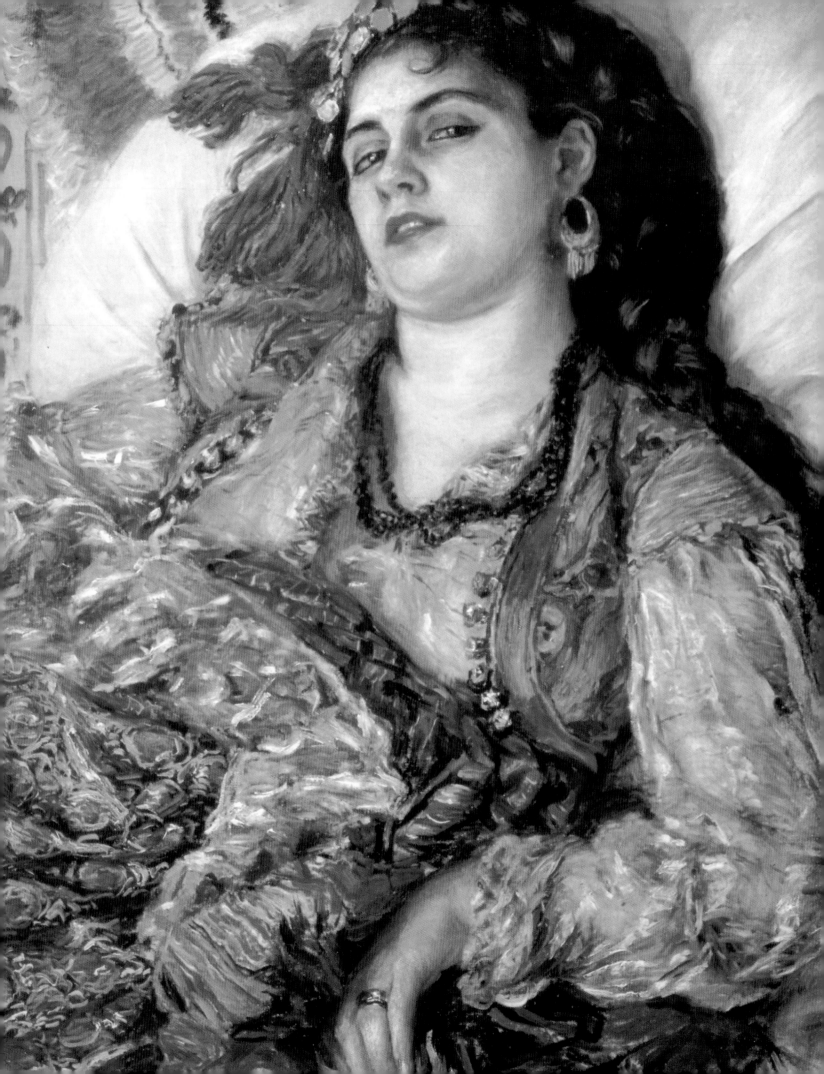

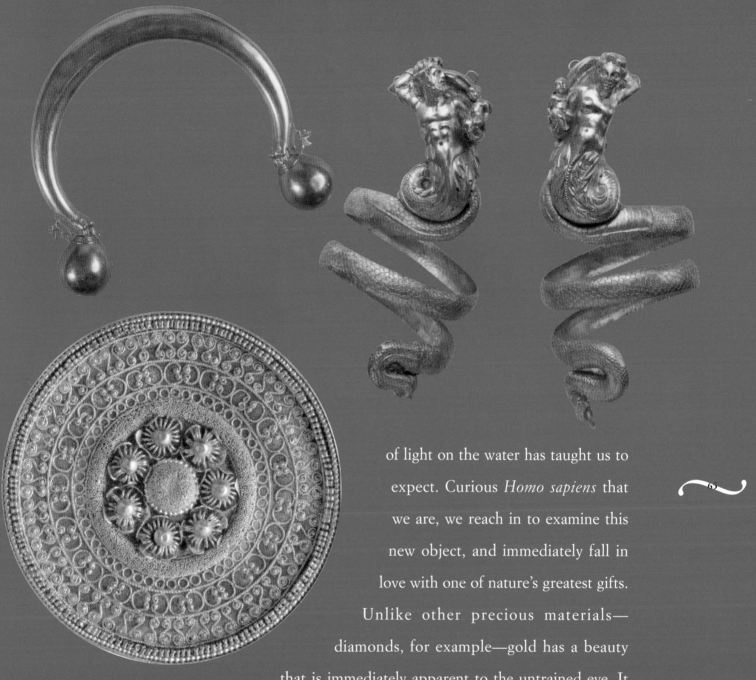

of light on the water has taught us to expect. Curious *Homo sapiens* that we are, we reach in to examine this new object, and immediately fall in love with one of nature's greatest gifts. Unlike other precious materials—diamonds, for example—gold has a beauty that is immediately apparent to the untrained eye. It shimmers like condensed sunlight even in its natural form, and needs very little processing to be worked into jewelry and other decorative items. Highly malleable and ductile, gold can be hammered into a whisper-thin sheet (one ounce of gold will cover a surface of 16 square meters) or a barely-

TOP German "gimmel" wedding ring, circa 1575.

CENTER Reliquary of Saint Elizabeth: the oldest section dates to the late Roman period, and the gold mount is from the 11th century.

BOTTOM Queen Mary of England's jewel casket, end of 17th century.

TOP *Three Princesses of Saxony: Sibylla, Emilia and Sidonia*, by Lucas Cranach the Elder.

CENTER Gold and sapphire ring that belonged to William Wytlesey, Archbishop of Canterbury, in the 14th century.

BOTTOM Front and back of gold locket, circa 1660.

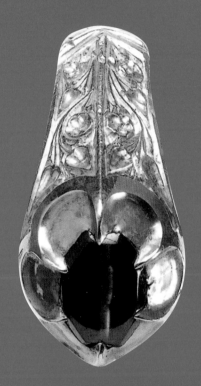

there wire (that same ounce of gold can be stretched into 50 miles of wire).

The extreme versatility and value of gold is its blessing, but also, in a way, its curse. Gold is endlessly recyclable and virtually indestructible, so cultures throughout the world have consistently chosen to melt down jewelry, figurines and other gold products when the need arose—or when fashions changed. In fact, over 85 percent of all gold ever mined is still in use today. In other words, it is entirely possible that the gold of the bracelet coiled around your wrist is a direct descendant of the material used to make an ancient Egyptian regal headdress...

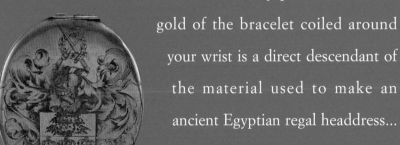

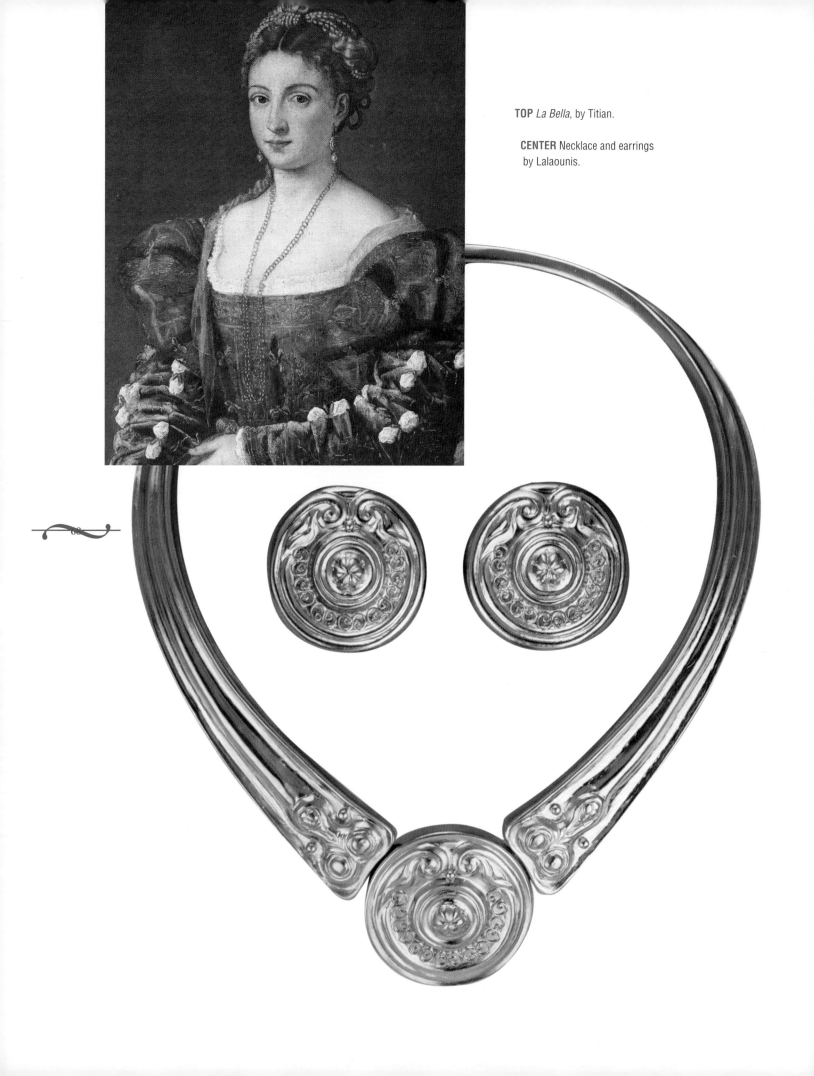

TOP *La Bella*, by Titian.

CENTER Necklace and earrings
by Lalaounis.

what a pedigree! Impressive though this is, one can hardly help thinking about all the priceless artifacts that have been destroyed over the millennia in the never-ending thirst for more, more, more gold.

We will trace the history of this ever-alluring material through the stories of those who have loved it, lived for it, risked everything for

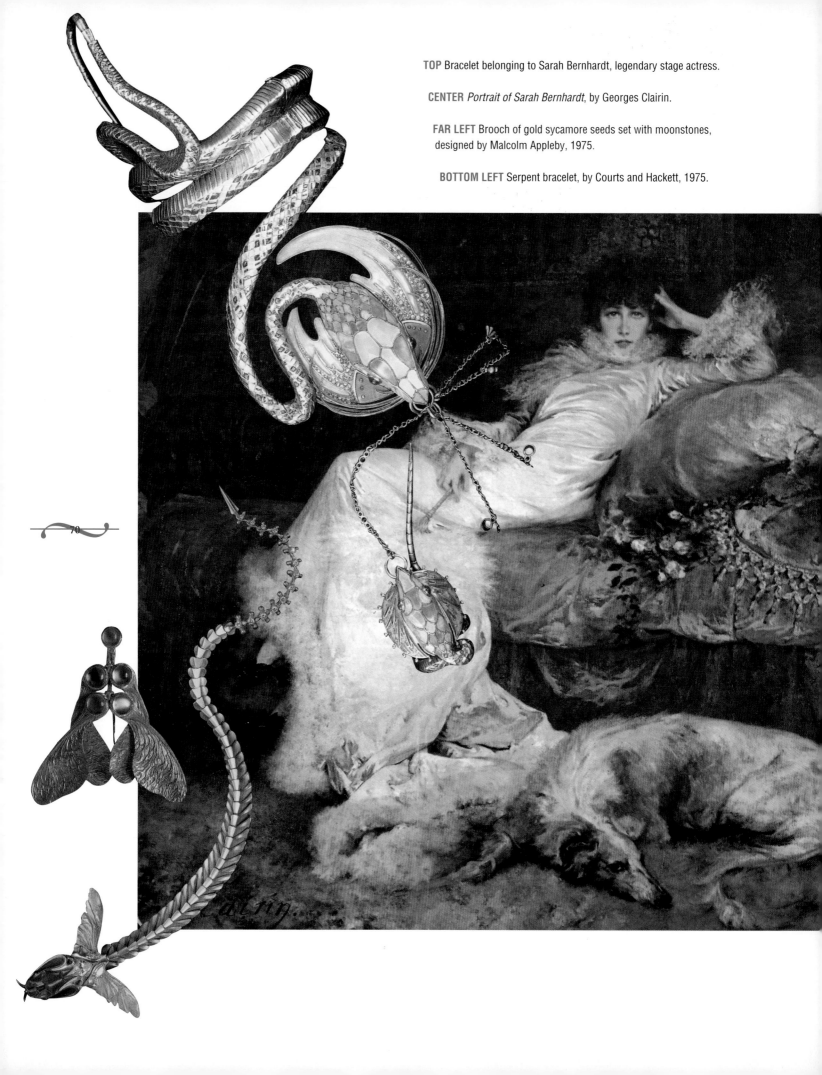

TOP Bracelet belonging to Sarah Bernhardt, legendary stage actress.

CENTER *Portrait of Sarah Bernhardt*, by Georges Clairin.

FAR LEFT Brooch of gold sycamore seeds set with moonstones, designed by Malcolm Appleby, 1975.

BOTTOM LEFT Serpent bracelet, by Courts and Hackett, 1975.

TOP Grape brooch by Elizabeth Treskow, circa 1941.

RIGHT Gold bangle by Giampaolo Babetto, 1988.

BOTTOM Sun mask by Johann Melchior Dinglinger, 1709.

it—even died for it. We will travel to shores of the ancient Nile and see how Cleopatra won back her rightful throne; we will journey to the New World and witness the devastation of cultures in the name of greed; we will explore the modern myths and developments that still surround this highly symbolic treasure. Come with us... there is much to see.

THE ANCIENT WORLD

EGYPT

Of all the ancient Egyptians, there are few that grip the modern public imagination as much as young Tutankhamen, the doomed boy king. But who was he, really? We know that he came to power in an age of tremendous political and religious unrest in Egypt. His predecessor, Akhenaten, had developed a monotheistic religion based on the sun deity Aten, often depicted as a golden disc (of course) streaming rays of life-giving light. As Akhenaten became more and more involved in his new faith, his country began to break down. The pharaoh shut down the traditional polytheistic shrines, undermining the stability of the Egyptian state; he left the running of the country to men who exploited their positions. Even his beautiful queen Nefertiti was not powerful enough to prevent the country from sliding into disarray, and her predicament was only exacerbated after Akhenaten died, leaving her without a male heir. She was succeeded by her stepson (or perhaps son-in-law), Tutankhamen.

As in many cultures—especially those that

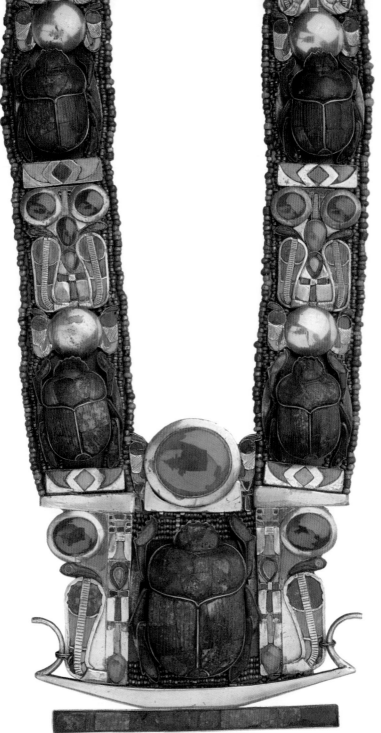

PREVIOUS SPREAD
LEFT Scarab pendant from the tomb of Tutankhamen.

RIGHT Gold relief from the tomb of Tutankhamen.

THIS PAGE
Pectoral with scarab motif, from the tomb of Tutankhamen.

FACING PAGE
Detail of golden throne from the tomb of Tutankhamen.

worshipped the sun—the ancient Egyptians revered gold as a sacred material, and described it in hieroglyphs as early as 2600 B.C. It was considered a divine, indestructible material, as the gods were believed to have bodies of gold that shone like the sun, their ancestor. After centuries of working with gold as an artistic medium, the Egyptians had raised it to the standard for international trade by 1500 B.C., and the world's oldest known treasure map (currently at the Museum of Turin) happens to coincide with this period, dating from 1320 B.C. This novel use for gold was followed in 1200 B.C. by new techniques for working with gold: this period is when Egyptians began to beat the precious metal into gold leaf, created alloys that were harder and

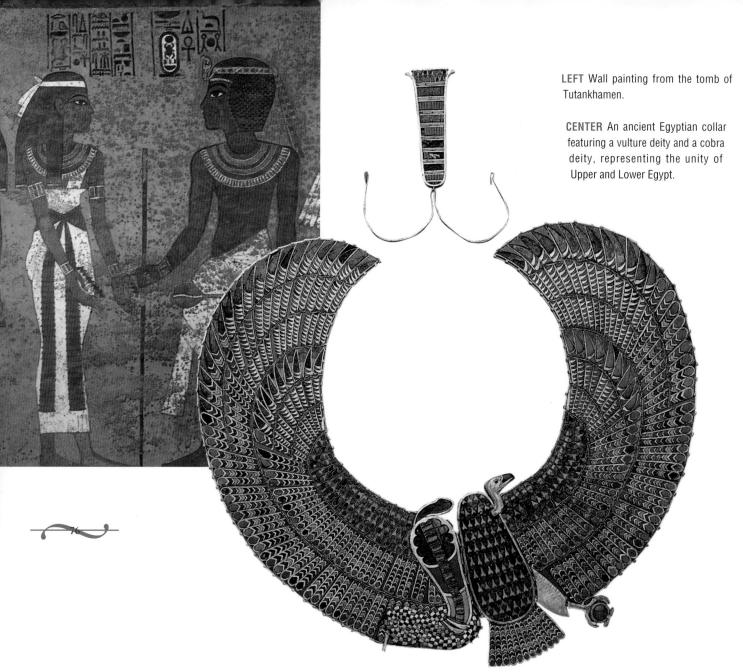

possessed a range of colors, and invented the "lost-wax" technique for sculpture. (This last technique was independently conceived by several different cultures; in it, a model is first sculpted in wax, then covered in sand and heated until the wax melts away, leaving a sculpture-shaped negative space into which molten gold is then poured.) Egyptian pharaohs were considered the living incarnations and descendants of the sun deities, and lived—and died—in splendor appropriate to this divine lineage. The tombs of the pharaohs were packed with precious objects that served the dual purpose of announcing the ruler's wealth and power, and equipping him for the journey into the afterlife.

Disgracefully, over the millennia that separate us from the ever-enthralling culture of ancient Egypt, the most splendid of these funerary monuments have been ransacked, looted and stripped of their unimaginable riches. What remains can give us only a hint of the incalculable wonders these tombs must have held.

But what a hint we have! On November 26, 1922, the British Egyptologist Howard Carter discovered the tomb of Tutankhamen:

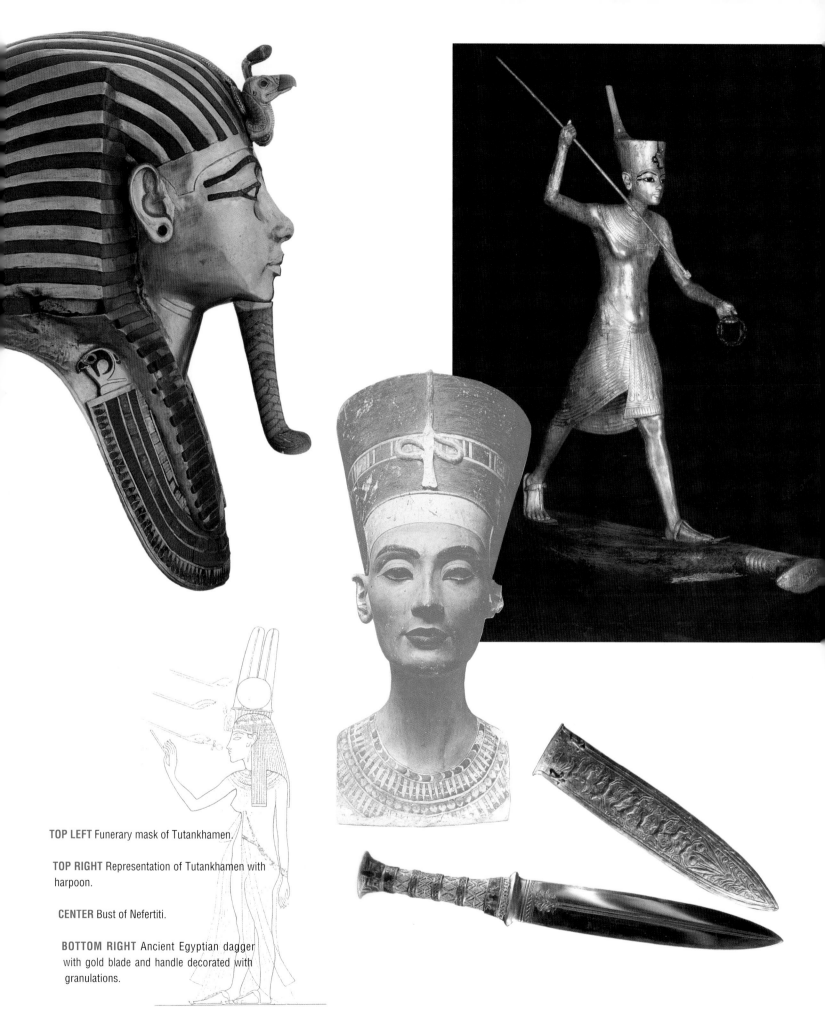

TOP LEFT Funerary mask of Tutankhamen.

TOP RIGHT Representation of Tutankhamen with harpoon.

CENTER Bust of Nefertiti.

BOTTOM RIGHT Ancient Egyptian dagger with gold blade and handle decorated with granulations.

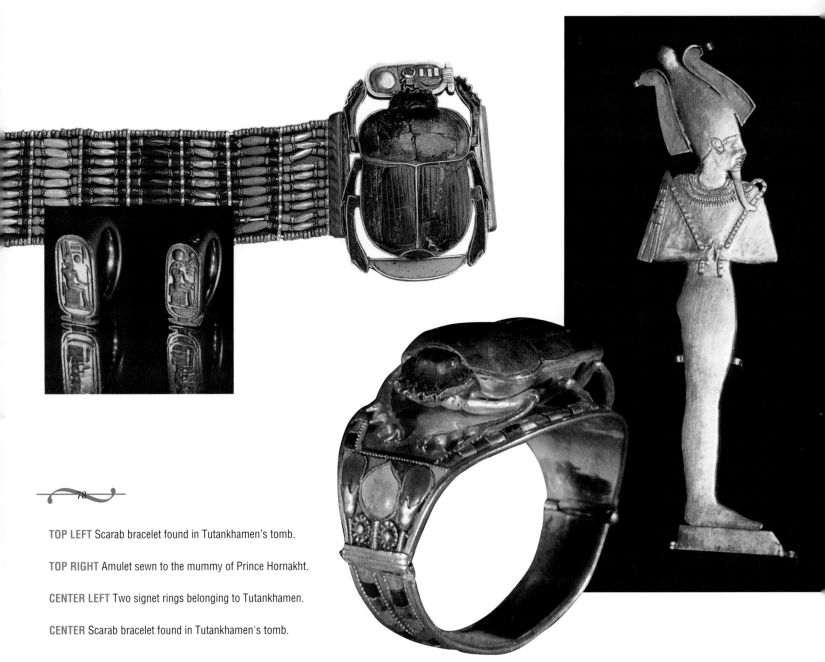

TOP LEFT Scarab bracelet found in Tutankhamen's tomb.

TOP RIGHT Amulet sewn to the mummy of Prince Hornakht.

CENTER LEFT Two signet rings belonging to Tutankhamen.

CENTER Scarab bracelet found in Tutankhamen's tomb.

I inserted the candle and peered in. . .
At first I could see nothing, the hot
air escaping from the chamber causing
the candle flame to flicker, but presently, as
my eyes grew accustomed to the light, details
of the room within emerged slowly from the
mist, strange animals, statues and gold—
everywhere the glint of gold. For the
moment—an eternity it must have seemed to
the others standing by—I was struck dumb
with amazement, and when Lord Carnarvon,
unable to stand the suspense any longer,

inquired anxiously, "Can you see
anything?" it was all I could do to get
out the words, "Yes, wonderful things."

Carter's speechlessness was well justified:
cataloguing and conserving all the objects found in
Tutankhamen's tomb was an enormous project,
occupying the next ten years of his life. Every piece
held sacred significance: Tutankhamen's famous
solid gold mask does a fair job of portraying his
basic features, according to research done on his
mummy, but more importantly, it represents the

serenity and eternal youth of the afterlife, as well as representing the divine aspect of the boy king. Royal symbols also adorn the mask, including the headcloth portrayed in gold and blue glass, the cobra and vulture (representing Lower and Upper Egypt, respectively) on the forehead, and the king's long false beard. Constructed in gold-covered wood, the Golden Throne found in the tomb portrays Queen Ankhesenamun anointing the young king, in a gorgeous, sophisticated combination of sheet gold and inlays of colored glass, faience and semiprecious stones. Between them floats a representation of the Aten, a sun deity depicted as a golden disc whose sun-like rays end in human hands. Every inch of the throne is covered in religious, regal and cultural allusions of this type. There is a pervasive mix of the secular and the religious, the mundane and the sacred throughout every object: chairs, beds and boxes were gilded and decorated with portraits of deities or scenes of the king performing various rituals.

THIS PAGE
Ointment box of Tutankhamen, in the form
of cartouches.

FACING PAGE
Funeral mask of Tutankhamen, 14th century BC.

Broad collar necklaces—which grew so large that they eventually also had to include counterweights that hung on the back to prevent the wearer from toppling over!—and pectorals were the main jewelry in use in ancient Egypt, and the most elaborate. The status placed on the necklace by the Egyptians, who usually left the upper part of their bodies exposed (both men and women), was such that when a system of awards was established in the New Kingdom, the most highly esteemed element of the award was the elaborate necklace, consisting of four rows of gold, disc-shaped beads, that the king placed around the honoree's neck.

Of course, the irony is that Tutankhamen was a short-lived ruler who reigned at a time when his great civilization had lost its way, at least temporarily. Akhenaten's insistence on Aten worship was reversed under Tutankhamen, as the Egyptians returned to their customary polytheism. The priceless artifacts in Tutankhamen's tomb are mere bagatelles compared to what must have been placed in the tombs of popular, powerful, long-reigning pharaohs. But that peek into the boy king's

TOP LEFT Earrings found in Tutankhamen's tomb.

TOP RIGHT Gold jewelry by Lalaounis.

CENTER Gold bracelet with protective wedjat eye, found on right arm of Tutankhamen.

golden funereal splendor is the only one we in the modern world would ever have before the door to that ancient, unknowable world swung shut forever.

The legendary Cleopatra also had a fondness for gold. Though her tomb is long lost to us, the extraordinary tales of her love of splendor form a cultural treasure far more valuable than a tomb of artifacts. We have the story of her seduction of Marc Antony, in which she dissolves an enormous pearl in a glass of wine to add some opulence to their dinner. We have descriptions of her living quarters by contemporary poets, so often envious of the charismatic queen's power and charm. Everything about Cleopatra seems to be bathed in the warm golden light of fantasy, intrigue and power—is it any wonder that one of her methods of transportation

TOP LEFT Artist's recreation of ancient Greek temple decorations.

CENTER LEFT Ancient Greek necklace, 4th century BC.

LEFT Gold pins from 4th century BC, found in a Cumaean tomb.

TOP RIGHT Death mask of a warrior (long thought to be Agamemnon), Mycenae, 16th century BC.

BOTTOM Jug shaped like the head of an Amazon, Greece, 4th century BC. Found in Bulgaria.

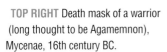

(and one that was sure to provide a spectacular entrance) was a golden barge? The beautiful queen, serenely floating along on her precious conveyance, must have been quite a sight to see...

GREECE & ROME

In ancient Greece, appreciation of gold took on a familiar face. In addition to being used primarily for jewelry and precious objects, gold became fungible—a form of currency. Pieces that have survived show the close relationship between goldsmithing and other forms of art. Greeks believed the precious metal to be a particularly dense blend of sunlight and water, an idea that makes perfect sense to anyone who has observed its fluid sparkle.

Everyone knows the petty beginnings of

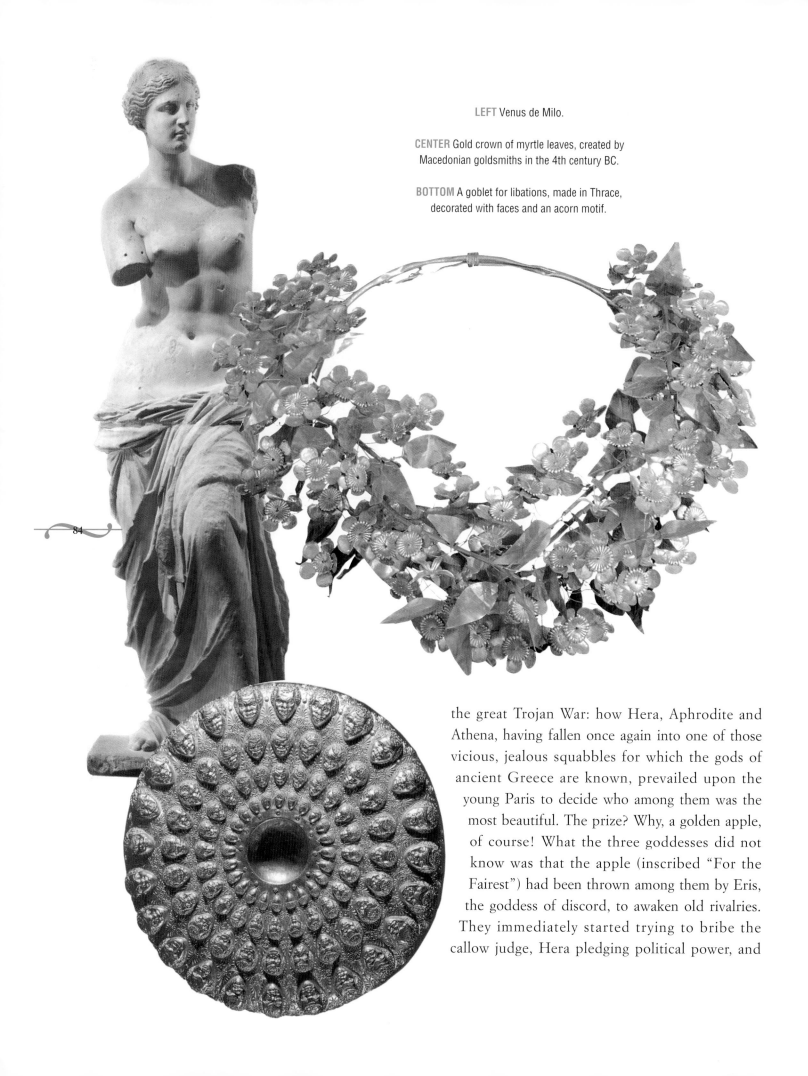

LEFT Venus de Milo.

CENTER Gold crown of myrtle leaves, created by Macedonian goldsmiths in the 4th century BC.

BOTTOM A goblet for libations, made in Thrace, decorated with faces and an acorn motif.

the great Trojan War: how Hera, Aphrodite and Athena, having fallen once again into one of those vicious, jealous squabbles for which the gods of ancient Greece are known, prevailed upon the young Paris to decide who among them was the most beautiful. The prize? Why, a golden apple, of course! What the three goddesses did not know was that the apple (inscribed "For the Fairest") had been thrown among them by Eris, the goddess of discord, to awaken old rivalries. They immediately started trying to bribe the callow judge, Hera pledging political power, and

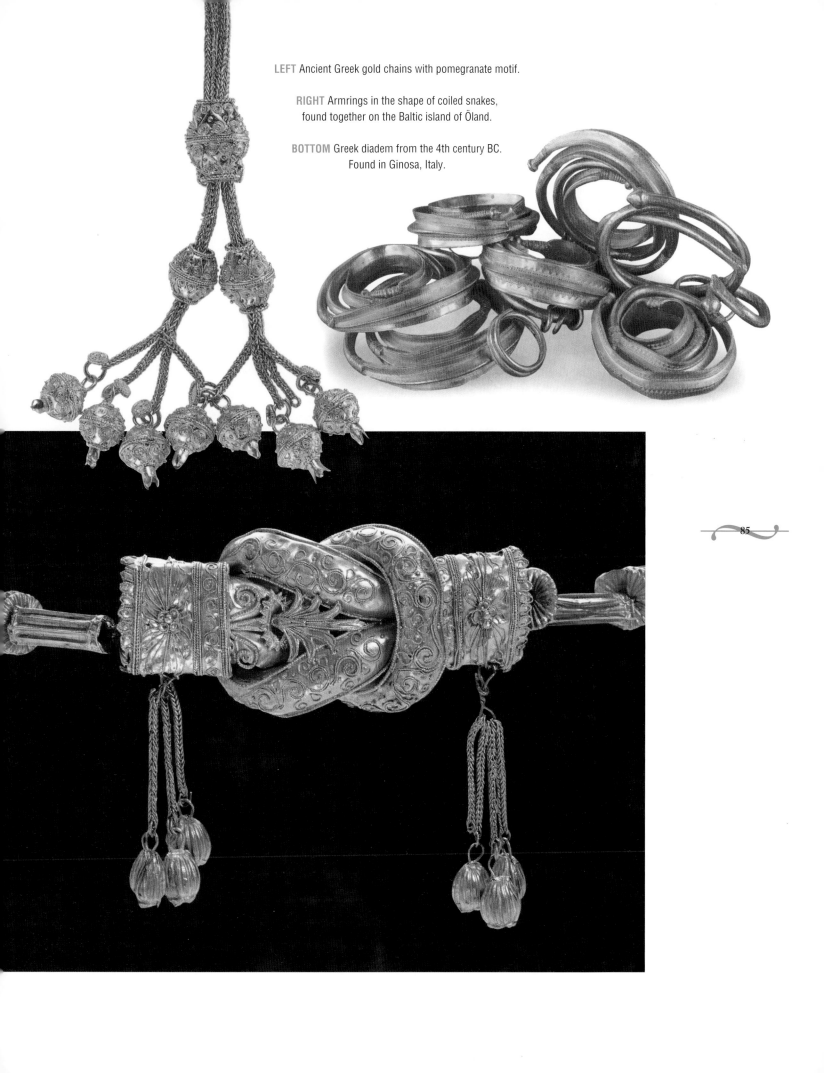

LEFT Ancient Greek gold chains with pomegranate motif.

RIGHT Armrings in the shape of coiled snakes, found together on the Baltic island of Öland.

BOTTOM Greek diadem from the 4th century BC. Found in Ginosa, Italy.

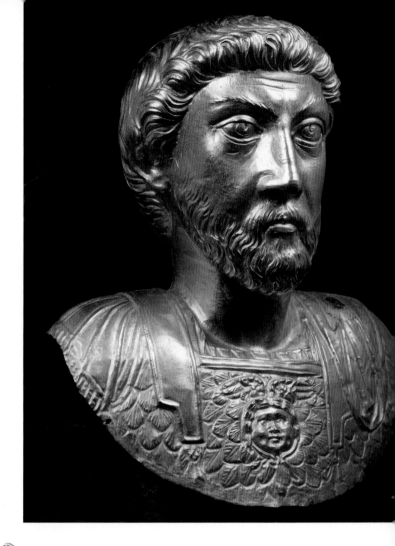

Athena promising success in battle, but it was Aphrodite who lured Paris to her side by offering the love of the most beautiful woman in the world. Unfortunately for all concerned, the woman in question, Helen, was already married to Menelaus. When Paris kidnapped Helen (with Aphrodite's help), their passionate love affair exploded into a war between Troy and Greece. After ten brutal years of bloody battle, the Greeks sailed away, leaving only a giant wooden horse as tribute to the victors... or did they? After the exultant Trojans dragged the horse inside their city walls and went to sleep, Greek soldiers swarmed out of the horse's hollow belly and slaughtered the Trojans, handily winning the war and coining the expression, "Beware of Greeks bearing gifts." What remains of the once-mighty kingdom of Troy, besides the story of the *Iliad*? Heinrich Schliemann, a 19th-century German archaeologist, came as close as anyone has ever come in our quest for the answer.

As in other cultures, gold jewelry—its

craftsmanship as well as its quality—
was a reliable indicator of status and wealth.
The Greek region of Mycenae—home to the first
Greek-speaking people—boasted one of the most
flourishing goldsmithing traditions in the world
until the civilization collapsed in the twelfth
century B.C. (Tellingly, this collapse put a halt to
the Greek artistic tradition for four hundred years.)
When Schliemann excavated the mound of
Hissarlik in the 1870s, he unearthed the ancient city
of Troy, ravaged by the Greeks' fire. Within the
remains of the Trojan palace, Schliemann found a

treasure trove of 250 gold objects,
which he immediately dubbed the "Treasure
of Priam." Schliemann's wife helped him protect
the artifacts and later smuggle them out of Turkey,
and one of the most famous images from the find
shows her in the same treasures that might have
been worn by Helen of Troy herself! Modern
historians have been able to flesh out our
understanding of the Mycenaean culture, using
artifacts from Heinrich Schliemann's discovery of
the ancient city in the 1870s and subsequent
excavations. Explorations of tombs have unearthed

THIS PAGE
Greek bracelet from 4th century BC.

FACING PAGE
Fragment of fresco from Pompeii, 1st century AD.

hammered gold funerary masks (like that reputed to be the mask of legendary king Agamemnon), services in gold plate, jewelry and arms (both ceremonial and functional). Mycenaean nobles wore ornate gold belt decorations and gold rings the size of grapes. Women wore it not only in necklaces and pendants, but also in small ornaments sewn onto dresses. Miniature scenes were painstakingly engraved on rings and rosettes—stylized images of nature, to be sure, but more complex tableaux as well: some rings found show women dancing among sinuous flowering plants, or powerful-looking horses drawing a chariot. These dynamic depictions of the natural world constitute a unique trend in the ancient world, separate from both the static style of Egyptian art and the later Greek idealization of the human form.

Gold informs the tale of Schliemann's famous find in one last way: when he and his wife smuggled the precious artifacts into Athens, Turkish authorities were furious at the theft of their cultural heritage. Schliemann "reimbursed" them for the trouble he had caused... with 50,000 gold francs.

GOLD WORLDWIDE

PRE-COLUMBIAN AMERICA

The arrival of the Spanish in the New World may have been fantastic for Europe, but it was a disaster for the existing cultures and those who wish to study them today. In thrall to their boundless lust for gold, the invaders melted down countless priceless artifacts that held immense cultural and religious significance to the native peoples of the continent. All they saw, in these countless figurines, urns, statues, masks, jewelry and ritual arms, was the riches represented by their material components: the cultural element was utterly discounted.

The Aztecs associated gold with the rainy season, which helped fertilize the ground and bring new life to the region every year. Xipe Totec, the Aztec god of the rains, also protected goldsmiths. The Incas placed silver, gold and coca leaves in the mouths of the dead to aid them in their journey to the afterlife: gold and silver represented the duality of sun and moon, as well as that of light and darkness. These two towering cultures, let us not forget, were themselves empires, conquering, subjugating and swallowing cultures of which nothing survives today—except, perhaps,

PREVIOUS SPREAD
LEFT Pectoral from Tolima culture of Colombia, AD 1-500.

RIGHT Traditional vessel used by the pre-Incan Quimbaya culture to hold hallucinogenic substances used in religious rituals.

THIS PAGE
LEFT Necklace from the Mayan culture, Iximiché, Chimaltenango, Guatemala.

CENTER Gold ornament from Colombian Nariño civilization, 650-1200 AD.

92

Large pin from Andean Colima civilization.

goldsmithing techniques or motifs that were incorporated into the dominant culture, leaving no trace of its origins.

Smaller cultures made their own profound mark on the history of pre-Columbian goldsmithing. The Chimú of northern Peru were noted for their expertise with gold, which coincided, interestingly, with a decline in the sophistication of their pottery. It was the Muisca and the Quimbaya, however, who represented the aesthetic peak of goldsmithing in the Americas. The Muisca, in particular, may have contributed to the legend of El Dorado—in one of their rituals, a leader was covered in gold dust (like the golden king of that mythical lost city)—and swam in a sacred lake, offering gold and precious stones to the gods. Both the Muisca and the

Pendant from Tairona
civilization of Colombia.

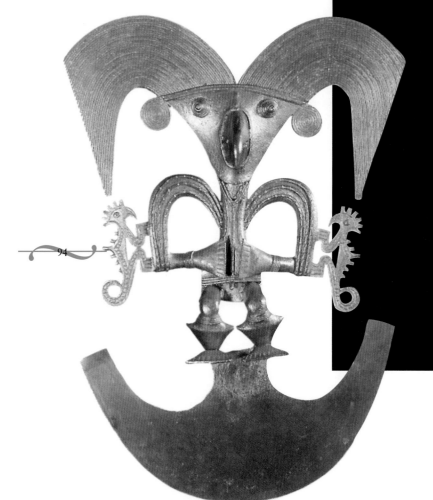

94

Quimbaya were highly sophisticated, using the lost-wax technique, gilding copper and silver, using platinum and gold alloys, dyeing gold and incorporating semiprecious stones and shells in their work. There were several strains and artistic currents in their work; before the arrival of the Spanish, the Muisca often used a very ornamentative style, with infinite repetition of selected motifs. Once the Europeans arrived, the indigenous style blended with the Spanish one, and colonial artwork truly became its own beast: the designs became emphatically baroque and ornate, with floral and zoomorphic designs taking the forefront. Taken as a whole, Latin American pre-Columbian goldwork shows an enormous esteem for birds of prey: eagles, probably worn as protective amulets, constitute the most common motif. Bats, crocodiles and fanciful invented (or were they?) creatures also abound, with symbolic significations that are still unclear.

The Incan Empire also had an overwhelming

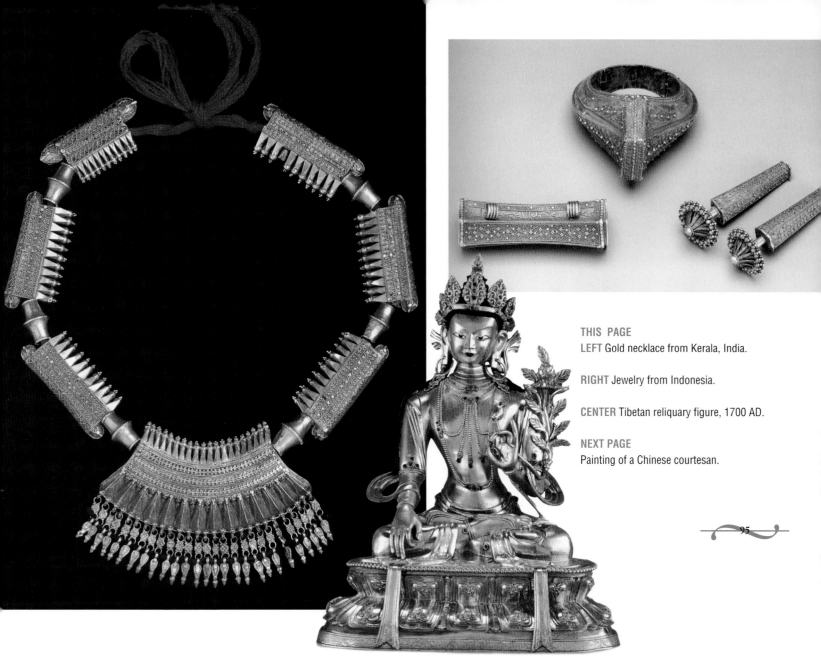

THIS PAGE
LEFT Gold necklace from Kerala, India.

RIGHT Jewelry from Indonesia.

CENTER Tibetan reliquary figure, 1700 AD.

NEXT PAGE
Painting of a Chinese courtesan.

95

fascination with gold: the oldest example of worked gold ever found in the Americas turned up in 2008 in southern Peru. The necklace, of cylindrical gold beads and small green stones, was found in a 4,000-year-old burial pit near Lake Titicaca. Much later examples of Peruvian goldwork startle with their finesse and delicacy: a spider web of golden thread decorates a nose ornament, traversed by four tiny spiders, and ear flares of hammered gold depict dancing bird-men. In 1532, the Inca had one of the largest gold collections ever amassed. When the Incan king Atahualpa was captured by Pizarro, the conquistadores demanded, as ransom, a 22-by-18-foot room filled with gold. Though Atahualpa offered up the ransom, Pizarro and his men killed the king anyway.

Today, what has been recovered of the golden treasures of these great lost civilizations lies in museums—most of the artifacts can be seen in the Museo del Oro in Bogotá, the Museo del Oro in Lima, and the Bruning Museum in Lambayeque, Peru.

INDIA

Many places in Asia have also been possessed by gold fever, most notably India. The Sanskrit word for

THIS PAGE
Tibetan brooch representing the Hindu deity Vishnu and
his winged mount Garuda.

FACING PAGE
Mamuli jewels from the Sumba region of Indonesia.

gold, *hiranya*, shows up in many religious names, such as Hiranyagarbha, "golden embryo" (the origin of all creatures) and Hiranyavakshas, "she with the golden breasts," another name for Vasudhara, goddess of the Earth. When gold and silver are used together in Indian jewelry, they represent the two sacred rivers of India—the Ganges and the Yamuna—and gold alone was considered to be pure sunlight, the noblest and purest of all metals.

Jewelry, especially gold jewelry, has always been a huge part of Indian culture; archaeologists can trace the evolution of jewelry designs and production through ancient statues and reproductions of necklaces, bracelets and earrings engraved on pillars and architraves of sacred buildings. Indian jewelry was not the only use they had for gold, however; Pliny the Elder complained about all the Roman gold given to pay for Indian goods, and modern-day India is second only to Rome for the ancient Roman gold coins found within its borders. This passion for gold continues to this day: there are strict limitations on private ownership of gold in India, but there is still

FACING PAGE
Indian necklace inspired by budding jasmine flowers.

THIS PAGE
TOP LEFT Bazaar oleograph of Minakshi-Devi, consort of Shiva.

TOP RIGHT Ceremonial pendant representing pre-Islamic traditions of Sumatra.

LEFT Sumatran pendant inspired by the Indian Makara monster.

RIGHT Gold pendant featuring Hindu deities Shiva and Parvati.

twice as much gold in private hands as in the reserves of the Bank of India. Much of this is due to the tradition of dressing young brides in a dowry's worth of gold jewelry. This jewelry is a safety cushion against the vagaries of fortune, being readily accessible in case of an emergency. Family gold is passed down through the ages, but it is considered bad luck to wear jewelry that once belonged to someone else; the gold is melted down and formed into new adornments for the next generation. Even in America, the jewelry shops of neighborhoods such as Jackson Heights, in Queens, New York, swarm with prospective Indian-American brides looking for dazzling pieces with which to adorn themselves on the big day.

AFGHANISTAN – THE BACTRIAN HOARD

Sometimes the quest to save golden cultural artifacts from would-be plunderers rivals the plot of the most thrilling adventure movie in its acts of daring and impossibly high stakes. One such story is that of the Bactrian Hoard, discovered in Afghanistan in the winter of 1978-79, mere months before the Soviet Army invaded. The treasure was rarely displayed in

104

the succeeding years, out of concerns
for its safety, as Afghanistan had become a
battlefield. In 1989, the gold was packed up
and moved to the vaults that contained the country's
gold reserves. During the civil war that broke out
after the withdrawal of the Soviet Army, the fate of
the Hoard was a mystery—some people feared the
worst. In the fighting, much of Kabul was destroyed,
including the National Museum, which was looted.
When the Taliban took control in 1996, they
demanded the opportunity to inspect Afghanistan's
gold bullion, which lay just yards from the hidden

Bactrian treasure. The ignorance
of the Taliban, who would have surely
destroyed this priceless piece of Afghanistan's
cultural heritage (they were committed to
demolishing all non-Islamic art), saved the Hoard;
they had no idea it was even there. As they left the
vault, a brave bank employee broke the key off in the
safe door, rendering all of its contents completely
inaccessible—and protected. Only a handful of
people even knew where the treasure was at this
point, and they all kept quiet. In 2004, a team of
Afghan and foreign museum experts broke into the

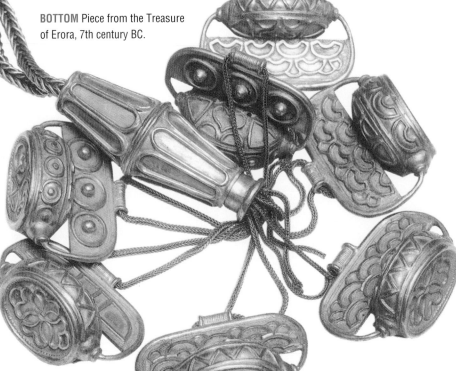

TOP *A Fellah Woman*, Charles Landelle.

CENTER Necklace from the Treasure of Carambolo.

BOTTOM Piece from the Treasure of Erora, 7th century BC.

safes inside the vault and began a long, intense process of cataloging and inventorying Afghanistan's hidden treasure. Throughout the 20 years of turmoil and heartache in Afghanistan, the artifacts were mostly undisturbed, after being completely so in the 2,000 years before their burial mound was unearthed. Rulers and whole cultures came and went over that millennial span. When the archaeologists first excavated the area in 1978, they found that coffins, clothes, flesh and even skeletons had rotted away and disappeared, but the gold jewelry still shined. Thousands of gold clothing appliqués lay where they used to decorate burial robes. Even as we face the essential impermanence of human life, gold persists, untouched and untarnished.

EUROPE

All over Europe, throughout human history, every member of society from the royal family on down hungered for gold; France is a perfectly representative sample. As in other European countries, France and its aristocracy could not get enough of the yellow stuff. The most historically renowned conspicuous consumer of all time, a man whose name

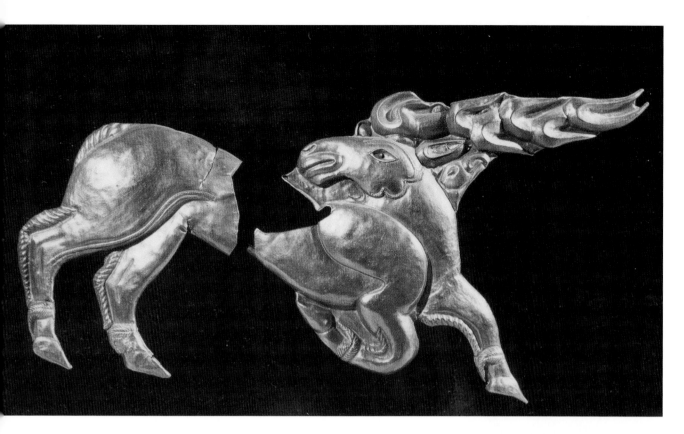

TOP Scythian jewelry from the 6th-1st century BC. Found in Hungary.

LEFT Beard comb from 5th-4th century. Found in Ukraine.

RIGHT Thracian decorative clasp from the Letnitsa find, 400-350 BC. Found in Bulgaria.

is synonymous with ostentation and stately luxury, is of course Louis XIV, the "Sun King"— a nickname that evokes not only the life-giving force of the sun, but also the resplendent gold he loved so. Though he passed edict after edict condemning extravagance (perhaps to avoid competition of the fashion-plate front), Louis XIV was surrounded by a court of aristocrats who were constantly angling to out-dress each other, and the undeniable luxury of gold was a huge part of the stylish nobility's aspiration. Like many other indulgences, gold cloth was restricted as a privilege for the royal family and the king's favorites; everyone else was forbidden to wear it. Those lucky enough to have the resources and the royal permission took full advantage of the situation.

One of those fortunate few was the famous—and infamous—Madame de Montespan. Breathtakingly beautiful, she became the favorite mistress of the Sun King and ruled the fashions of his court until her dramatic downfall, when she was accused of using black magic to gain the king's affections. One of her admirers was the noted writer Madame de Sévigné, who lovingly described a dress that Madame de

Montespan wore to a court function: "a gown of gold on gold, embroidered in gold, bordered with gold, and over that gold frieze stitched with a gold mixed with a certain gold which makes the most divine stuff that has ever been imagined." Other noblewomen enjoyed the fashion of wearing transparent lace gowns over dresses in gold brocade.

Of course, women and men resplendent in golden clothes and jewelry had more than just each other with whom to compete. As befits anyone nicknamed the "Sun King," Louis XIV wanted his palace to sparkle. Soured on Paris, perhaps because of a traumatic childhood memory of being forced to flee Paris with his mother, the absolute monarch set his sights on Versailles, a few miles from the capital, where his father had maintained a hunting lodge. This was where the Sun King built himself a palace worthy of the name. The most stunning area of the Versailles Palace, of course, is the dazzling Hall of Mirrors, in which a wall of mirrors faces seventeen arcade windows, making for a ravishing show of glimmer and glamour as the French sunlight shimmered off the gilt walls and

LEFT *Portrait of Louis XIV*, by Hyacinthe Rigaud.

CENTER A clasp from the royal cloak, made in France between the 13th and 14th centuries.

BOTTOM The "Sword of Charlemagne" part of the French Crown Jewels.

bounced around the magnificent corridor. Gilt and gold leaf covered the palace, and the king's own bedroom was a perfect example, with gold everywhere. In an allusion to the centrality of the sovereign in the absolute monarchy, this bedroom was situated in the exact center of the Versailles palace, at the point where all the roads leading to the palace would converge. Unfortunately for us, the vast treasures of Louis XIV's reign have mostly been lost, melted down for resources or destroyed by the revolutionaries. The rooms of Versailles, however, remain, retaining an aura of their erstwhile splendor, whenever we imagine golden women and men in a room of sunlight and gilt.

MONEY AND TREASURE

Until very recently in human history, the use and ownership of gold jewelry has been restricted, sometimes by law, to the very wealthy or the aristocracy. However, in one form gold has always been a little more accessible: when struck into coins and used as money. Recognizing the inherent value of gold as a result of its rarity, cultures began to use the precious metal as currency almost as soon as the idea of abstract currency began to replace the barter system.

King Croesus, king of the Lydian empire in the sixth century B.C., was wealthy beyond imagination—his treasures led to the familiar phrase, "rich as Croesus." Croesus has also gone down in history as the originator of coined money. Excavations in Sardis, the seat of Croesus's ancient empire, have turned up coins with heads of lions and rams, and once the Lydians caught on to making alloys, they began to mint gorgeous coins in mixtures of silver and gold, which depicted animals and gods on their faces. Laws spread throughout the land, governing exactly how much of each metal should be used to make the coin alloys. For the first time in history, regular citizens had a chance to handle precious metals.

Octadrachma coin with head of Berenice II,
minted in Ephesus 246-221 BC.

FROM LEFT
Macedonian coin with head of Apollo, minted circa 336 BC; Pantikapaion coin with head of Pan,
minted circa 320 BC; coin with head of Zeus, minted in Asia Minor circa 340 BC.

Phanes stater, possibly minted in Ephesus circa 630 BC.

Besides images of gold bullion in Fort Knox or Scrooge McDuck's swimming pool of gold coins, the most prevalent mental pictures we have today of gold currency might be of the overflowing Spanish chests of gold doubloons and pieces of eight, sunk forever at the bottom of the ocean. Or are they? Adventurous gold-seekers have always scoured the bottom of the ocean floor looking for centuries-old wrecks, but recent advances in technology have meant that treasure-hunters can go further out and deeper than ever before. Imaging technology can make the whole process quicker and more profitable. As always in the history of gold, however, the procedure can be rife with conflict. Archaeologists team up with the treasure-hunters for the access to sixteenth-century Spanish ships, but sometimes find themselves horrified by the measures taken to get at the gold, which can destroy important—and valuable—artifacts. And, of course, the governments to which these ships belonged are not ready or willing to let their contents go without a fight...

Coin representing Darius the Great,
minted in Babylon circa 330 BC.

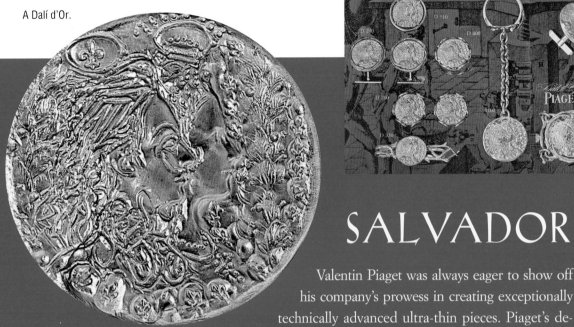

A Dalí d'Or.

SALVADOR DALI

Valentin Piaget was always eager to show off his company's prowess in creating exceptionally technically advanced ultra-thin pieces. Piaget's designers threw themselves into ever more intriguing challenges, such as fitting an entire movement inside an apparently intact gold coin. News of this accomplishment reached the ears of legendary Surrealist Salvador Dalí. In typical (for him) megalomaniacal yet self-mocking fashion, he offered to join forces with Piaget in the creation of a brand-new form of currency.

The Dalí d'Or was a new kind of project, providing a wry commentary on the relationship between art and commerce. The pocket-sized artworks were crafted in 24-karat yellow gold, and the coins came in denominations of one-half, one, two and five Dalís d'Or. Stamped with the face of the artist himself, these limited edition pieces were a huge success, and helped to solidify Piaget's reputation as not just a watchmaker, but a brand that contributed to the wider culture's ongoing artistic dialogue. The partnership with Dalí was particularly apt—who better, after all, to collaborate with Piaget, than an artist best known for painting clocks?

PIAGET
1874
La Côte-aux-Fées and Geneva

The Gold Dali

From the genius of SALVADOR DALI, his palette and his crucible, a new coinage has come to us — the GOLD DALI.

The obverse bears the famous mustachioed 'lucky antennae' profile, inseparable from the effigy of wife Gala: 'my Gravida — queller of terrors and conqueror of desire'.

On the reverse, in the likeness of our own earthly sphere — the hard yet soft element — are the eggs, teeming with life in process of formation — the world of tomorrow. For Salvador Dali, the egg is so replete with meaning that it is to be found in most of his keyworks.

Enthralled by these captivating gold coins, emblems of art absolute from Dali's alchemistic smithy, PIAGET, the master-jewellers, have secured the sole right to combine them with their own 'haut luxe' production. And so you will now find '5 Dali' — '2 Dali' — '1 Dali' — '½ Dali' pieces converted, as is done with antique coins, into pendants, bracelets, rings and other exclusive items. We may add that each and every Dali coin has a 900/1000 gold content and bears a serial number. Mintage is, of course, limited.

Ancient Celtic coins minted circa 200 BC. Found in Bavaria.

LEGENDS AND SYMBOLISM

The cultural significance of gold has always been twofold. On the one hand, we have the obvious, literal interpretation of gold as a stroke of great good fortune—the luckiest among us might hit "the mother lode" or come across "the pot of gold at the end of the rainbow." However, many of the legends surrounding gold expose the darker underbelly of human nature. Take, for example, the legend of Rumpelstiltskin. The king overhears a miller bragging about his daughter, who can "spin straw into gold," and taking the boast literally, marries the talented girl as quickly as possible.

Once the nuptials are over, he locks her in a room full of straw and orders her to get to work. Even for those with a rather cynical view of matrimony, this is extreme. Terrified by her new husband's greed, is it any wonder the poor miller's daughter promises her firstborn to the mysterious gnome that appears before her? Greed is also the motivating force in Aesop's fable of the goose that laid the golden eggs, which has passed into our language as shorthand for the triumph of avarice over patience. Elated by the newfound riches

PREVIOUS SPREAD
LEFT Aurillac bracelet, 4th-1st century BC.

RIGHT *Lady at her Toilette*, School of Fontainebleau.

THIS PAGE
LEFT Funeral mask of Tutankhamen.

CENTER Gold ceremonial hat almost 30 inches tall, found in Germany, made in 1000-800 BC.

BOTTOM Ancient Egyptian earrings.

provided by their otherworldly fowl, the farmer and his wife sharpen their knives opt for what they think will be an incomparable egg collection and slice their goose wide open, only to find... nothing. Their goose, we might say, was cooked.
King Midas was another prime example of human shortsightedness. Already rich, he loved his regal treasure so much that he asked Dionysus to grant him one wish: that everything he touched would turn to gold. Dionysus, perhaps ready for the slightly sadistic enjoyment the Greek gods always seemed to take in the travails of mortals, granted it. At first, Midas was overjoyed, touching tiny flowers, fruits and blades of grass in his garden to see them rendered in the precious metal. With every stroke of his fingertip, his wealth increased exponentially. But, as the saying goes, be careful what you wish for. The trouble started almost immediately; when the king sat down at his golden table, on his golden throne, and took his golden spoon in hand to begin his dinner, the soup turned to gold when it touched his lips: hard, bright and utterly inedible. The worst was

TOP LEFT Pendant of the Baule people from the Ivory Coast.

RIGHT Round and rectangular gold beads made in the Ivory Coast.

BOTTOM The heavy twisted gold earrings of the Fulbe women of Mali are symbols of tribal identity as well as sought-after pieces of jewelry.

TOP LEFT Earring from the tomb of the Señor de Sipán from the Moche civilization of Peru.

TOP RIGHT Dagger with inlay decoration, Mycenae, 16th-15th century BC.

RIGHT Ancient Greek cup, possibly the work of a Mycenaean goldsmith, 15th century BC.

BOTTOM Pectoral from the Tairona culture, 900-1600 AD.

yet to come—when the young daughter of King Midas ran to greet him, she was also instantly transformed into lifeless gold. Stricken by the realization that his blessing had become a curse, Midas begged Dionysus to undo his wish. Dionysus agreed to lift the curse upon Midas bathing in the Pactolus River, in modern-day Turkey. Midas's predicament and its solution are rumored to be the origins of the real gold now present in the river. The legend has also given us the rather misleading expression, "the Midas touch."

The seductive power of gold was a huge part of Greek myths and legends—just remember the golden apples of the Hesperides, which figure in the stories of Heracles, Atlas, Atalanta and the Trojan

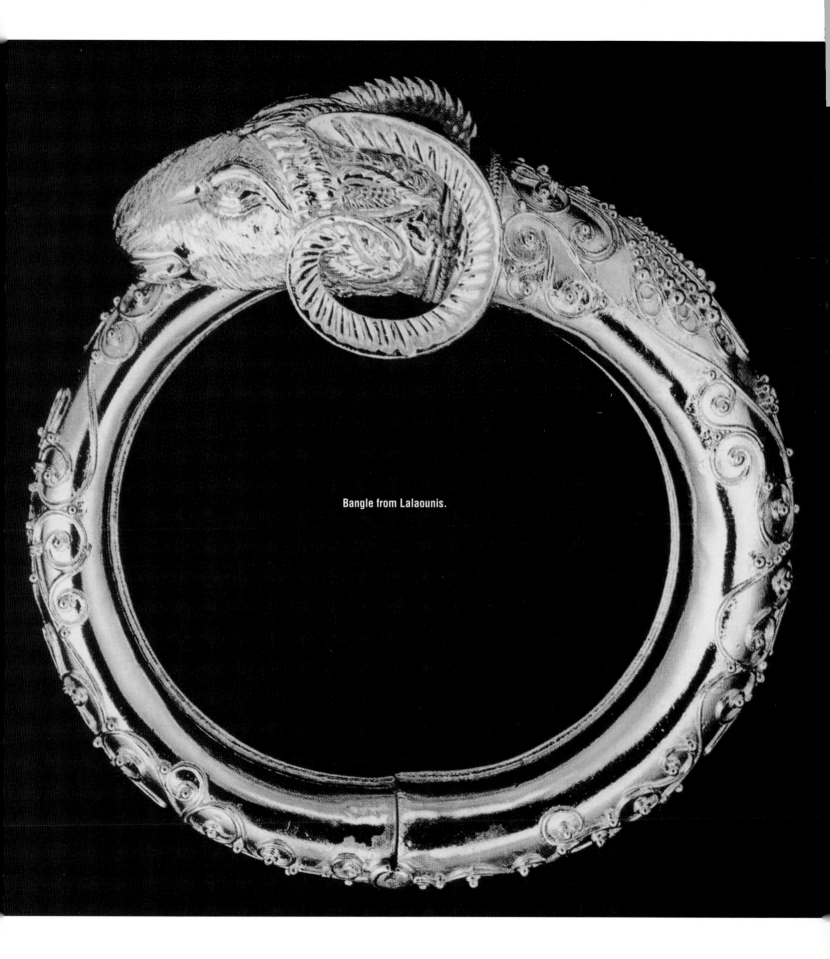

Bangle from Lalaounis.

THIS PAGE
TOP Pair of Roman snake bracelets, 1st century AD.

LEFT *Scene of the Harem*,
by Théodore Chassériau.

CENTER Armlet from medieval Iran,
11th century.

FACING PAGE
Gold binding for a copy of the Koran from the late
16th or early 17th century.

War, which was triggered when Paris awarded a golden apple to Aphrodite, who had promised him Helen of Troy in return. One such compelling story is that of Jason and the Golden Fleece. Cheated out of his rightful claim to the throne, Jason was sent away at birth for his own protection. When he returned to his homeland, the usurper, Jason's half-uncle Pelias, recognized him as the man who was to be his doom (according to a prophecy). Pelias sent Jason on a mission to retrieve the Golden Fleece of Colchis. The king of Colchis, Aeetes, promised Jason the Fleece if he could complete (as is usual in these cases) three difficult

TOP LEFT *The White Slave*, by Jean Lecomte du Nouy.

TOP CENTER Early Byzantine wedding ring, 6th century.

RIGHT Jewish wedding ring, 17th-18th century.

CENTER Ancient Greek bracelet from the Olbia Treasure, 1st century BC.

and dangerous tasks. With the help of Medea, the king's daughter, who had fallen in love with him, Jason completed the tasks and escaped from Colchis, returning in triumph to Pelias's court. There, Medea tricked Pelias's daughters into dismembering him, promising to perform a spell that would regain his youth. Some modern historians believe in that the mission can be interpreted as an historical one, with Jason's quest for the Fleece as a metaphor for gold needed to overthrow his uncle. Others have remarked that the ancient kingdom of Colchis was located on the shores of the Black Sea, where prospectors dipped woolly sheepskins into the river to collect the alluvial gold dust in its current. Actual or metaphorical, the Golden Fleece determined the fate of a man and a nation.

As a stand-in for all that is cherished, gold plays a huge role in the Romanian fairy tale of Tarandafiru, in which a princess searches for her vanished husband. The days of the week, in human form, offer their otherworldly help: Mother Wednesday presents the princess with a gold-spinning distaff, Mother Friday gives her a golden bobbin that winds gold thread, and a golden hen and golden chicks that lay golden eggs are gifts from

Reproduction of Etruscan jewelry,
created by Giacinto Melillo in the 1860s.

TOP Late 10th-century gold brooch, discovered in the Treasure of Gisela.

CENTER The Iron Crown, the most celebrated object in the Monza Treasure, possibly dating from the 5th century.

Mother Sunday. When the princess finally finds her husband, they have two golden children, and live, presumably, happily ever after. Note how the very objects that can bring misery in more cautionary tales—golden-egg laying fowl, the ability to spin straw into gold, and golden children—are transformed here into unmixed blessings, untainted with the sin of greed.

Based on rumors of the religious rituals of the Muisca tribe in Colombia, where the ruler would ritually cover himself in gold dust and make offerings to the gods, the Spanish conquistadores persuaded themselves of the legend of El Dorado. Originally a reference to the tribe's ruler ("the golden one"), "El Dorado" came to signify a mythical place where gold lay thick upon the ground, awaiting only a ready hand to scoop it up. In the 16th century, the conquistadores searched for the elusive city high and low, always convinced it lay just beyond the horizon. Plundering as they went, the Spaniards eventually reached as far as modern Western New Mexico, but had to classify El Dorado in the same category as Shangri-La or Ponce de Leon's Fountain of Youth. The legendary town is

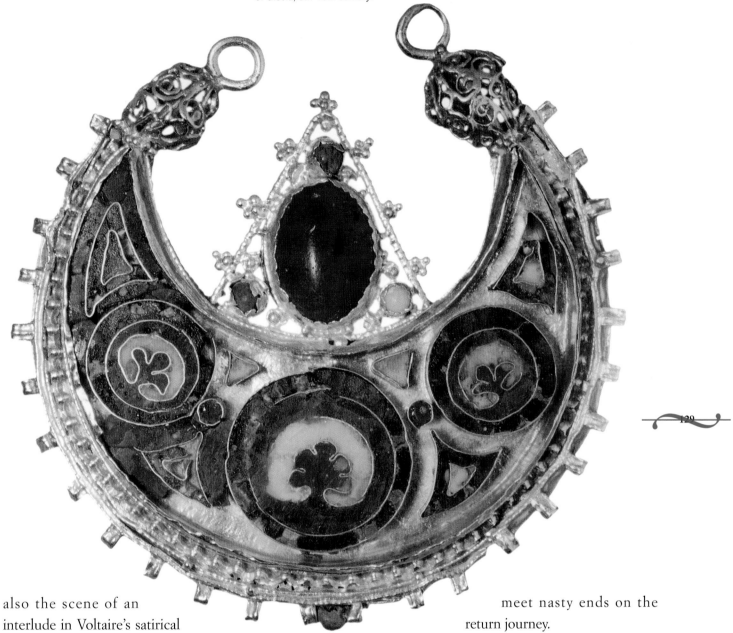

also the scene of an interlude in Voltaire's satirical novella "Candide"—in Voltaire's notion of a utopia, the streets are paved with heaps of precious stones, there are no priests, and the king's jokes are actually funny. When Candide insists on leaving to continue his search for the lovely Cunegonde, the king gives him 100 sheep laden with gold and other treasures. However, just as this ideal society can only exist in complete isolation, so Candide and his companions find it impossible to salvage any of El Dorado's treasure, as the sheep all meet nasty ends on the return journey.

Of course, the presence of gold as a catalyst for unimaginable greed can also be turned on its head: what would a world without gold be like, or a world in which gold was robbed of its power? In his seminal work, *Utopia*, Sir Thomas More imagined such a world:

While they eat from earthenware dishes and drink from glass cups... their chamber pots and all their humblest vessels, for use in the

THIS PAGE
LEFT Salt cellar by Benvenuto Cellini, 1540-1543.

RIGHT *Princess Augusta*, by William Beechey.

CENTER Massive sideboard dish depicting Bacchus
and Ariadne, made 1814-1815.

130

FACING PAGE
Perpetual wall calendar with
6 adjustable concentric circles,
made in Augsburg circa 1670.

FOLLOWING PAGE
Interior of the dome of San Marco,
12th century, gold mosaic.

*common halls and even
in private homes, are
made of gold and silver.
Moreover, the chains and heavy
shackles of slaves are also made of these
metals. Finally, criminals who are to bear the
mark of some disgraceful act are forced to wear
golden rings in their ears and on their fingers,
golden chains around their necks, and even
golden headbands. Thus they hold up gold and
silver to scorn in every conceivable way.*

Students of Greek
(or etymology) will
notice that the word
"utopia" is a riff on *topia*,
"place" and the prefix *ou-*, meaning
"not," so utopia literally means "no place," perhaps
a comment on More's optimism regarding his
fictional project. More hopeful types might point out
that utopia could also derive from *eu-topia*, meaning
"good place." Either way, we have yet to achieve the
enviable tranquility of More's Utopian inhabitants.

CELLULOID SHINE

Besides serving as an endless source of fascination for human cultures throughout history, gold happens to be extremely photogenic. It mimics pure sunlight in photographs, recalling ancient beliefs worldwide of the precious metal's special relationship with the source of all life. Even in its most utilitarian form—the unadorned ingots that sit in Fort Knox and other strongholds—gold gleams irresistibly, seductively. Small wonder, then, that it has always been a source of cinematic inspiration, starring in countless heist movies and twisty thrillers, as well as in the dark, Shakespearean drama of HBO's program "Deadwood."

The Italian Job and *Three Kings* are just two films whose plots—and the passions of their protagonists—revolve around the yellow metal. Somehow, one suspects, the considerable value of the material is not the only thing motivating the crafty criminals and grizzled prospectors. In today's world, plenty of things could be more profitable—plutonium comes to mind—but gold exerts a strange force on our psyches, explained by the luscious shots of the bounty of the crime. Even

that triumphs over trust and friendship. Three friends team up to prospect, but when they strike it rich, the problems begin. As one of them says, "Ah, as long as there's no find, the noble brotherhood will last but when the piles of gold begin to grow... that's when the trouble starts."

Sometimes, as occasionally happens in post-Code heist movies, the criminals win, and we cheer. We have no doubt that Michael Caine will figure out a way to walk away with his spoils at the end of *The Italian Job*—and we are glad of it, for who among us cannot sympathize with the golden attraction he

when the gold is never seen, or if the movie is in black and white, every filmgoer has an immense store of mental images that call to mind—in Technicolor—the precise, atavistic lure of the yellow stuff.

Like many cautionary legends that feature the corrosive effects of greed on the human soul, *The Treasure of the Sierra Madre* features a lust for gold

LEFT Earrings with a griffin motif, from the 4th century BC.

RIGHT Rudolph Valentino in *The Sheik*.

BOTTOM Gold jewelry by Lalaounis.

THIS PAGE
Gold necklace by L. Gaillard, Paris.

FACING PAGE
TOP LEFT French brooch, circa 1900.

TOP RIGHT Rita Hayworth.

CENTER Pearl and gold ring by René Lalique.

BOTTOM LEFT Publicity shot of Marlene Dietrich
for *Shanghai Express*.

BOTTOM RIGHT Gold bracelet by Mauboussin.

feels? Other crimes are unforgivable. In the James Bond movie *Goldfinger*, the titular villain stores up a sizable stockpile of gold, but those accumulated riches are not enough for him. Rather than go to the trouble of stealing even more gold, he hatches a sinister plot to increase the value of his hoard by irradiating all the gold in Fort Knox, rendering it untouchable for the next six decades. Destroying gold, taking away not just its availability but its inherent worth and appeal—this could not go unpunished, and Auric Goldfinger meets a predictably lethal end.

Interestingly, contemporary physicists have explained that Goldfinger's plan would have worked, but not exactly in the way he intended. In theory, a cobalt-iodine atomic device could irradiate gold by introducing an extra neutron into the gold atom. However, radioactive gold is extremely unstable—once irradiated, it would become liquid mercury within days! Transforming gold into another element: not exactly what the world's alchemists have dreamed of, but they would probably be intrigued nonetheless.

THIS PAGE
TOP LEFT Singer Rihanna in Piaget.

TOP RIGHT Actress Demi Moore in Piaget.

CENTER RIGHT Actress Becki Newton in Piaget.

CENTER Oliva ring.

FACING PAGE
TOP Actress Maggie Cheung in Piaget.

CENTER Yvel necklace.

THIS PAGE
TOP LEFT Charlize Theron in Bulgari.

TOP RIGHT Audrey Hepburn entering
the Bulgari store in Rome, circa 1967.

BOTTOM RIGHT Martin Sheen outside
of Bulgari, circa 1964.

BOTTOM CENTER Necklace by Bulgari.

FACING PAGE
Actress Anne Hathaway in Bulgari.

142

THE THIRST
FOR GOLD

Gold does not tarnish—it is indestructible, and so is our desire for it. Leaving aside simple thievery, there are really only two ways of getting at this yellow treasure: mining, and creating it from another element, or alchemy. Alchemy has dashed as many hopes as it has raised (in an exact one-to-one ratio, given its impossibility). Mining, however, has been slightly more fruitful—and thus far more popular. In fact, in the 19th century, every discovery of gold was immediately followed by a Gold Rush, in which hordes of would-be prospectors descended upon the brand-new mining operation, hoping to be one of the lucky ones who would literally strike gold.

The most famous American Gold Rush was sparked off in January of 1848, when a carpenter named James Marshall came across a bit of gold at John Sutter's lumber mill in Northern California. Though Marshall and Sutter tried to keep a lid on their discovery—Sutter had plans for an agricultural empire that a gold rush would ruin—the only thing that travels faster than bad news is a rumor of quick and easy golden riches. Once the

word got out, miners from all over America—and all over the world—swarmed the area in search of a quick payday. The newspapers called them "Argonauts," after the men who accompanied Jason on his quest for the Golden Fleece.

The route to California was not an easy one: prospectors could travel overland via stagecoach, sail around South America's Cape Horn, or sail to Panama, cross the isthmus on mules, and set sail again. Nonetheless, hundreds of thousands of "forty-niners" made the trip, many of them eventually returning home with little more than the shirts on their backs. California, however, was utterly transformed. From a sleepy port of 1,000 people, San Francisco had exploded into a boomtown, the center of trade for all the goods and services any prospector could want. By 1850, the easy-to-find alluvial gold was exhausted, and mining called for more sophisticated techniques and equipment. The transformation, however, was complete. California had gone from an isolated strip of land that had just been won from Mexico, to a full-fledged state in the Union. This may have been the most permanent result of the Rush—in general, the gold never lasted very long.

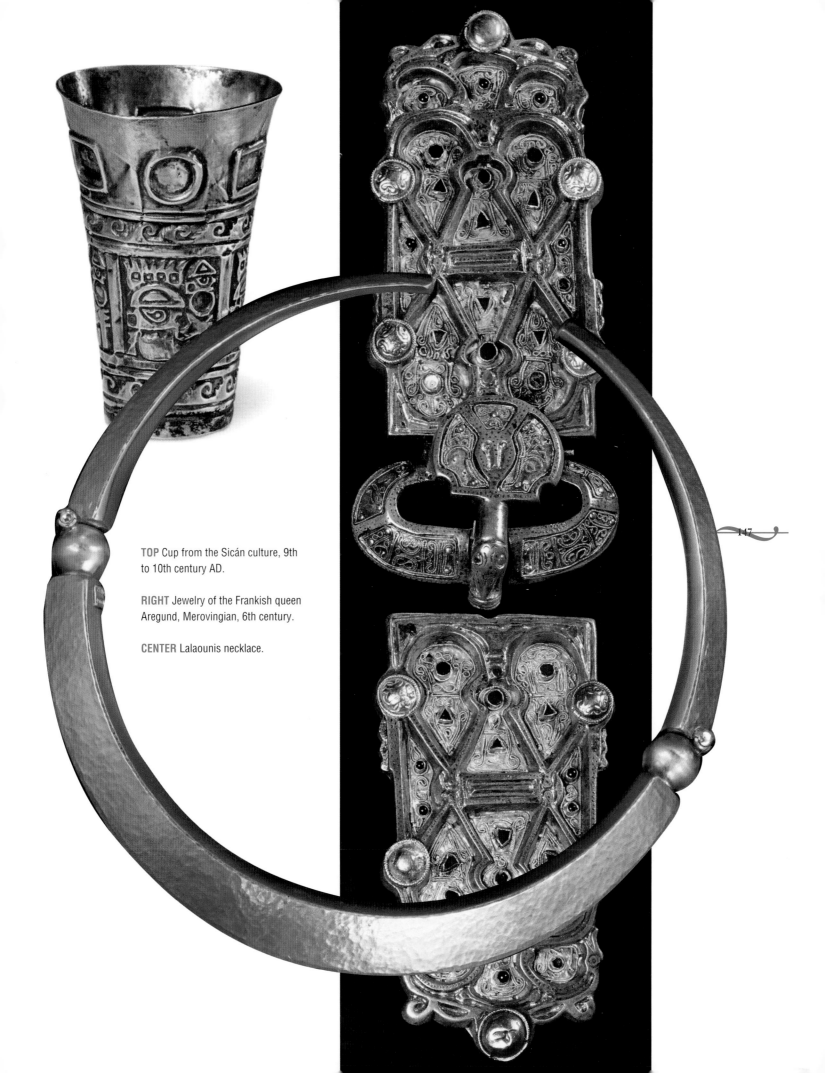

TOP Cup from the Sicán culture, 9th to 10th century AD.

RIGHT Jewelry of the Frankish queen Aregund, Merovingian, 6th century.

CENTER Lalaounis necklace.

Prospecting was hard work: crouching in promising streams, panning through never-ending troughs of gravel, living in makeshift tents and without the company of women. Nonetheless, there is some chance of success—out of the hundreds of thousands of prospectors, at least some did strike it rich with gold. The same cannot be said of the thousands of alchemists over the centuries.

For 2500 years, alchemists investigated the underpinnings of the natural world, building upon a mixture of art, astrology, chemistry, medicine, metallurgy, mysticism and physics. The alchemists had several goals; the best known were the "elixir of life" and the ability to transform lead and other base metals into gold. In the Middles Ages, European alchemists became convinced that finding the "philosopher's stone," a substance that would magically expand their understanding of alchemy to the point where any undertaking would be possible. Understood metaphorically, the alchemists' goals could be seen as the single quest to take whatever is base, common, fallible and mortal, whether it be metal of human flesh, and raise it to a state of refined, imperishable enlightenment.

FACING PAGE
Dutch bodice ornament circa 1630.

THIS PAGE
LEFT Portrait of Empress Eugénie.

RIGHT *Portrait of Eleonora Gonzaga*, by Titian.

BOTTOM LEFT One of a pair of gold shoulder clasps
from a royal ship burial at Sutton Hoo, England,
early 7th century.

BOTTOM RIGHT A bracelet in gold,
black enamel and lapis lazuli, circa 1870.

The population of alchemists included both committed scientists and utter charlatans, and rulers with money troubles were only all too happy to welcome both into their circles. However, despite the many contributions to the human experience that alchemists have made—inventing gunpowder and contributing to the fields of metalworking, glassworking, ceramics and cosmetics among them—they eventually had to admit that transforming one element into another was not within the realm of possibility.

FACING PAGE
Detail of *Judith with the Head of Holofernes*, by Lucas Cranach the Elder.

THIS PAGE
TOP LEFT French Sainte-Foy gold statue, 9th century.

TOP RIGHT Gold breast ornament of the late 12th or early 13th century, decorated with lions, a dog, a leopard and two griffins.

CENTER Box of Theodoric. Merovingian, 7th century.

THE MODERN AGE

The use of gold in medicine and technology has a long and illustrious history. Like many other precious materials, gold was considered to have an array of medicinal uses. As far back as the 7th century B.C., Roman dentists were using gold wire to attach false teeth, and the use of gold fillings for cavities was pioneered in the 16th century. Even in modern times, we use gold medicinally—for more than 70 years, doctors treated rheumatoid arthritis by regular injections containing gold, which acts as an anti-inflammatory. Despite its efficaciousness, doctors still don't know why it works. Because it is non-toxic and non-reactive, gold readily lends itself to medical applications, from the gold surgical tools that surgeons use to clear coronary blockages, to the gold pellets used to treat prostate cancer.

Gold's versatility has led to its use in all sorts of technical applications. It has played a role in some of the proudest moments in American history: NASA's engineers wrapped the precious metal around Apollo lunar landing modules, protecting the astronauts from radiation. A golden miniature model of the Apollo 11 lunar module wittily juxtaposes gold's space-age uses with its traditional role as recognition of a signal achievement: French newspaper *Le Monde* commissioned three to present as gifts for the Apollo astronauts when they made a visit to Paris.

Outer space continues to be an extra-terrestrial forum for gold's usefulness. Even today, astronauts use a thin gold film on their visors to protect their eyes from the sun's glare, just as they did on the Apollo missions. The planets of Neptune and Uranus got their turn in the spotlight when scientists using the Keck telescopes, which incorporate giant gold-coated mirrors, to capture the most detailed images of those planets ever created. Gold-coated mirrors were also crucial in the development of the laser in 1960, an invention of seemingly limitless application.

Increasingly environmentally conscious building techniques have explored the use of gold in making windows: the metal helps reflect sun away in the summer and hold in heat in chilly winters. However, any use of gold in "green" efforts must contend with the harmful environmental effects of gold mining, which uses cyanide to leach the metal from the ore. To greenify the yellow metal, Australian researchers have discovered that some tiny microorganisms ingest trace amounts of gold in rocks, concentrating them in larger nuggets. This biotechnology holds great promise for the future of gold mining.

Mercury Venus Earth Mars Jupiter Saturn Uranus Neptune

A GOLDEN RAINBOW

Throughout most of human history, the color of gold has been constant, immutable. Depending on its origin and pure gold content, the brilliant metal has always been coyly, boldly, flirtatiously, unwaveringly, steadfastly, joyfully, longingly, faithfully one shade and one shade only: a gleaming yellow. It was this unmistakable hue that led our ancestors to associate the metal with our sun, which resembles nothing so much as a shining gold coin of inestimable value. However, times are changing, and our insatiable thirst for novelty and artistic expression is beginning to wear away at the old atavistic lure of yellow. The possibilities are endless, or nearly so, with carefully calibrated alloys. The gold we wear is never pure gold—the metal alone is too soft to make the immortal jewelry that we treasure and pass down the generations. The alloy described as 24-karat gold, which contains 99.7% pure gold, is the highest purity used in jewelry—much more common is 18-karat gold, which contains 75% pure gold. Within that other 25%, however lies a whole world of metallurgical science in the service of

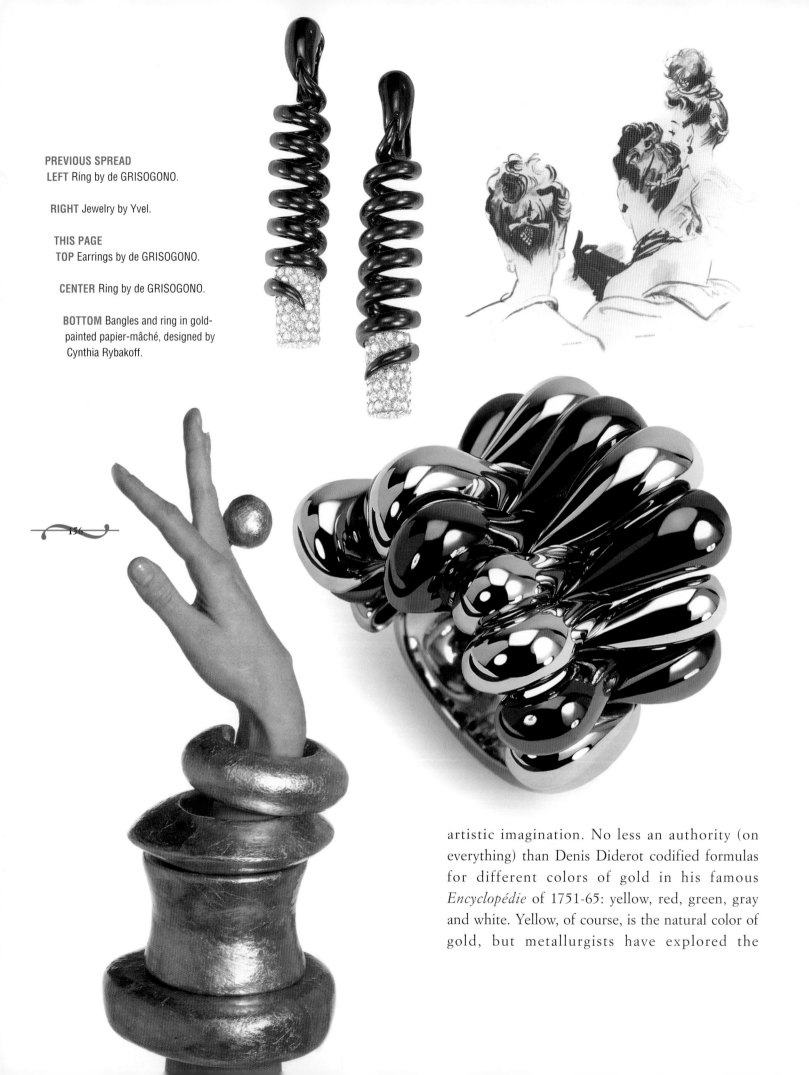

artistic imagination. No less an authority (on everything) than Denis Diderot codified formulas for different colors of gold in his famous *Encyclopédie* of 1751-65: yellow, red, green, gray and white. Yellow, of course, is the natural color of gold, but metallurgists have explored the

Bracelet by Bulgari.

possibilities of Diderot's other four colors... and more besides.

There is a theory that humans are predisposed to be attracted to warm colors—the pinks, reds and oranges that signal the ripeness of fruit, the nearness of fire or the ruddy undertones of many people's skin. Given the newfound off-the-charts popularity of rose gold, there may be something to this. Mixing pure gold with copper and a smaller amount of silver adds a warm, almost fleshy glow to delicate jewelry, and designers are increasingly incorporating rose gold and its cousins pink gold (with more silver, less copper) and red gold (an alloy of pure gold and copper) into dramatic, lively pieces.

The popularity of green gold—pure gold mixed with silver alone—hit its zenith with Art Nouveau and its nature-inspired forms. Blue gold—an alloy of gold with steel or arsenic—was used in much the same way, mimicking the rivers in which gold miners toiled or struck it rich. A slightly different proportion of the elements used for blue gold

TOP LEFT Platinum necklace by LEVIEV.

TOP RIGHT Anne Hathaway in Piaget.

LEFT White-gold rings by Bulgari.

CENTER Platinum ring by Boucheron.

would result in gray gold, with a softer, more subdued sheen than white gold. The inventively geometric use of monochrome materials has always appealed to modern designers with a flair for the beauty that such stark lines possess. Art Deco signaled the modern birth of this aesthetic, with its insistence on white and black motifs, but for some time, gold was not invited to this particular party. The days of gold's exclusion are, thankfully, over. The purest, most stunning diamonds can now be proudly set off by white gold, pure gold combined with platinum or palladium and nickel and zinc.

PLATINUM

Of course, no discussion of monochromatic jewelry and the perfection of white stones on white metal would be complete without singing the myriad praises of platinum, gold's ever-elegant sister in the world of jewelry design. The history of platinum does not share the unending triumphant march of gold—it is, rather, more of a Cinderella story. The word "platinum" comes from the Spanish for "little silver," and for millennia, platinum was treated as silver's unwanted relation. Around 100 B.C., the Incas and other pre-Columbian Native Americans worked platinum and other metals

Platinum parure by Cartier.

into ceremonial jewelry, but the precious metals lapsed back into obscurity, and remained completely unknown in Europe until it annoyed the conquistadores in the mid-16th century. Irritated by the unworkable white metal nuggets that kept cropping up in the gold mines of Colombia, the Spanish miners called it "platina del pinto," considered it to be unripe gold, and left it in the rivers in hopes that it would mature into something more desirable. In the mid-18th century, the Spanish astronomer Antonio de Ulloa wrote about the mysterious metal. At this point, platinum started to pick up in popularity among

European alchemists, who believed that platinum could bring them one step closer to their ultimate goal of turning lead into gold. In 1751, Swedish scientist Theophil Scheffer categorized platinum as a precious metal and its appeal for royalty immediately skyrocketed. King Louis XVI of France declared it was the only metal fit for kings, and had his jeweler fashion several pieces in platinum for him. Of course, the rampant royal rivalries of the time meant that King Carlos III of Spain had to surpass the French king's enthusiasm for the rare metal—he commissioned an ornate foot-tall platinum chalice, which he then gave to

Ring and earrings by Cartier.

the pope, in a properly ostentatious show of generosity. The alluring yet intransigent material continued in near-anonymity for another two and a half centuries—its rarity, difficulty and the necessity of alloying with iridium, an even more expensive metal, all worked against it. Despite its appealing, sturdy luster, platinum required extremely high temperatures to melt—much higher than anyone could use until relatively recently. Diamonds were often set in silver to play up the white light within, but these pieces often required settings that look heavy to the modern eye.

In fact, platinum did not really hit its stride until the very beginning of the 20th century, when fashion and technological advancements combined to make platinum the preferred setting for diamonds. A few decades later, when the fashions of the 1920s and 30s called for diamonds in designs in which the mounting seemed to vanish from view, the strong, untarnishable, brilliant platinum was the natural choice. Today, platinum is sometimes considered even more exclusive and prestigious than gold—these days, almost anyone can have a "gold" credit card, but only the elite enjoy the privileges of platinum.

DIAMONDS
POWER AND BEAUTY

PREVIOUS SPREAD
LEFT Cartier jewelry.

RIGHT Bulgari diamond necklace.

THIS PAGE
TOP LEFT Muslim bride in Hyderabad
wearing gold ornaments typical of the region.

TOP RIGHT Indian necklace
in gold and diamonds.

CENTER Pendant of necklace that belonged
to an Indian princess in the 19th century.

TOP The 128.51-carat Tiffany Diamond.

BOTTOM Indian bangles dating from the 18th century.

The year was 1914, the place was Russia, and revolution was in the air. Centuries of imperial privilege were being swept away before the grand, implacable tide of history.

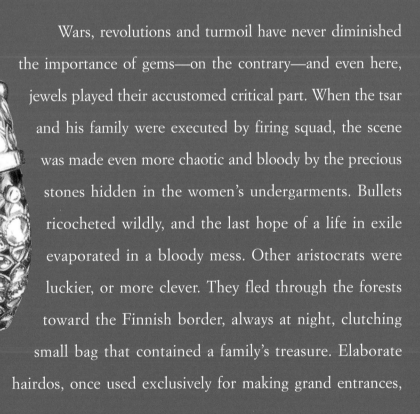

Wars, revolutions and turmoil have never diminished the importance of gems—on the contrary—and even here, jewels played their accustomed critical part. When the tsar and his family were executed by firing squad, the scene was made even more chaotic and bloody by the precious stones hidden in the women's undergarments. Bullets ricocheted wildly, and the last hope of a life in exile evaporated in a bloody mess. Other aristocrats were luckier, or more clever. They fled through the forests toward the Finnish border, always at night, clutching small bag that contained a family's treasure. Elaborate hairdos, once used exclusively for making grand entrances,

LEFT Portrait of Empress
Sissi of Austria.

RIGHT Cartier lace bow
brooch, 1906.

TOP LEFT Fabergé egg set with
diamonds, 1899.

TOP RIGHT Detail of *A Muslim Prince*,
by Jean-Joseph Benjamin-Constant.

LEFT European ring from the late
18th or early 19th century.

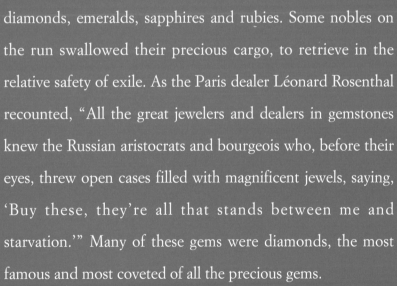

now served an ironically utilitarian
function; within the suspiciously full coifs,
tucked behind fussy ringlets, lay a fortune in
diamonds, emeralds, sapphires and rubies. Some nobles on
the run swallowed their precious cargo, to retrieve in the
relative safety of exile. As the Paris dealer Léonard Rosenthal
recounted, "All the great jewelers and dealers in gemstones
knew the Russian aristocrats and bourgeois who, before their
eyes, threw open cases filled with magnificent jewels, saying,
'Buy these, they're all that stands between me and
starvation.'" Many of these gems were diamonds, the most
famous and most coveted of all the precious gems.

The history of the word "diamond" testifies to the
extraordinary qualities of the stone. "Adamas" from the

162

TOP Princess Margarete von Thurn und Taxis as Marie Antoinette.

CENTER Diamond necklace belonging to the von Thurn and Taxis family.

TOP Empress Josephine often wore jewels from Chaumet.

CENTER Boucheron ring with engraved diamond, 1900.

BOTTOM European ring from the 18th or 19th century.

Greek, originally meant "unconquerable," before its definition shifted to include "an imaginary stone of impenetrable hardness." The meaning shifted once again in the first century A.D., to accommodate the real-life equivalent of this "imaginary" stone, and the "adamas" of times past spawned not just our "diamond," but also "adamant," a word used to describe a stance of passionate, unwavering intensity—words that can also be used to describe humanity's love affair with diamonds, a love affair that shows no signs of slackening. Exceptionally hard, a diamond can scratch anything without getting scratched itself, a quality that has been

LEFT French diamond sautoir circa 1930.

CENTER Mrs. Cornelius Vanderbilt wearing necklace and brooch acquired from Cartier in 1904.

BOTTOM Art Deco ring circa 1925.

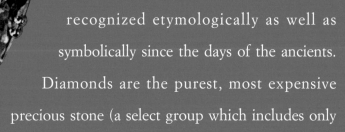

recognized etymologically as well as symbolically since the days of the ancients. Diamonds are the purest, most expensive precious stone (a select group which includes only diamonds, rubies, sapphires and emeralds).

Every diamond has its own particular charm and allure, and though charm and allure are generally considered to be unquantifiable, we humans are a taxonomical sort. We rate and judge and order, and we have devised four categories by which diamonds can be rated and their value determined. We humans also have a great love of mnemonics, leading us to the "Four C's": carat, clarity, color and cut. The Four C's

TOP Scroll tiara commissioned from Cartier by Elisabeth, Queen of the Belgians, in 1910.

BOTTOM Elisabeth, Queen of the Belgians, wearing scroll tiara.

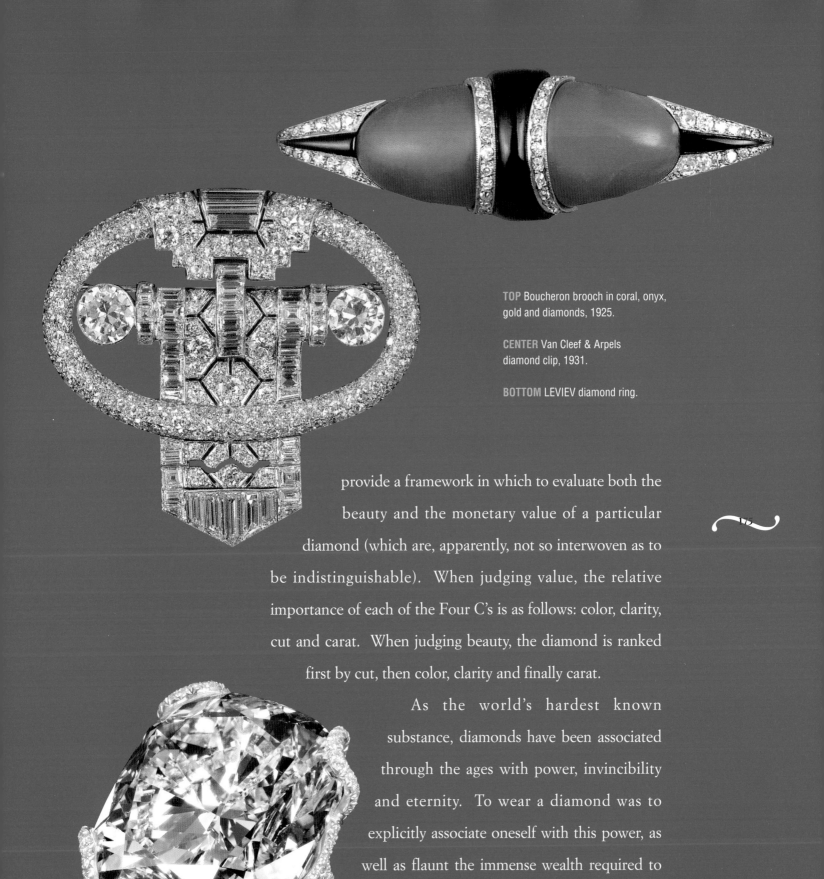

TOP Boucheron brooch in coral, onyx, gold and diamonds, 1925.

CENTER Van Cleef & Arpels diamond clip, 1931.

BOTTOM LEVIEV diamond ring.

provide a framework in which to evaluate both the beauty and the monetary value of a particular diamond (which are, apparently, not so interwoven as to be indistinguishable). When judging value, the relative importance of each of the Four C's is as follows: color, clarity, cut and carat. When judging beauty, the diamond is ranked first by cut, then color, clarity and finally carat.

As the world's hardest known substance, diamonds have been associated through the ages with power, invincibility and eternity. To wear a diamond was to explicitly associate oneself with this power, as well as flaunt the immense wealth required to

LEFT Ingrid Bergman
in Bulgari jewelry.

RIGHT Cartier
diamond earrings.

Diamond and platinum bracelet from
Van Cleef & Arpels circa 1937.

buy one. The supernatural
properties ascribed to
diamonds could fill a book of their
own: they protected against plagues,
witchcraft, poisons, nightmares, sickness and insanity. To
ancient Egyptians, diamonds represented the sacred sun, and
it was accordingly placed in the middle of the sacred ankh.
Early Hindus used diamonds to protect against fire, poison,
theft, water, snakes and evil spirits; they brought the wearer
good luck, equilibrium and loyalty, especially if given as a
gift. Romans wore diamonds set in steel to protect against
insanity, and Roman soldiers wore them against the skin for
fortitude and strength in battle. Early Christians believed
diamonds could prevent harm from lightning. Jewish high

Van Cleef & Arpels diamond and
platinum clip and necklace, 1928.

priests used diamonds when acting as judges—if the stone lost its brilliance when held in front of the accused, guilt was declared, but continuing to sparkle was seen as proof of innocence of the accused. Of course, there were limitations on these impressive powers: they held only if the diamond was given freely. If the gem had been stolen or lent, it would be useless—or worse—to its wearer. In India and Persia, diamonds were considered poisonous, but in the Middle Ages in Europe, they were held to be an antidote to poison. References to diamonds in ancient literature and myth

182

TOP The "Louis Cartier" diamond, one of very few D-flawless gems to weigh over 100 carats.

CENTER Cartier diamond necklace.

LEFT LEVIEV diamond earrings.

RIGHT Bayco ring set with
a pink sapphire flanked by
diamonds, with diamond pavé.

abound. According to Ovid, Zeus turned his childhood friend Celmis into a diamond. One story, whose particulars vary over cultures and over time, has Alexander the Great confronting a valley of poisonous snakes fiercely guarding the mounds of diamonds at the bottom. Noticing circling eagles overhead, Alexander and his men slaughtered some sheep and threw their fatty carcasses to the bottom of the valley. The birds wasted no time in swooping to the bottom of the valley to pick up the meat, diamonds clinging to the bottom. Alexander and his men immediately began to make as much noise as they could, startling the eagles into dropping their precious cargo. This story of ingenuity turns up in the writings of Marco Polo as well as in 1,001 Arabian Nights,

Bulgari necklace in white gold,
set with diamonds, emeralds,
spinels and an aquamarine.

LEFT Bulgari diamond ring.

RIGHT Chopard diamond earrings.

and closely follows Hindu myths of battles between the Nagas, mythological diamond-guarding serpents, and Garuda, an eagle-like deity.

One ancient passage makes explicit claims for the diamond's power, while also accounting for the caveat of human weakness: "He who carries a diamond on the left side shall be hardy and manly; it will guard him from accidents to the limbs, but nevertheless a good diamond will lose its power and virtue if worn by one who is incontinent, or drunken." Another anonymous verse makes even bolder claims: "The evil eye shall have no power to harm him that wears the diamond as a charm. No king shall thwart his will and even the gods shall his wishes fill."

THAT RARE
JOY OF OPULENCE

HISTORY OF DIAMONDS

Surprisingly, given their prominence in the last dozen or so centuries, diamonds are not as prevalent in early history as other gems. Whereas a ruby or an emerald still gives a hint of its allure in its rough state, diamonds look like dull rocks until they are polished and cut. The precious stones are, however, mentioned by Plato and Aristotle, and Pliny ("The diamond, that rare joy of opulence...") agreed that they prevented poisoning and brought victory to the wearer, as well as noting their clarity, colorlessness and heat resistance.

INDIA

In sharp contrast to the prestigious jewelry houses of today, in India, jewelers were low-caste and anonymous, more concerned with creating for the greater glory of the Divine than for personal recognition. Diamonds were often used in temples to adorn idols, or to be used as ornaments for the priestly Brahmin class. Until 1729, India was the sole source of world's diamonds. As in Western cultures, diamonds in India have always been symbols of power and wealth; they could be given to retain or regain a lover's or ruler's lost favor, they could serve as symbols of

tribute or expressions of fidelity in exchange for concessions and protection. Mughal emperors often inscribed names and titles on them, ensuring that the content of the inscription would last as long as the precious stone itself—that is, for eternity. As they have been all over the world since, diamonds were used to acquire military equipment, finance wars, foment revolutions and tempt defections. In an intrigue worthy of a spy novel, one Indian ruler was murdered when he ate diamond powder sprinkled on his food.

Indians recognized early on the diamonds were the world's hardest material, naming it for the deity Indra's magic weapon, the Vajra, which was extremely hard and generated bolts of lightning. In Sanskrit, the word for diamond, *hira* or *hiraka*, also means thunderbolt.

MIDDLE AGES

Throughout the Middle Ages in Europe, it was thought that the best way to identify a diamond was to try to smash it to pieces. Much like the crude medieval methods of determining guilt or innocence, this was not highly effective, and many genuine diamonds were shattered in the process. However, it was during this time that the first diamond was used as in an

187

OPENING SPREAD
LEFT
Diamond ring from Cartier with 50-carat center stone.

RIGHT
102.9-carat Type IIa diamond, owned by LEVIEV.

THIS PAGE
LEFT State portrait of Queen Charlotte,
by Allan Ramsay, 1761-62.

RIGHT Cartier diamond breast ornament
designed as two sprays of lilies, 1906.

BOTTOM LEFT Pair of jeweled ornaments,
French circa 1770.

BOTTOM RIGHT Portrait of Queen
Victoria by Thomas Sully.

LEFT The Cullinan I and Cullinan II diamonds, cut from the largest diamond ever discovered.

RIGHT Crown used for the coronation of Louis XV, 1722. It contains the Regent Diamond and the Grand Sancy.

CENTER Boucheron ring with carved diamond, 1900.

engagement ring. The couple that inaugurated this tenacious tradition was Maximilien of Austria and Marie of Bourgogne, in 1477.

The diamond had such standing in the Middle Ages that it was often given as a gift to further diplomacy, such as the diamond ring given by Edward III of England to the King of France in 1362. Mary Queen of Scots gave Elizabeth I a heart-shaped diamond ring 1584; an accompanying poem expressed her hope for a friendship that "neither suspicion, nor rivalry nor envy nor hatred nor old age" would tear asunder. (It was a nice idea, anyway...)

FRANCE AND THE DIAMOND

Louis XIV, as befits the Sun King, adored diamond buttons and buckles—he bought 118 diamond buttons in 1685 alone. He also filled out his jewel collection with stones from English Crown Jewels bought by Cardinal Mazarin during the English Civil War. He is said to hold the record for wearing the most diamonds carats at once, making him a "shining" example of the aristocracy's adoration of diamonds. Anyone who has been paying attention to the violent passions that diamonds arouse should not be surprised that they contributed, indirectly, to the downfall of the

TOP LEFT AND RIGHT Epaulette
containing 76 diamonds, designed to be
worn on the shoulder to secure a sash,
as seen in portraits of Portuguese
monarchs.

CENTER European ring from the
18th or 19th century.

French monarchy. The Diamond Necklace
Affair is widely recognized as historically
significant for adding to the disillusionment that
the French populace had already begun to feel toward
the monarchy. Banking on Louis XV's indulgence for
his mistress's desires, the Parisian jewelers Boehmer
and Bassenge made a diamond festoon necklace for
Madame du Barry, but the king died before he could
pay for it. The jewelers then offered it to Louis XVI as
a gift for Marie Antoinette, but the queen demurred. A
few years afterward, in 1784, Jeanne de Valois,
Comtesse de la Motte, initiated an elaborate con game
targeting Cardinal de Rohan, who had fallen into

disfavor with Marie Antoinette. Through an
complicated deceit involving forged love letters
and lookalikes, Comtesse de la Motte convinced
Cardinal de Rohan to buy the necklace "on behalf of"
Marie Antoinette. Instead of presenting it to the
queen, however, the comtesse took the necklace to
England and broke it up, selling the precious stones
separately. Despite Marie Antoinette's complete
ignorance of these actions, the general public believed
she had bought it for herself, and the unfortunate
queen was charged in the court of public opinion with
unseemly extravagance.

Napoleon Bonaparte and Josephine understood the

symbolic power of jewelry, resetting the state jewels in Neo-Classical style, in an explicit nod to ancient Greece, Rome, and France's new imperial age. The symbolic effect of diamonds was also taken into account. The Regent Diamond, which had been used as collateral for several loans (the aristocratic equivalent of being in and out of hock), was permanently redeemed by Napoleon, and he wore it on his sword hilt—legend had it that the possessor of that diamond was unconquerable. Unfortunately for Napoleon, this turned out not to be the case. During France's Restoration, the French Crown Jewels were reset in the style of the ancien

régime, emphasizing once again the links of the current establishment to their past role models.

Jewelry was not only the source of rivalry, it was also sometimes the medium through which that rivalry could be conducted. The actresses known as "La Belle Otéro" and Liane de Pougy were both Boucheron devotees, who used the house's jewelry to compete with each other. As the story of their most famous battle goes, La Belle Otéro showed up at Maxim's covered in Boucheron diamonds, a gauntlet thrown down to her rival, a non-verbal "beat this, if you can." When Liane de Pougy arrived, she was

FACING PAGE
Crown created by the jeweler of the
Russian court, set with diamonds,
pearls and a ruby spinel, 1762.

THIS PAGE
LEFT Detail, *Fondation de l'Académie
des Sciences*, H. Testelin, 1667.

RIGHT Van Cleef & Arpels
gold and diamond clip.

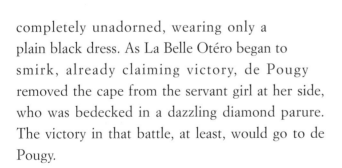

completely unadorned, wearing only a
plain black dress. As La Belle Otéro began to
smirk, already claiming victory, de Pougy
removed the cape from the servant girl at her side,
who was bedecked in a dazzling diamond parure.
The victory in that battle, at least, would go to de
Pougy.

FAMOUS DIAMONDS

Some diamonds go down in history simply because
of their impressive size, color, or intrinsic value.
Others figure in tales of wealth, power, prestige,
class, murder, robberies and unsolved mysteries.

Koh-I-Noor

The Koh-I-Noor, whose name means "Mountain
of Light" in Persian, is the oldest known large
diamond. According to legend, the Koh-I-Noor was
found on the riverbanks next to Karna, newborn son
of the Sun God. After Karna's death, the Koh-I-Noor
was given to the deity Shiva to use as a third eye.
Shiva's assessment of the diamond was prescient: "He
who possesses this diamond will rule the world but
have nothing but sorrow—only a god or a woman can
wear it without fear."
The Koh-I-Noor makes its first appearance in history
in the memoirs of Babur, the first Mogul ruler of India,

when he claimed the great diamond from a vanquished foe. After Babur's death, his son Humayun refused to sell the stone, maintaining, "Such precious gems cannot be bought; either they fall to one by the judgment of the flashing sword, which is an expression of divine will, or else they come through the grace of mighty monarchs." After 1547, the trail of the famous diamond runs cold until 1739, when Nadir Shah captured Delhi. A member of the defeated Mohammed Shah's harem revealed the secret hiding place of the gem to Nadir Shah; it was in Mohammed Shah's turban. Nadir Shah restored Mohammed to the throne and

threw a feast in his honor—then, during the feast, as casually as he could, he suggested switching turbans, a gesture signifying eternal friendship. When he unwrapped his new turban later that night in private, Nadir gave the diamond its name, exclaiming "Mountain of Light!" When Nadir was murdered, the Koh-I-Noor followed the fortunes of the region, landing in the hands of whichever pretender to the throne was currently in power, though never for very long. Through constant internecine warfare, the Koh-I-Noor changed owners again and again. Eventually, when the British claimed power over

194

the Punjab region in India, the Koh-I-Noor was again treated as part of the spoils of war, and given to Queen Victoria. After its perilous, cholera-ridden voyage back to England, some of Victoria's more superstitious subjects were wary of accepting such a gift, pointing to the ominous legends that surrounded it.

In the twentieth century, India, Afghanistan and Iran all made bids to have the Koh-I-Noor returned to their respective governments. However, the history of the stone is so peripatetic, so tortured, that it seems nearly impossible to determine who the rightful owner should be. Seeing as India was the birthplace of the

"Mountain of Light," that country would seem to have the strongest claim, but no less a personage than Jawaharlal Nehru, the first Prime Minister of independent India, renounced his country's claim, saying, "Diamonds are for emperors, and India does not need emperors."

Hope

If many diamonds seem to lead somewhat tumultuous existences, passing from owner to owner under shadow of war, bankruptcy, despair, political upheaval, unthinkable betrayal, and heartbreak the blue diamond now called "Hope" takes the million-dollar

196

prize in the sweepstakes of ruined lives, at least according to the popular myths that have arisen around it. Its early life remains shrouded in mystery until it fell into the hands of Jean-Baptiste Tavernier, a well-known explorer and lover of jewels in the seventeenth century. Tavernier sold the stone, called, at this point, the "Tavernier Blue," to Louis XIV in 1668. In 1792, when Marie Antoinette and Louis XVI were already on the outs with the French populace, the Crown Jewels went on display in the Garde Meuble. This was a mistake for several reasons, not the least of which was the theft of the priceless stones. Here, the history of the Blue Diamond of the Crown comes to an abrupt, shuddering stop. While we contemplate what could have happened to the precious gem during the years of its disappearance, let us note one germane legislative development that occurred in the meantime: in 1804, the French Assembly passed a law of amnesty, decreeing that all crimes committed during wartime would be forgiven after 20 years had passed. Two days after the statute of limitations expired, as if by magic, the Blue Diamond turned up at a London dealer's.

The Blue Diamond led a somewhat reclusive existence until, in 1839, it turned up in the collection of Henry Philip Hope. When Henry Philip Hope died, he left

LEFT Boucheron pectoral ornament created for the Exposition des Arts Décoratifs, 1925.

RIGHT Dragonfly brooch, France, circa 1900.

BOTTOM Green diamond set in a ring pavé with black diamonds, from de GRISOGONO.

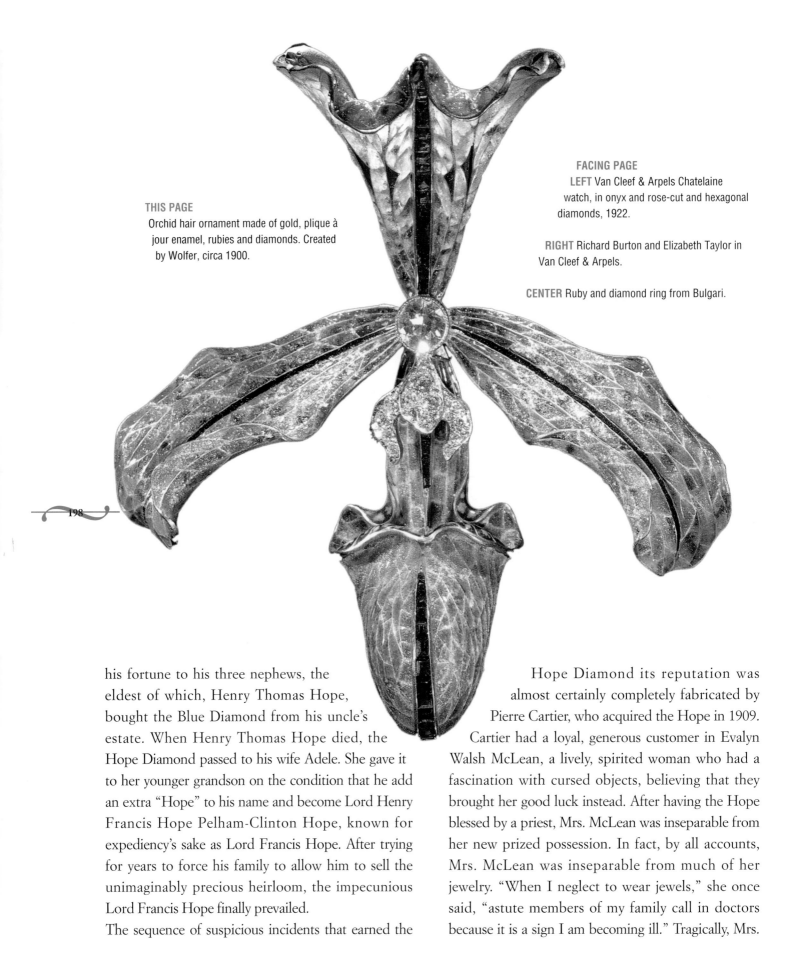

THIS PAGE
Orchid hair ornament made of gold, plique à jour enamel, rubies and diamonds. Created by Wolfer, circa 1900.

FACING PAGE
LEFT Van Cleef & Arpels Chatelaine watch, in onyx and rose-cut and hexagonal diamonds, 1922.

RIGHT Richard Burton and Elizabeth Taylor in Van Cleef & Arpels.

CENTER Ruby and diamond ring from Bulgari.

his fortune to his three nephews, the eldest of which, Henry Thomas Hope, bought the Blue Diamond from his uncle's estate. When Henry Thomas Hope died, the Hope Diamond passed to his wife Adele. She gave it to her younger grandson on the condition that he add an extra "Hope" to his name and become Lord Henry Francis Hope Pelham-Clinton Hope, known for expediency's sake as Lord Francis Hope. After trying for years to force his family to allow him to sell the unimaginably precious heirloom, the impecunious Lord Francis Hope finally prevailed.

The sequence of suspicious incidents that earned the Hope Diamond its reputation was almost certainly completely fabricated by Pierre Cartier, who acquired the Hope in 1909. Cartier had a loyal, generous customer in Evalyn Walsh McLean, a lively, spirited woman who had a fascination with cursed objects, believing that they brought her good luck instead. After having the Hope blessed by a priest, Mrs. McLean was inseparable from her new prized possession. In fact, by all accounts, Mrs. McLean was inseparable from much of her jewelry. "When I neglect to wear jewels," she once said, "astute members of my family call in doctors because it is a sign I am becoming ill." Tragically, Mrs.

McLean's subsequent history lends the most credence to theories of a curse. After a relentless string of personal tragedies, Mrs. McLean succumbed to pneumonia at the age of 60. We can only imagine if she blamed her blithe acquisition of the Hope Diamond for the heartbreaking turn of events that followed it. In April of 1949, Harry Winston bought Mrs. McLean's entire jewelry collection, and presented Hope Diamond to the Smithsonian in 1958. Four years later, the Smithsonian loaned the stone to the Louvre, where it was reunited with the Sancy and the Regent, for the first time since that fateful night of September 16, 1792.

Regent/Pitt Diamond

The Regent's history, unsurprisingly, involves foul play. As the story goes, a slave found the diamond and smuggled it out of India by inflicting a wound on his own calf and hiding the gem among the bandages and torn flesh. He escaped to the sea and took an English sea captain into his confidence, getting murdered and thrown overboard for his trouble. The captain sold the diamond to the merchant Thomas Pitt and later killed himself. Pitt did not know a moment's rest while he had this jewel; he never spent two nights in the same place and traveled in disguise and without notice.

LEFT Brooch by Givenchy, 1954.

RIGHT Mauboussin Lasso
diamond necklace.

CENTER LEVIEV diamond ring.

Tormented by the fear of being
robbed of his treasure, Pitt
tried to sell it, but the jewel was
literally priceless: at 140.5 carats,
it was so much larger than any

other diamond on the market that no one could set a
value on it.

After the death of Louis XIV, when Louis XV was
still too young to rule, the Regent of France, the
Duke of Orleans, bought the Pitt diamond from its
English owner, changing its name in the process, to
the Regent. Louis XV wore it as a shoulder
ornament at his coronation. As with many
other diamonds, the Regent was used again
and again as security on loans for the military,
until Napoleon redeemed most of the diamonds
that had been used as collateral. Throughout the
political turmoil in France, as the country tried to
decide whether it would be monarchy, empire or
republic, the Regent changed hands as well. Though
it stayed with the Bourbons through Napoleon's

Bulgari necklace with diamonds.

return to France and his defeat at Waterloo, by the time of the Second Empire, Napoleon III had presented it to his Empress Eugénie, who wore it often. At the beginning of the Third Republic, the French government decided to sell the Crown Jewels of France, but excluded the Regent and other diamonds of historical interest from the sale. It is now on permanent display in the Louvre.

Orlov

The Orlov diamond's history illustrates the ineffable power diamonds hold over the human mind, and the lengths to which the unscrupulous have gone in an attempt to grab some of that power for themselves. The beginning of the story of the Orlov, which now weighs 189.6 carats, does not begin with "Once upon a time." In fact, it begins with a question mark.

The most widely circulated origin story for the Orlov places it in the eye of an idol in a temple in Srirangam, one of the most sacred shrines in southern India. As the story goes, a French soldier gone AWOL learned that the temple contained a celebrated idol of a Hindu deity with diamond eyes, and he resolved to gouge out these priceless, sightless eyes, however long it took. The major stumbling block he faced was the

prohibition of all Christians in the temple's inner sanctum. The would-be thief opportunistically converted to Hinduism and found a job in the temple itself, eventually becoming the guardian of this innermost shrine. One dark and stormy night, the French faux-Hindu prized out one of the idol's diamond eyes, then lost his nerve and fled before getting the other. The thief then scaled the walls of the temple, swam the river and ran through the jungle before making it to the English army base at Trichinopoly.

From there, the stone made its way to Count Grigory Grigoryevich Orlov, who had caught the eye of Catherine the Great while she was still a Grand Duchess. After the death of her husband Peter (a death orchestrated in part by Count Orlov), Catherine raised Orlov to the rank of count. At one point, Catherine thought of marrying her favorite, but was dissuaded from her plan. Unfortunately for Orlov, the empress cooled in her ardor, and he returned home from a failed diplomatic mission to find himself replaced in her affections. To try to win her back, Count Orlov presented her with the diamond that now bears his name. Though Catherine had it

Bulgari diamond necklace.

mounted in the Imperial Scepter, Orlov did not succeed in regaining his position at court and died not only in exile from his love, but insane.

The Sancy

The Sancy's history spans four centuries, and the widely varying accounts of its story have led Edwin Streeter to call it "the very sphinx of diamonds." There are at least three diamonds that have been called "Sancy," but the authentic Sancy weighs 55.23 carats and owes its name to Nicolas Harnay de Sancy, a

bloody conflicts between Protestants and Catholics of his time by changing his religion to suit the prevailing mood. How the diamond came into Sancy's possession is not known, though several stories have made the rounds over the centuries.

When Henry IV took the French throne, he appointed Sancy to the post of Superintendent of Finance. Sancy repaid this trust by using his own diamond on several occasions as collateral for loans to finance his king's army. At the end of the sixteenth century, Sancy sold it to James I of England. James I took steps to insure that

Salma Hayek wearing de GRISOGONO necklace pavé with white and cognac diamonds.

piecemeal as a financial stopgap, but this policy proved unworkable once his son Charles I took power. Charles I was chronically short of money, and the civil war that broke out during his reign did not help matters. His wife, Queen Henrietta Maria, used the Sancy as collateral on several loans, and when she defaulted on them, the stones were sold to Cardinal Mazarin. Upon his death, Cardinal Mazarin bequeathed both stones to the French Crown, and Marie Antoinette wore the Sancy in more delicate pieces. It was later pawned to raise money for the army (a theme in this diamond's life story).

In 1867, the diamond was exhibited by the French jeweler Bapst, and offered for one million francs, a sum the Maharajah of Patiala was all too happy to pay. Lucien Falize, archaeologist, goldsmith, historian and painter, also briefly owned the diamond before it was purchased by William Waldorf Astor for his wife. Somewhat miraculously, the Astor family managed to refrain from using the Sancy to finance any wars, and it was not until 1978 that William's great-grandson sold it for one million dollars to the Banque de France and Musées de France. It is now in on display in the Louvre, though not for the first time. In 1962, the

Sancy was exhibited next to its old companions the Regent and the Hope Diamond in the Louvre's exhibit "Ten Centuries of French History."

Cullinan

At 3,106 carats, the Cullinan diamond burst into public consciousness as an absurdly large stone—so large, in fact, that the miner who found the extraordinary gem was mocked and disbelieved by everyone at the mine. He insisted, however, on the authenticity of his find until it was proven. Such widespread incredulity can be understood when we consider that the largest diamond found until that point, the Excelsior, weighed 995.2 carats, less than a third of the weight of the Cullinan.

The Cullinan has a blue-white color, and is of exceptional purity. This exceptional stone measured four inches by two and a half inches by two inches, and everyone knew it would be extremely difficult to find a buyer for such a large diamond. Eventually the South African legislature introduced a motion that the Cullinan diamond be bought by the South African government and presented to King Edward VII of England. The motion passed, despite the qualms of those who felt the gift was unseemly in light of the grinding poverty of many South Africans.

The largest gem cut from the Cullinan, the Cullinan I, was dubbed "The Great Star of Africa" by Edward VII, and remained the largest cut diamond

THIS PAGE
LEFT Maggie Cheung in Piaget.

RIGHT Kelly Rowlands in de GRISOGONO.

BOTTOM Bulgari earrings set with diamonds.

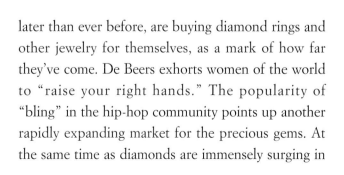

207

FACING PAGE
TOP LEFT Oliva diamond earrings.

TOP RIGHT Audemars Piguet Carnet de bal collection.

LEFT Chopard diamond bracelet.

RIGHT de GRISOGONO rings.

in the world until 1988, when the Golden Jubilee was cut. Unlike so many other diamonds, the Cullinan has led a relatively peaceful existence, neither inciting murder nor being endlessly sold to pay for various wars, nor bringing tragedy down upon all who touched it.

In today's diamond world, we see a confluence of intriguing trends, both stylistically and societally. Diamonds are more popular than ever, that is for certain. No longer does a diamond ring signify the passive acceptance of a lover's gift; well-educated, financially independent women, who are marrying later than ever before, are buying diamond rings and other jewelry for themselves, as a mark of how far they've come. De Beers exhorts women of the world to "raise your right hands." The popularity of "bling" in the hip-hop community points up another rapidly expanding market for the precious gems. At the same time as diamonds are immensely surging in

A Criminal Passion

In the history of many famous jewels lies at least one theft, testament to the irresistible temptation exerted by the divine gifts of the earth. The audacity and cleverness of the thieves often leads to a grudging admiration from those of us who would never dream of such an escapade.

Carlton Hotel, Cannes, August 1994

A gang armed with machine guns burst into the Carlton Hotel jewelry store in Cannes in 1994 just as it was closing, threatening the terrified staff, shooting rounds into the ceiling, and eventually making off with $45 million of jewels. After the excitement calmed down, the police noticed that the ceiling was entirely free of bullet holes...the thieves had been shooting blanks.

Antwerp, March 2007

A man calling himself Carlos Hector Flomenbaum (not his real name) frequented the ABN Amro bank, in Antwerp's diamond district, for almost a year before making his move. "Flomenbaum" bought bank employees chocolates, and slowly gained their trust with his charm. He was such a trusted customer, in fact, that bank employees gave him his own electronic card to access the bank's vault, which he used to steal $28 million of uncut diamonds—over 120,000 carats in all, including 41 blue diamonds and two extremely rare green stones.

Harry Winston, Paris, December 2008

Fourteen months after the storied jewelry store was robbed of $14 million worth of jewels, a gang of jewel thieves that authorities are calling the Pink Panthers struck again, in December of 2008. Just before closing time, four members of the gang—some of them in feminine wigs and scarves—were buzzed in to the exclusive shop, and lost no time in smashing display cases and scooping up precious stones. The whole event took less than 15 minutes, and the thieves slipped back into the night with emeralds, rubies and diamonds worth more than $105 million. Robberies attributed to the Pink Panthers have occurred all over the world, including Dubai, Tokyo and London. Though investigators have nabbed some of the members, many more are still at large, and much of their loot—as is typical with jewel heists—will never be recovered.

Cartier brooch.

popularity, consumers are educating themselves about where their stones are coming from. Just as we have started buying organic food in greater and greater numbers, consumers of jewelry are beginning to insist that their diamonds be "conflict-free." Diamond dealers have created the Kimberley Process as a way to ensure that none of their stones come from war-torn areas, where the presence of diamonds may only aggravate the conflict. Amnesty International encourages consumers to buy diamonds that are certified through the Kimberley Process.

Another emerging trend is the suddenly ravenous taste for colored diamonds. Also known as fancy diamonds, they are beginning to come into their own alongside their transparent cousins as a way to add personality, liveliness and interest to a setting. Pink and yellow fancy are both especially popular, but red and blue diamonds are among the most valuable, because the most rare. The most expensive diamond ever, in dollars per carat, was a stunningly blue 6.04-carat diamond. Sold for $7.98 million, its per-carat price was a shocking $1.32 million! Fancy colored diamonds, though not all as valuable as the new record holder (or even the former record holder, the Hancock Red), are beginning to reach the same

exposure and recognition
as white diamonds.

Black diamonds are also gaining fast,
mostly due to the efforts of Fawaz Gruosi of de
GRISOGONO, a true visionary of black diamonds.
Cut, polished, and given pride of place, black
diamonds easily prove their value to any setting they
inhabit. Where white diamonds symbolize purity and
innocence, black diamonds insinuate sensuality and
sophistication. They are extremely hard to facet and
polish to bring out their brilliance, not giving up
their secrets as easily as other stones might. More
and more jewelry wearers are falling under the spell
of the black diamond, making it a stone to be
reckoned with in years to come.

RUBIES

STONE OF COURAGE, STONE OF PASSION

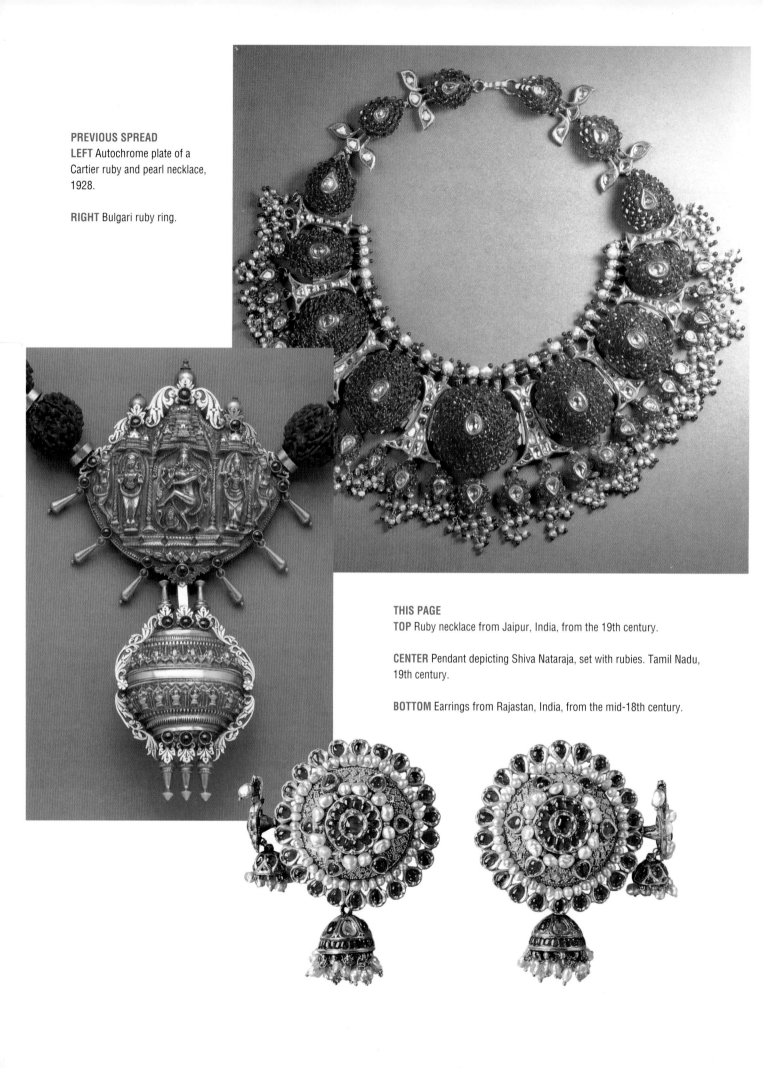

PREVIOUS SPREAD
LEFT Autochrome plate of a
Cartier ruby and pearl necklace,
1928.

RIGHT Bulgari ruby ring.

THIS PAGE
TOP Ruby necklace from Jaipur, India, from the 19th century.

CENTER Pendant depicting Shiva Nataraja, set with rubies. Tamil Nadu,
19th century.

BOTTOM Earrings from Rajastan, India, from the mid-18th century.

TOP A 19th-century cabochon ruby and emerald bracelet made in Jaipur.

BOTTOM "Gimmel" ring, possibly from Germany, 1631.

For Jean-Baptiste Tavernier, famed gem dealer of the seventeenth century, a perfect ruby of six carats or more was the absolute ideal, the supreme prize for him to bring back to the French court of Louis XIV, the Sun King.

Tavernier, who also acquired some of history's most exquisite diamonds, traveled through India and the Far East, making six journeys that could last years. He described the opulent splendor of the gem-obsessed courts, the intricate, months-long haggling sessions that were routine among Eastern traders, and the untouchable, quantifiable perfection of the ruby. "When a ruby exceeds six carats and is perfect," he wrote, "it is sold for whatever is asked for it." Nothing is more precious to us than the blood that flows within our veins, and the ruby is the quintessential manifestation of that in the external world. If blood is first, rubies might be second. Is

215

FACING PAGE
Detail, *The Mystic Marriage of Saint Catherine*, by Lorenzo Lotto.

THIS PAGE
TOP Ruby and emerald belt worth $1 million.

CENTER Armband centerpiece from Northern India in the 17th-19th century.

BOTTOM European ring from mid-18th century, set with a diamond and a ruby.

it any coincidence that the most highly prized and sought-after color, ruby's richest hue of all, is named for the blood that falls from the nostrils of a freshly killed pigeon? It was only in the thirteenth century that the Latin "ruber" lent itself to the striking red corundum for which so many have risked all.

The ruby is rich in symbolic value by virtue of its deep hue. "I'm here!" red announces, pushing its way to the front of the line. Perhaps we are drawn immediately to red because of our shared evolutionary history—the reddest strawberries are the juiciest and most delicious, and if one of our tribe (or our prey) is bleeding, that must take priority over all else. Whatever the reason, it is no accident that rubies, which evoke both the furious heat of passion

TOP LEFT Pair of ruby and diamond earrings, part of the Russian Crown Jewels.

TOP RIGHT Ruby and diamond flower spray for hair or bodice, made for the Russian royal collection.

CENTER Necklace and brooch from Tipu Sultan's treasury at Seringapatam.

and the life-giving properties of fire, have been cherished throughout the ages, associated even today with courage, romantic love and protection from harm (just remember Dorothy Gale's powerful ruby slippers in *The Wizard of Oz*).

In a pure state, corundum is perfectly colorless and transparent. Like perfection in so many forms, this is boring, though extremely rare. The drama begins only when the imperfections are taken into account—the tiny trace of chromium that lends a crimson glow to the crystal. (The combination of titanium and iron leads to the blue flame of the sapphire, ruby's close kin.)

Rubies stand at 9 on the Mohs scale, second only to diamonds in hardness. This sign of

TOP LEFT Brooch-pendant with two-headed eagle that belonged to Duchess Anne of Bavaria. It dates from the mid-16th century.

TOP RIGHT 1603 portrait of the Princess Royal by Robert Peake.

BOTTOM A bracelet given by Queen Elizabeth I to her cousin Lord Hunsdon.

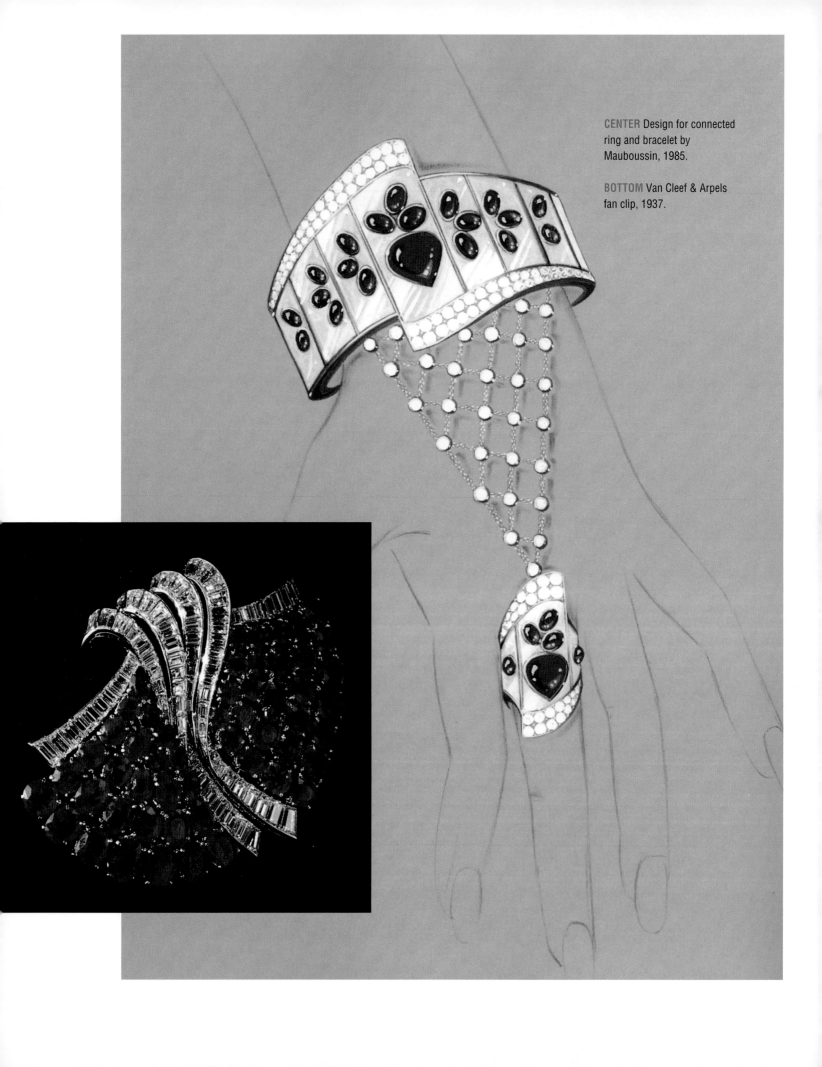

CENTER Design for connected ring and bracelet by Mauboussin, 1985.

BOTTOM Van Cleef & Arpels fan clip, 1937.

TOP Marlene Dietrich wearing Van Cleef & Arpels, circa 1937.

LEFT Cartier palm tree ruby brooch, 1957.

indestructibility lends to the aura surrounding the precious gem; its legends of protection and invincibility possess a certain persuasiveness. If the stone in your pocket can be scratched only by the hardest of substances—a diamond—it seems entirely possible that some of the stone's strength could be transferred to its possessor. When ancient peoples first took a second look at the glittering pebbles in their streams and rivers, and began to wear them as ornamentation or amulets, they used the stones in their natural state. Even if the idea of faceting the stones had occurred to them, they had neither the technique, nor the theory, nor the tools to do it properly. Ancient jewelry shows, however, our ancestors were not immune from the constant drive we have to build upon natural beauty. They ground gems into crude

TOP de GRISOGONO necklace in rubies and white diamonds.

CENTER Bulgari ruby and diamond necklace.

shapes—asymmetric

circles, ovals, squares, rectangles—and shaped them into
cabochons to show off the color. Sand could be used to polish
most gems, except for those—rubies, sapphires, topaz, spinel
and of course diamonds—with a Mohs hardness of over 7. No
fools they, ancient peoples must have remarked upon the effect
of heat upon the gems they found around them, and heat
treatment has been documented as early as 2000 B.C. Heating
rubies heightens their color and dissolves some rutile needles,
making it an effective, inexpensive and nearly universal
method of treating gems.

LEFT Sophia Loren wearing a Van
Cleef & Arpels ruby and diamond
necklace.

RIGHT LEVIEV ruby and
diamond ring.

A PRICE ABOVE RUBIES

HISTORY AND SYMBOLISM

The Bible contains several references to rubies and their value—wisdom is valued "above rubies," as are virtuous women. However, not all stones referred to in ancient writings as "rubies" really were—the ancients classified stones by color, and lumped rubies in with garnets, spinels and other red gems under the term "carbuncles." It was not until first-century Rome that Pliny noted that rubies were in a class of their own, distinguishable from other red stones by their weight and their inclusions.

Rubies—real rubies—are believed to have reached the Mediterranean and Europe in Greco-Roman times, after a long and illustrious history in Asia. The island of Serendip (now Sri Lanka) was so absurdly rich with rubies and sapphires that jewels were said to wash down from the mountains after every heavy rain. Marco Polo wrote that the king of Serendip had a ruby as big as his finger and over four inches long. Rubies were sacred in nearby India, and especially beloved of the Hindu deity Krishna. Those seeking to better their odds in the metempsychosis lottery would

offer rubies at his temples: a splendid stone would guarantee rebirth as an emperor, while lesser rubies led to mere kingdoms. An old belief held that all rubies began pale and transparent, their color deepening and richening over time. People often buried pink sapphires to let them "ripen," and rubies with many flaws and inclusions were said to be "overripe," like a mushy strawberry.

The undisputed champion in the world ruby Olympics would have to be the mountainous region of Upper Burma, in the country now known as Myanmar. The king of Pegu, according to Elizabethan traveler Ralph Fitch, led his troops into battle in battalions that included three hundred thousand men and five thousand elephants, many of which wore gem-encrusted regalia. Fitch also described Pegu's four treasure houses, which were covered in rubies and sapphires and held the royal jewelry collection. Every king, after his coronation, would dismantle his finery and place its gems on top of the treasure houses, for the

TOP LEFT Detail of *The Annunciation*, by Hans Memling.

TOP RIGHT Ruby ring from the mid-18th century.

CENTER Portrait of Sir Henry Guildford, favorite of Henry VIII, by Hans Holbein.

BOTTOM Jewel of enameled gold set rubies and diamonds, probably made in Prague circa 1615.

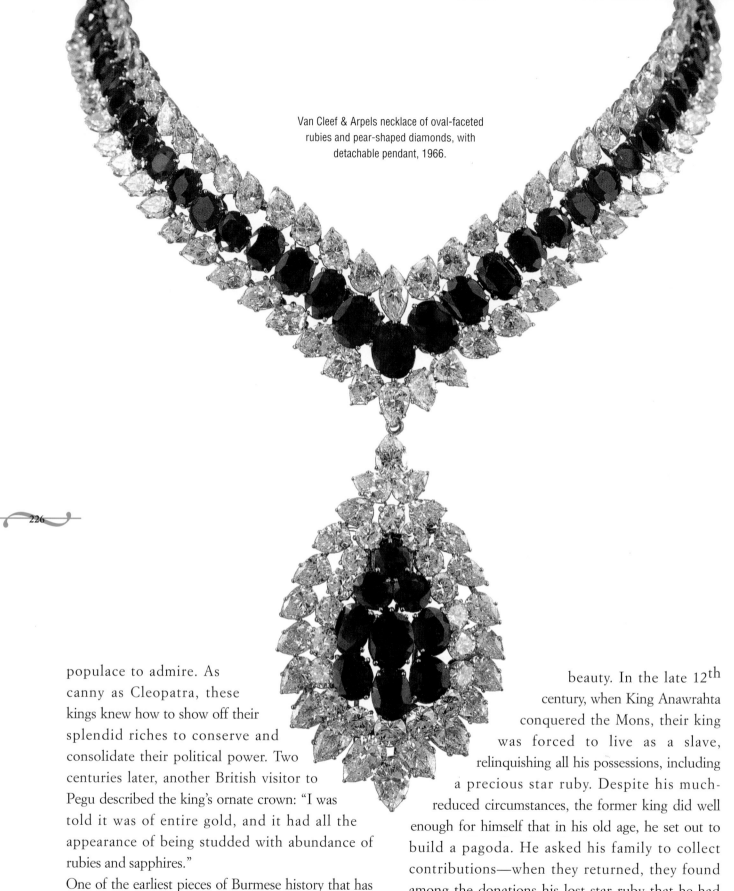

Van Cleef & Arpels necklace of oval-faceted rubies and pear-shaped diamonds, with detachable pendant, 1966.

populace to admire. As canny as Cleopatra, these kings knew how to show off their splendid riches to conserve and consolidate their political power. Two centuries later, another British visitor to Pegu described the king's ornate crown: "I was told it was of entire gold, and it had all the appearance of being studded with abundance of rubies and sapphires."

One of the earliest pieces of Burmese history that has come down to us illustrates the everlasting potency of the ruby as status symbol, valued object and thing of

beauty. In the late 12th century, when King Anawrahta conquered the Mons, their king was forced to live as a slave, relinquishing all his possessions, including a precious star ruby. Despite his much-reduced circumstances, the former king did well enough for himself that in his old age, he set out to build a pagoda. He asked his family to collect contributions—when they returned, they found among the donations his lost star ruby that he had prized so. King Anawrahta had returned it anonymously to finance the pagoda of his former rival.

TOP LEFT Ruby and diamond parure by Chaumet.

TOP RIGHT Double clip brooch by Cartier, 1929.

227

"Secret" ruby ring by Boucheron.

For centuries, Burmese miners toiled under a law that chafed and irritated them: any stones they found above a certain weight had to be offered first to the king. As anyone with the slightest knowledge of human nature could have predicted, this law resulted in the needless destruction of what were likely the largest rubies the world had to offer. Disinclined (to say the least) to offer up this precious bounty to their ruler, who would likely pay quite little for it, miners who came across large rubies would surreptitiously destroy them, breaking them into several smaller stones that could be legally sold to anyone the miner wished. One villager who did turn an exceptional stone over to the king did not get quite the reaction he was

TOP Van Cleef & Arpels ruby, diamond, emerald and onyx bracelet, 1924.

LEFT Photograph from *Vogue*, 1931. The models are wearing Mauboussin.

BOTTOM Cartier sautoir with rubies, pearls and diamonds, 1930.

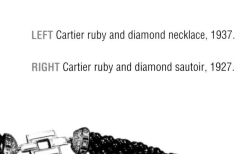

229

looking for. In 1661, a fisherman named Nga Mauk found a splendid ruby in the stream by his village— various accounts place its size anywhere from 61 to over 150 carats!—that shone with a perfectly pure, fluorescent scarlet. He brought it to the king, who according to the story, placed it in a glass of milk. The milk turned bright red, its creamy whiteness no match for the ruby's insistent fire.

Unfortunately for Nga Mauk, the king found himself with an itch he couldn't quite scratch. Though extremely pleased to have acquired such an impressive stone, he couldn't stop himself from wishing he had another stone exactly like the first. A traveling gem dealer heard of the king's wish and presented him with his finest stock, a ruby he had acquired just over Burma's Indian border. Rather than falling at the dealer's feet for fulfilling his latest fondest desire, the king was shocked into silence. This new stone was the same extraordinary color as Nga Mauk's ruby, and a bit larger. The two rubies fit together perfectly—the king soon realized that Nga Mauk had found a truly enormous ruby and split it in two, saving the bigger half to sell for his own profit. Furious, he sent soldiers to Nga Mauk's tiny village,

LEFT Van Cleef & Arpels ruby and diamond necklace.

RIGHT Design in the 1939 catalog for Van Cleef & Arpels, which was never printed due to the outbreak of war.

CENTER Bulgari ruby ring with emeralds and diamonds.

where they locked all the villagers into one house and set fire to the whole community. Such are the passions that rubies arouse among the pampered and powerful. The second ruby, the dealer's ruby, was never seen again. As the renown of rubies spread throughout Europe, so did the Asian beliefs that ascribed to them magical powers. Burmese soldiers carried rubies on their person (or even cut into their skin!) as protection against enemy fire. Like many gems, rubies were thought to have various magical and healing powers— they were the prescription for any circulation disorder

or melancholia, as well as providing or ensuring courage, wisdom, health and good luck (especially in love). Once in Western Europe, rubies also acquired the power to serve as warnings to their owners: if a formerly bright stone turned dull and dark, trouble was ahead. Catherine of Aragon, the first wife of Henry VIII, was said to have received such a warning—though it does not seem to have done her much good. On the other hand, she did survive the marriage, so maybe the warning was a useful one! On a darker note, Elizabeth, the wife of Franz Joseph of Austria, was assassinated on the day

OUTER Mauboussin multicolored gemstone necklace set with rubies, emeralds, sapphires and diamonds, 1967.

INNER Van Cleef & Arpels ring in polished gold with bead motif in faceted rubies, circa 1940.

LEFT Gouache design by René-Sim Lacaze for a commission by Countess Camargo to Van Cleef & Arpels.

TOP Mauboussin necklace in pearls, rubies and diamonds, 1931.

CENTER Rose brooch with 25 petals of rubies set invisibly. Van Cleef & Arpels, 1938.

she left home without her ruby, which she always wore as talismanic protection.

Just as alchemists schemed fruitlessly to turn lead into gold, so have people dreamed of creating their own rubies. Only once in history has anyone succeeded, with near-disastrous consequences for the gem industry. In the 1890s, Auguste Verneil described his technique for growing synthetic rubies, and when he introduced them to the market in 1902, confusion reigned. Consumers had no way of telling natural rubies from the new synthetic ones, and prices plummeted as supply exploded. It took years for natural rubies to regain the prestige—and the prices—they had had before Verneil's innovation.

FAMOUS RUBIES

The ruby's rich rarity makes it even more highly prized than diamonds—a must-have in the crowns and Crown Jewels of royalty all over the world. Interestingly, some of the most famous "rubies" are actually a similar-looking stone, the red spinel. The Black Prince's Ruby has a long history of political intrigue and even treacherous murder behind it, as well as a link to world-changing events, having been

Cartier palm-tree necklace, set with ruby beads
studded with diamonds.

worn by King Henry V during the Battle of Agincourt. Despite its current setting above the Cullinan II diamond in the Imperial State Crown, the noteworthy stone is actually a spinel the size of a chicken egg.

The Delong Star Ruby was involved in an extraordinary jewel heist as daring as it was preventable. After having seen the movie *Topkapi*, which depicted a robbery in Istanbul's Topkapi Museum, Jack "Murph the Surf" Murphy decided that the American Museum of Natural History could be robbed in much the same way. Murph and his accomplices entered through a window that had been left open for ventilation, avoiding the sparse security staff. The only stone that had a burglar alarm was the Star of India, and its battery was dead. The thieves grabbed handfuls of rubies, diamonds and sapphires, including the 100.32-carat De Long Ruby, the Star of India and J.P. Morgan's Midnight Sapphire. Most of the collection was insured, but the three large stones were—literally—priceless, and thus uninsurable. Noting that the famous sapphires and ruby were much too well known to be fenced, and that the thieves had neglected to help themselves to hundreds

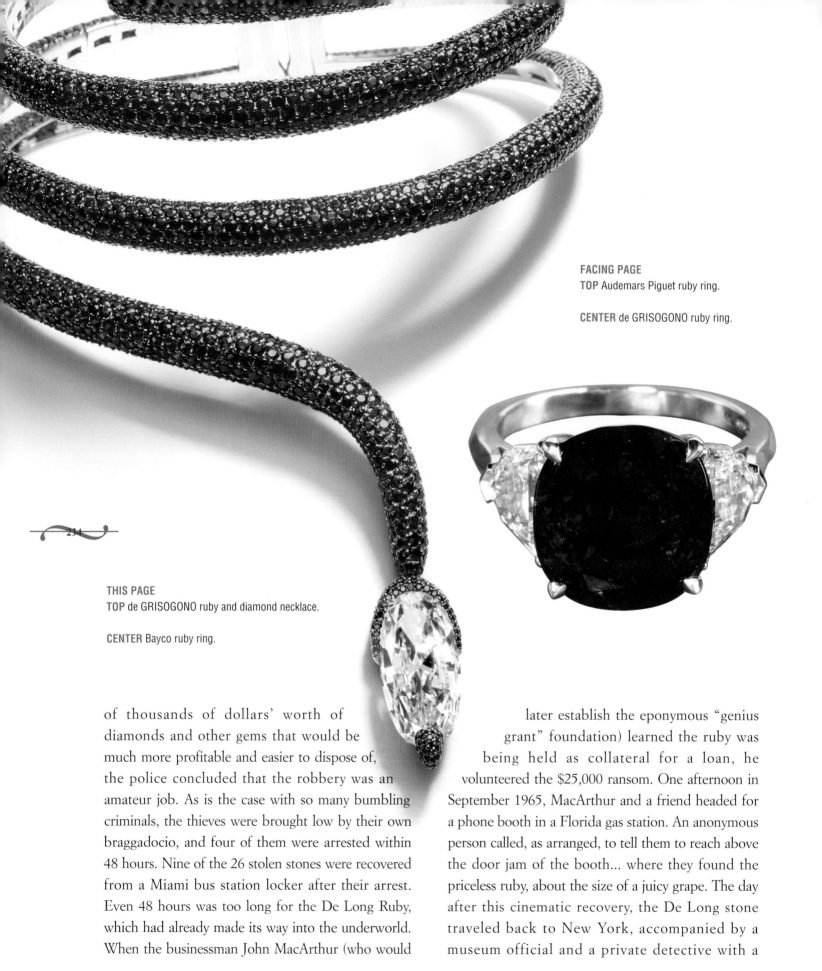

FACING PAGE
TOP Audemars Piguet ruby ring.

CENTER de GRISOGONO ruby ring.

THIS PAGE
TOP de GRISOGONO ruby and diamond necklace.

CENTER Bayco ruby ring.

of thousands of dollars' worth of diamonds and other gems that would be much more profitable and easier to dispose of, the police concluded that the robbery was an amateur job. As is the case with so many bumbling criminals, the thieves were brought low by their own braggadocio, and four of them were arrested within 48 hours. Nine of the 26 stolen stones were recovered from a Miami bus station locker after their arrest. Even 48 hours was too long for the De Long Ruby, which had already made its way into the underworld. When the businessman John MacArthur (who would

later establish the eponymous "genius grant" foundation) learned the ruby was being held as collateral for a loan, he volunteered the $25,000 ransom. One afternoon in September 1965, MacArthur and a friend headed for a phone booth in a Florida gas station. An anonymous person called, as arranged, to tell them to reach above the door jam of the booth... where they found the priceless ruby, about the size of a juicy grape. The day after this cinematic recovery, the De Long stone traveled back to New York, accompanied by a museum official and a private detective with a

briefcase handcuffed to his wrist. While the media circus descended on the private detective and his mysterious briefcase, the museum official slipped in the back door of the Museum of Natural History, having carried his precious cargo from Florida underneath his shirt.

On the whole, of course, famous rubies are better known for their own qualities than their checkered pasts. It is usually an extraordinary size that makes a name for a ruby, such as the Eminent Star Ruby, the largest ruby known. If its size of 6,456 carats makes you gasp, just consider that before cutting, it weighed a whopping 30,000 carats! Cut into an oval cabochon, the gem is considered to be of mediocre quality, though such a compromise is only to be expected, with such an incredible size. The largest known gem-quality ruby weighs in at 250 carats, and shines in splendor on the crown of Charles IV of Luxembourg, King of Bohemia (1316-1378). He had ordered the remarkable gem for the reliquary containing the skull of Saint Wenceslas.

Washington, D.C.'s stately Smithsonian Museum is the worthy home of the 137-carat Rosser Reeves Ruby, the largest fine star ruby in the world. Rosser Reeves, a legendary ad executive who coined M&M's famous slogan, "Melts in your mouth, not in your hand," considered the luminous beauty a lucky charm—his "baby"—and brought it with him everywhere he went—a modern example of the talismanic power ascribed to the ruby since ancient times.

The honor of the most expensive ruby ever goes to the exquisite Alan Caplan Ruby (also know as the Mogok Ruby). The untreated 15.97-carat Burma beauty was sold by Sotheby's of New York in $3,630,000—equaling $227,301 per carat! Famed gemston dealer Graff of London purchased the stone and then reportedly sold it to the Sultan of Brunei for an engagement ring.

LEFT Yvel pin in rubies, pink sapphires and diamonds.

RIGHT Emmanuelle Béart in de GRISOGONO.

CENTER LEFT Liv Tyler in Piaget.

CENTER RIGHT de GRISOGONO earrings.

BOTTOM LEVIEV earrings with rubies and diamonds.

TOP LEFT Bulgari ruby and diamond brooch.

TOP RIGHT Bulgari rings with ruby and diamonds.

CENTER Bulgari ruby and diamond necklace.

EMERALDS

THE COLOR OF LIFE

PREVIOUS SPREAD
LEFT Madonna in Bulgari.

RIGHT de GRISOGONO orchid brooch.

TOP Emerald necklace dating from the
1st century BC, found in Pompeii.

RIGHT Ceramic figure with drilled
emerald from the Sinú culture in
northern Colombia. 500-1000 AD.

BOTTOM 18th-century Iranian snuff
box made of a huge emerald crystal.

TOP Carved emerald ring that belonged to the head of the East India Company in 1797.

BOTTOM Emerald choker from 19th-century Jaipur, India.

*I*t was the most important day of the young woman's life. On December 21, 1959, Farah Diba, a young architecture student, married the love of her life, Mohammed Reza, other wise known as the Shah of Iran.

The wedding took place amid indescribable pomp and luxury, including Farah's adornment of white diamonds from the Iranian Crown Jewels. However, the most opulent celebration was yet to come: eight years later, on October 26, 1967, the shah and his wife were officially crowned. Teheran was illuminated by 60,000 light bulbs and 100,000 roses bloomed on every street corner. Farah's crown, however, put all the other splendid trappings of the occasion to shame.

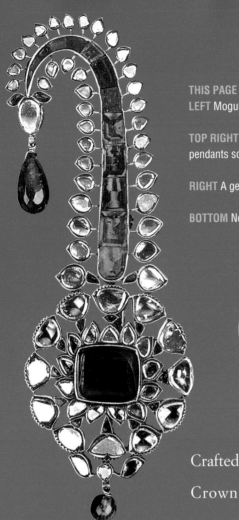

THIS PAGE
LEFT Mogul turban ornament.

TOP RIGHT A pair of antique carved emerald drop pendants sold at Christie's Geneva.

RIGHT A gem-studded box from Iran.

BOTTOM Neo-Renaissance ring by Chaumet.

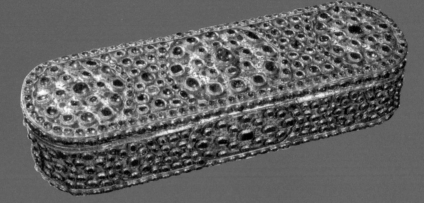

FACING PAGE
Painting of Raja Savant Singh and Bani Thani as the deities Krishna and Radha, circa 1780.

Crafted entirely of emeralds, diamonds and pearls from the Crown Jewels, the crown was instantly legendary. The esteemed house of Van Cleef & Arpels created the piece, as well as the other exquisite jewels with which the new empress wore it: dazzling regal luxuries in diamonds and lush, verdant emeralds. (The emerald was an especially important element in the festivities, as green is the color of Islam.) Public reaction to this marvelous crown was so enthusiastic that Van Cleef & Arpels displayed a replica in its store window, allowing any curious onlookers to take a closer look. Such has been the accustomed fate of the emerald for centuries: used in symbolically laden rituals, privy to the most intimate moments of power, against the skin of

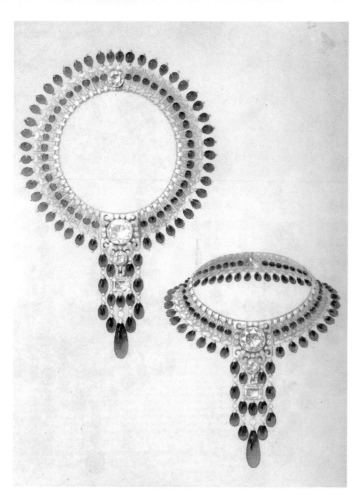

LEFT Two views of a design for an emerald and diamond necklace made by Boucheron for the Maharajah of Patiala in 1928.

RIGHT Cartier bracelet, created in 1930 for the Aga Khan.

BOTTOM Léon Bakst's costume design for the Ballets Russes.

LEFT Emerald and sapphire necklace made by Cartier in 1927 for the Aga Khan.

RIGHT Wife of the Aga Khan, wearing emerald tiara and necklace by Cartier.

BOTTOM Cabochon emerald and diamond bangle by Mauboussin.

the most beautiful and powerful women in the world, and proudly displayed for the delectation of the many. How could it not be one of the most treasured stones in history?

Through the cracks in a city sidewalk, a seed blows, anonymous, unnoticed. Left to its own devices, the seed sprouts and a tiny shoot springs into the world—one more example of the persistence of green. Is it any wonder that green is the color of hope, of renewal and longevity? The verdant green of the emerald suggests all this and more.

Emeralds are among the most coveted precious gems—more expensive, per carat, than diamonds! Perhaps their popularity is due to their soothing, lush

Parure by Piranesi.

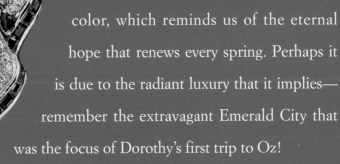

color, which reminds us of the eternal hope that renews every spring. Perhaps it is due to the radiant luxury that it implies—remember the extravagant Emerald City that was the focus of Dorothy's first trip to Oz!

The gorgeous green stones have another association with the otherworldly and the magical: in ancient Roman times, they were said to be the gemstone of Mercury, the god of commerce, journeys—and dreams. It is said that emerald mines cause strange dreams in those sleeping nearby—a link between the Emerald City and the possibility that Dorothy's visit there was just a particularly vivid dream is almost impossible not to draw.

TOP Illustration from *La Gazette du Bon Ton*, 1923.

LEFT Mauboussin earrings set with diamonds, emeralds, rubies and sapphires,

RIGHT Statuette with emerald lode, created circa 1724.

TOP Cabochon-cut emerald necklace by de GRISOGONO.

BOTTOM Diamond and emerald ring by de GRISOGONO.

248

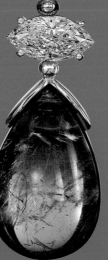

There is a certain paradox contained within every emerald: its unchanging green color, caused by trace amounts of chromium or vanadium in the mineral beryl, evokes new life in a cycle of constant growth, change and even death. Reminiscent of a pliant leaf or a lush, soft bed of grass, the emerald scores an impressive 8 on the Mohs scale of hardness. Despite its durability and hardness, every emerald contains inclusions that undermine its structural integrity—one good whack can ruin a beautiful, valuable stone.

TOP Emerald necklace and sapphire and emerald brooch by Mauboussin.

CENTER Emerald drop earrings by Bulgari.

THE IMPERIAL GEM

HISTORY AND SYMBOLISM

Queen and lover of rulers, perhaps part divinity with an indisputable flair for spectacle and the dramatic entrance (as well as, it must be said, the dramatic exit), Cleopatra could be the most famous emerald lover in all of human history. Her seduction of Julius Caesar owed quite a bit to her frequent awe-inspiring displays of her wealth and power, all carefully orchestrated to play up both her royal blood and feminine wiles. Remember, if you will, her famous entrance on that golden barge.

Contemporary Roman writers thoroughly described her lavish living quarters, which screamed of royal power even though her brother had deposed her. The hallways were clad in ivory, the roof held up with agate columns, the floor tiled in onyx and porphyry, and to top it all off, according to Marcus Annaeus Lucanus:

And fixed upon the doors with labor rare
Shells of the tortoise gleamed, from Indian seas,
With frequent emeralds studded.

PREVIOUS SPREAD
LEFT Art Deco clip with diamonds and emeralds,
made in 1928 for Princess Hohenlohe by Van Cleef & Arpels.

RIGHT Cartier jewelry from the Inde
Mystérieuse collection.

THIS PAGE
LEFT Moroccan earrings from the 17th-18th century.

RIGHT Gold mask with emerald eyes from
Chimú civilization in northern Peru.

CENTER Gold and emerald pendant,
found in Panama.

Emeralds were by far the flashiest, most expensive gems of the ancient world, and Cleopatra's very visible affection for them sent a twofold signal. First of all, like any socialite worth her salt, she had an image to maintain. Her people loved to see their queen decked out in her regalia; anything less would have compromised her popularity and her power. Secondly, emeralds symbolized Egypt, and so the queen killed two (or three) birds with one stone: she could demonstrate her wealth and her patriotism at the same time, all the while playing up her feminine allure. It is only fitting that the most famously adorned woman in ancient history should loan her name to an emerald mine that had been supplying the world with these luscious gems since 2,000 years before she was born. The rich deposits known as Cleopatra's Mines provided almost all of the stones used in the earliest emerald jewelry. Romans fell head over sandals for the intriguing gems, and they had lost none of their dramatic appeal one thousand years after the fall of the Roman Empire, when Marco Polo returned from his legendary trip to China bearing emeralds.

As with all precious stones, emeralds were ascribed near-miraculous healing powers. They could retard or hasten childbirth, prevent snakebite, improve

TOP Byzantine mural from the 6th century depicting Empress Theodora and her court.

CENTER German "gimmel" ring from 1631, set with an emerald and a ruby.

BOTTOM Spanish colonial emerald brooch, with a diameter of 6 cm.

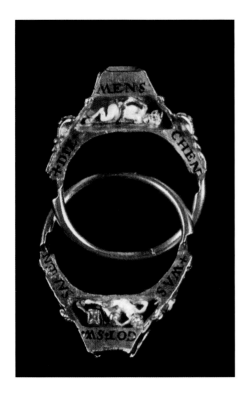

Van Cleef & Arpels sautoir with a faceted
53.85-carat center emerald, from 1975.

memory, cure dysentery, prevent epilepsy and stop bleeding.

In what is now Colombia, unrivalled source of the world's finest emeralds, the indigenous people used the gems in jewelry and religious rituals for millennia before the rapacious conquistadores arrived. On the Peruvian coast, there was a tribe whose people worshipped an emerald rumored to be as large as an ostrich egg. The priests would parade it through the streets on holy days, showing it to pilgrims who had walked long distances to see it. The priests built up quite a healthy collection of emeralds by convincing their people that the huge stone had daughters (the smaller emeralds), and the offering that would please it the most was to be reunited with its children. Long after the "mother" stone had disappeared, the smaller offerings were held in the temple, until the Spanish arrived and demanded to know their source. These emeralds had come from what is now called Chivor, but as the Europeans soon learned, there were even better stones to be found in Muzo.

The Muzos started using emeralds as jewelry and in religious ceremonies sometime around 500 A.D. One local legend of the jewels' origin involves Fura and Tena, the region's first people, who were granted

LEFT Bracelets illustrated in a
Van Cleef & Arpels catalog, 1925.

RIGHT Barbara Hutton wearing an emerald
tiara by Cartier. Photograph by Cecil Beaton.

CENTER Cartier emerald necklace
commissioned by
Merle Oberon in 1938.

Cartier parure in emeralds, sapphires, rubies,
diamonds and gold.

eternal youth on the condition of eternal fidelity. As they so often are in legends like these, this single, all-important rule was broken by Fura, who fell in love with a handsome blond, blue-eyed foreigner named Zarbí. Like the picture of Dorian Gray, Fura's guilt showed on her person, as she began to age for the first time. Tena immediately understood what had happened, and what would have to follow. Though the sin had been hers alone (sound familiar?), the god Are punished them both. Tena killed himself, leaving Fura to sit by his decomposing corpse and bathe it with her endless tears. Those torrents of tears

became the region's emeralds, and Fura's screams of pain and sorrow became brightly colored butterflies. Are took pity on the couple and turned them into the two mountains that stand over the region today.

Though the European arrivals did not value emeralds as highly as other cultures did, they recognized their importance for trade and often exchanged them for more gold. Taking advantage of the Spaniards' relative gemological ignorance, the native Colombians told them that real emeralds would not shatter when hit with a hammer. Of course, due to emeralds' natural

LEFT Emerald and diamond tiara worn at the coronation of George VI in 1936 and Elizabeth II in 1952.

RIGHT Queen Sylvia of Sweden.

Cartier emerald necklace commissioned by Lady Granard in 1932. The center stone weighs 143.23 carats.

inclusions, they can be quite fragile, despite their hardness; the invaders smashed countless emeralds to smithereens before catching on. The flood of high-quality Colombian emeralds on the European market threw the nascent trade into disarray. Royals are often noted for their extravagant tastes and lust for jewels, but even they could not keep up with Colombia's extraordinary output, and as the rarity of emeralds decreased, so did the implied status of those who wore them.

History would change that. Napoleon Bonaparte was fascinated by the green stone: the association it held with ancient Rome mirrored his own ambition to recapture the triumphs of the Romans. Besides, green was his favorite color! When Napoleon swept through Rome and looted the Vatican, one of the treasures he spirited away was a large green emerald that he held onto for several years. He eventually returned it to Pope Pius VII, in a gesture that was both magnanimous and insulting: the gorgeous gem was set in a lavishly decorated tiara—which did not fit on the pope's head.

LEFT Emperor and Empress of Iran at coronation in 1967.

RIGHT Crown of Empress Farah Diba Pahlavi, designed by Van Cleef & Arpels.

BOTTOM Boucheron's design for the crown of Empress Soraya, 1951.

Emeralds were often Napoleon's choice for more personal gifts as well. He gave a splendid emerald necklace to the Empress Josephine, which she was later painted wearing. According to the artist who painted her, Jean-Baptiste Isabey, when she came to sit for her portrait, Josephine had just found out that Napoleon was going to divorce her. She insisted on wearing her emerald jewelry, which represented a happier time in their relationship—but there was also a deeper significance, of which Josephine was aware. Some English women who had been left by their husbands wore green to symbolize their sad state; as Josephine said to Isabey, "I want [the emeralds] to represent the underlying freshness of my grief." That same necklace was stolen not long after Isabey painted Josephine's portrait. Afraid of being accused of engineering the theft himself, Napoleon ordered the director of police to exert all his efforts to find it. The police department turned to legendary criminal Eugène François Vidocq for help, and he tracked down the missing finery in three days. Napoleon gratefully pardoned him, and Vidocq later became one of France's most famous detectives. In ways small

THIS PAGE

TOP Boucheron design for an aigrette set with diamonds, rubies and engraved, pear-shaped emeralds, 1928.

CENTER Boucheron design for a belt set with cabochon emeralds and diamonds on woven gold.

BOTTOM 142.2-carat emerald pendant from Cartier. The emerald is carved with an Islamic prayer.

FACING PAGE

TOP The famous Topkapi dagger.

CENTER The Maharajah of Dhranghadra wearing a Cartier emerald turban ornament, 1935.

BOTTOM Emerald and ruby globe that Nasir ud-Din Shah had made to reduce palace theft.

and large, emeralds have a way of changing the world.

Napoleon's affection for the stone ensured that demand would more than catch up with supply. When Napoleon made green the "imperial" color, those eager to express their solidarity (or simply catch the emperor's favor) contributed to the emerald's immense popularity between 1852 and 1871. Just as Princess Diana's sapphire engagement ring sparked interest in that gem, Princess Mary's choice of an emerald engagement ring in 1922 set off an emerald boom in 1920s England. After centuries of playing

second (or even third) fiddle to diamonds and rubies, emeralds became the most expensive gem per carat in the late years of the 19th century.

FAMOUS EMERALDS

One of the most tenacious legends of the Middle Ages concerned Prester John, the mythical Christian king of a realm in the East. It was said that he carried a scepter with an enormous emerald in it, as evidence of his vast wealth. The rumor of a Christian stronghold in the middle of what medieval Christians considered

enemy territory was sufficient to spark crusade after crusade. Other emeralds, though their reputation was less fantastic (if more reality-based) have similarly captured the public imagination and inspired far-fetched fantasies of ownership. Though rulers would often instigate wars as an excuse to seize another sovereign's jewels, occasionally the opposite was true: a valuable gift could seal an otherwise tenuous alliance. In the 18th century, Persian ruler Nadir Shah gave Turkish Sultan Mahmut I an Indian-made gem-studded gold throne. Not to be outdone in generosity, the sultan commissioned a gift in return: the 13-inch Topkapi Dagger, whose hilt is studded with three enormous emeralds, a fourth emerald covering a hidden watch. Unfortunately for the budding friendship, as the dagger was on its way to its intended recipient, the emissaries learned that Nadir Shah had been assassinated. As the purpose for their trip was now moot, the emissaries returned to Turkey with their precious cargo, which is now on display in Istanbul's Topkapi Museum.

Despite the loss of the breathtaking Topkapi Dagger,

263

the Iranian treasury—where national treasures live as collateral for Iran's monetary system—contains more than its share of spectacular emeralds. Among the precious paintings, clocks, urns and other treasures in the Melli Bank Museum lie jeweled thrones, objets d'art—and, of course, crowns. The crown worn by the last shah of Iran and husband of Farah Diba, Mohammed Reza Pahlavi, is bedecked with thousands of diamonds and hundreds of pearls, but gives pride of place to five large emeralds, which total almost 200 carats! The shah's father had chosen emeralds both to recall the Persian kings who ruled from the third to the seventh century, and because green is the color of Islam.

The most dazzling exhibit in the Iranian treasury, however, is neither a crown, nor a throne, nor regal finery. In the 1860s, Shah

264

Nasser ud-Din was enraged by his slowly dwindling (though still enormous) store of precious gems. As long as the stones were lying around loose, her realized, they would be a constant, irresistible temptation to petty thieves. As a kind of anti-theft cum inventory system, he commissioned his jewelers to create a stunning globe, made entirely of gold, with the continents depicted in rubies and the vast seas in emeralds. Not only were the royal jewels now safe from harm, but they could easily be displayed and admired in all their ostentation.

All crowns are created for ceremonial purposes, but the Crown of the Andes has never been worn by any ruler. It was crafted by the people of Popayan, Colombia, after a plague that had originated in Ecuador stopped short of their borders. The people attributed their great good fortune to a combination of two mystical elements: the emerald's well-known ability to protect against illness, and the intervention of the Virgin Mary, who prevented the plague-carrying vermin from reaching their city. Twenty-four goldsmiths and gem workers labored for six years, creating the crown that would be the symbol of their gratitude to the Virgin out of

Cartier jewelry.

268

100 pounds of gold and 447 emeralds that were originally owned by the Incas. The largest emerald was named Atahualpa, for the Inca king murdered by Pizarro. The Crown was first presented to the public in a religious parade in 1599. Over the course of its checkered history, it has been stolen, recovered, and sold to raise money for humanitarian endeavors. Eventually an anonymous American foundation purchased it, and the Crown of the Andes remains there to this day.

The Mogul Emerald is one of the world's largest, weighing in at 217 carats. Like so many of India's finest emeralds, it has its origins in Colombia, and like many emeralds owned by Indian royalty, it has been beautifully engraved, carved with tiny flowers and a Shiite prayer. Emperor Aurangzeb, who had tiny holes drilled in the stone so that it could be sewn to his sleeve or turban, was the last great Mogul ruler in India.

Most uncut emeralds are six-sided, but the Patricia Emerald, currently at New York's Museum of Natural History, has twelve sides—just one more example of its stunning uniqueness. At 632 carats, the Patricia Emerald is one of the largest uncut

TOP LEVIEV emerald and diamond necklace.

RIGHT Naomi Campbell in de GRISOGONO.

BOTTOM Emerald ring by de GRISOGONO.

emeralds in the world, and its quality is remarkable. It was named for the daughter of the owner of the Chivor Mine, in the Colombian Andes, where this extraordinary stone was found. For many years, the Duke of Devonshire Emerald was the largest uncut emerald in existence, weighing in at 1,383.95 carats. Emperor Dom Pedro of Brazil gave it to the sixth Duke of Devonshire, who led a life of freewheeling bachelordom and accepted the generous gift for his family's collection in 1831. The deep green gem is completely transparent in some areas, and quite flawed in others.

SAPPHIRES

THE CELESTIAL GEMSTONE

PREVIOUS SPREAD
Sapphire, emerald and diamond necklace by Cartier.

THIS PAGE
TOP LEFT The Knyvett Seal,
set with a large sapphire
engraved with the coat of arms
of the Knyvett family.
Made in England circa 1580.

CENTER Detail, *The Three
Youngest Daughters of George
III,* by John Singleton Copley.

BOTTOM Early 7th-century
Byzantine bracelet, excavated
in Upper Egypt.

274

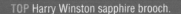

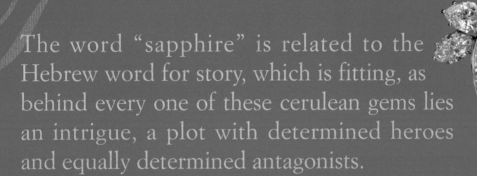

The word "sapphire" is related to the Hebrew word for story, which is fitting, as behind every one of these cerulean gems lies an intrigue, a plot with determined heroes and equally determined antagonists.

The Old Testament relates that in the days before the great flood that was to (almost) wipe out humanity, God sent Noah a book with "all the secrets and mysteries of the universe." This book contained everything that anyone could possibly want to know, from medicinal secrets to the tricks for controlling demons. This book, which was the most valuable object in the world, was made of sapphire, a stone that has symbolized power and knowledge ever since. In fourteenth-century England, every bishop was given a sapphire ring when he took office. The deep blue color of the ring symbolized the powers of Heaven, divine forces that were now to operate through the Church's new representative.

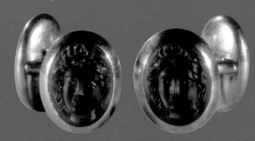

TOP LEFT Boucheron design for necklace
in sapphires and diamonds, 1878.

TOP RIGHT Boucheron Salome bracelet of sapphires
on blackened gold.

BOTTOM Portrait of Princess Bagration, one of
Chaumet's loyal customers, by François Gérard.

TOP LEFT Van Cleef & Arpels sapphire and diamond bracelet, 1921.

TOP RIGHT The 98.57-carat Bismarck sapphire, donated to the Smithsonian by Countess Mona von Bismarck.

BOTTOM French chalcedony ring with gold and sapphires, circa 1930-40.

As shockingly different as they appear, the fiery ruby and the coolly elegant sapphire are as close as sisters. The sapphire's rich blue comes from the presence of titanium and iron in corundum—though it is possible for corundum to be completely colorless, it very rarely is. Sapphires come in all colors of the rainbow: a minute amount of a particular element determines with which stunning hue we will be graced. Iron alone leads to a sunny yellow sapphire, and vanadium creates a purple sapphire. Besides the archetypical blue color, sapphires are also often found in hues of pink, peach, orange, lavender, purple, green and a striking pink-orange known as *padparadscha* (Sinhalese for "lotus flower").

Just as "ruby" derives from the Latin word for red, sapphires get their name from the Latin *sapphiros*, a

TOP RIGHT Cartier panther clip brooch sold to the Duchess of Windsor, featuring a 152.35-carat cabochon sapphire. Made in 1949.

LEFT Van Cleef & Arpels diamond and sapphire necklace with 38-carat sapphire pendant, 1960.

BOTTOM Mauboussin sapphire brooch from the 1970s.

derivation of the Greek word for blue, and in ancient times, any attractive blue stone was called a sapphire. Researchers have surmised that what the Bible refers to as "sapphire" was actually most likely to be lapis lazuli. The name that Romans assigned to actual blue sapphires, confusingly enough, was hyacinth. Sapphires are mined all over the world, from "Gem Island" of Sri Lanka to Tanzania to the alarmingly productive mines of Australia. The most surprising find might be in our own backyard: Montana produces stunning gems, which were originally disdained, discarded and viewed as an impediment to the serious business of gold mining. That is, of course, until one enterprising miner sent a packet to Frederick Kunz, a New York gemologist in the 1880s, and received a handsome check in return. A delicate cornflower hue, which

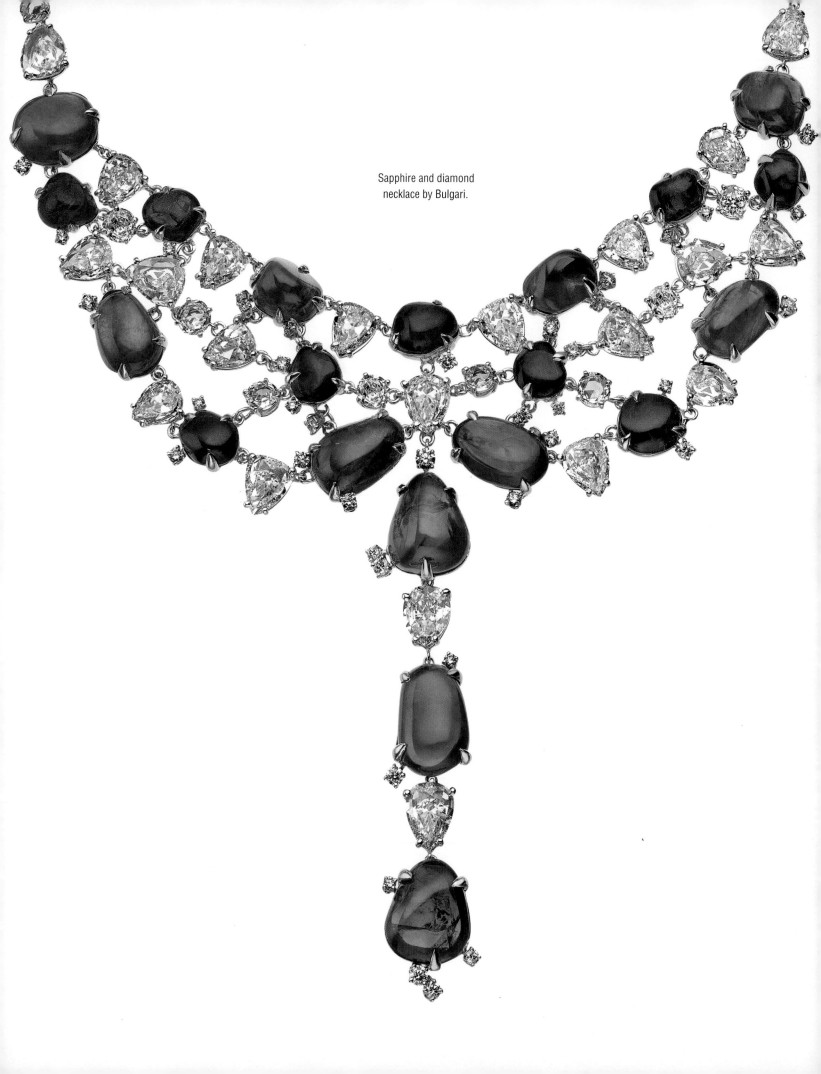

Sapphire and diamond
necklace by Bulgari.

holds its color in low light, is the trademark of Yogo Gulch, Montana's most famous mine.

Though a perfect diamond contains no flaws or inclusions, these can actually make sapphires and rubies even more beautiful and mysterious. Microscopic rutile needles within the stone dissolve upon being heated, but if left alone, they occasionally align along perfect 60-degree angles. When this happens, the play of light on these interior inclusions forms a six-rayed star pattern within the gem— and no matter how many times the stone is cut in half, each smaller star sapphire shows the same perfect pattern. Many of the most famous rubies and sapphires are stars.

THE STONE OF DESTINY

HISTORY AND SYMBOLISM

Sapphire is known as the "celestial" gemstone, due to its uncanny resemblance to the sky at any time of day. Ancient Persians held that the Earth itself rested upon a giant sapphire whose hues were reflected in the sky. According to this belief, sapphires found in the ground are chips from this giant pedestal. The Vatican elite, in allusion to the stone's symbolism of purity of purpose and of deed, wore sapphires in their rings and on their scepters. Like many precious stones, sapphires were believed to protect the wearer from harm. In the

Middle Ages, sapphires were used to treat eye ailments and as an antidote to poison; medieval lapidaries also held that sapphires in water would reveal the unknown to the questioning eye. In India, sapphire was used as a sort of mineral antivenin: an elixir made by immersing the gem in water was believed to counteract the bites of snakes and scorpions. Eastern cultures believe the gem wards off evil. In the West, the star sapphire is also known as the Stone of Destiny: the star's three rays represent Faith, Hope and Charity.

Wearing sapphire was said to lead to exceptional clarity of mind. Is it any wonder that the Titan Prometheus (whose name meant "forethought") was said to wear a sapphire ring? The ring of Prometheus was actually a form of punishment for him—after stealing divine fire from the gods to bring to mortals, the Titan's furious fellow deities sentenced him to be chained to a rock for all eternity, an eagle tearing out his liver every day, the organ regenerating itself every night. After a few eons of this torture, Zeus killed the eagle, but insisted that Prometheus wear a ring made from his chains and the mountain's rock, to remind him never to challenge the gods again. The ring was forged in the iron of the chains, and set with a sapphire from the mountain. Greek mythology holds that this was the first ring ever created.

When consulting the famously cryptic Oracle of Delphi, ancient Greeks wore sapphires, which not only helped to open the psychic gateways between this world and the next, but hopefully aided the advice-seekers to make sense of the oracle's enigmatic pronouncements. It was also believed that sapphires would help their wearers find the solutions to any knotty challenges.

OPENING SPREAD
LEFT Cartier necklace commissioned in 1936 by Daisy Fellowes.

RIGHT Detail, *The Venus of Urbino* by Titian.

FACING PAGE
Sapphire and diamond breast ornament by Cartier, 1907.

THIS PAGE
TOP LEFT Gouache design for a necklace of sapphires and diamonds, circa 1932 by Van Cleef & Arpels.

TOP RIGHT 57.63-carat cabochon sapphire brooch by Cartier, 1924.

CENTER Mauboussin advertisement in *Harper's Bazaar*, December 1930.

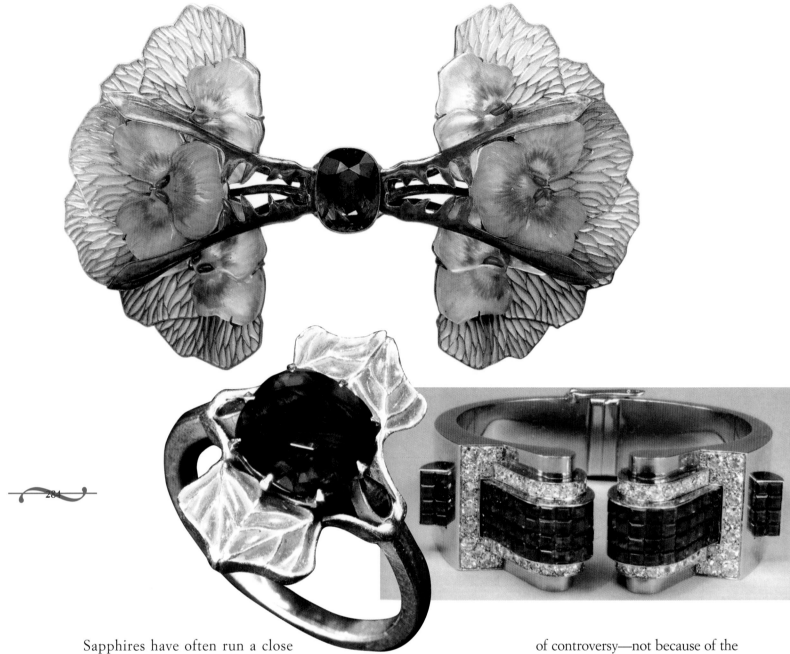

Sapphires have often run a close second to diamonds as the stone of choice for engagement rings, perhaps because they symbolize truth, sincerity and faithfulness, three crucial aspects of any long-term relationship. (Their use may also be linked, in a somewhat underhanded way, to the 18th-century belief that a sapphire could detect feminine fidelity. If the wearer was unfaithful, the superstition held, her sapphire would change color.) The engagement ring that Prince Charles gave to Princess Diana featured a brilliant center sapphire and reawakened mass demand for the lovely stone. The ring was from Garrard Jewelers and aroused a bit of controversy—not because of the sapphire itself, which everyone agreed was exquisite. Nor was it the jeweler—Garrard had been a royal jeweler for centuries, and the pristine quality of its stones was undisputed. What the young couple had done, however, was to choose a "ready-to-wear" ring directly from the Garrard catalog, instead of asking for a custom design, as most royal customers were (and are) wont to do. Though shocking at first, this choice attested to the refreshing breath of unpretentious glamour that Princess Di would bring to the somewhat stuffy royal family.

The steady popularity of sapphires over the centuries

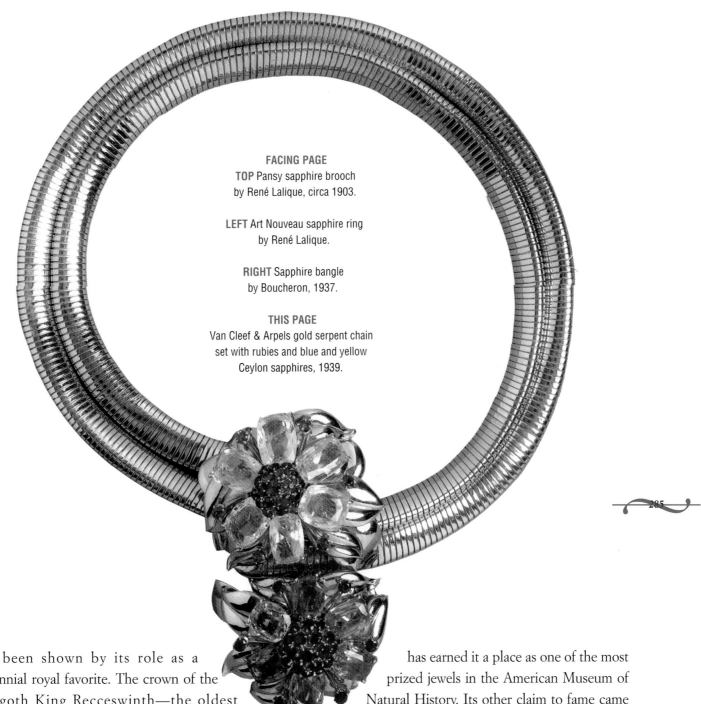

285

has been shown by its role as a perennial royal favorite. The crown of the Visigoth King Recceswinth—the oldest European crown that has survived—contains sapphires, and their association with royalty continues to this day: the so-called "Wedding Ring of England" has been used in every English coronation (save Queen Victoria's) since 1831.

FAMOUS SAPPHIRES

The handsome Star of India, cut as a cabochon to highlight its asterism (what some might call "star" quality), weighs an impressive 563.35 carats; its size has earned it a place as one of the most prized jewels in the American Museum of Natural History. Its other claim to fame came in 1964, when it was stolen, along with the De Long Star Ruby and 24 other precious stones, in a daring heist. The Star of India was quickly recovered.

The Stuart Sapphire, like many Crown Jewels, has a history stretching back hundreds of years. Its early history is shrouded in obscurity, but it was definitely among the jewels King James II of England carried with him when he fled to France, and James passed it down to his son Charles Edward. Once the Stuart cause was definitively over, the 104-carat stone was

286

cut diamonds weighing 16 carats in total.

Cartier first came across Queen Marie of Romania's Sapphire in 1913, when it was added to seven other sapphires to create a stunning sautoir. Later that year, the necklace was altered, dropping the smaller stones to focus on the magnificent sapphire drop, attaching it to a pendant ring of calibré-cut sapphires. In 1921, King Ferdinand of Romania fell in love with the sumptuous gem, now suspended on a diamond necklace, and bought it for his consort, Queen Marie, then in her mid-forties. At the King's coronation the following year, the Queen wore her 478-carat sapphire necklace, which perfectly complemented her equally stunning sapphire tiara. Queen Marie of Romania's sapphire is the largest known faceted sapphire.

The unique Ruspoli Sapphire is renowned not so much for what it has much of, as it is for what it has little of: nearly flawless, the gem was cut with only six facets, like a huge sapphire prism. Now in the Paris Musée au Jardin des Plantes, the Ruspoli took a circuitous route there, narrowly avoiding disaster. In the 17th century, a Roman prince named Ruspoli sold

given to King George III. The sapphire was set in Queen Victoria's State Crown, just below the Black Prince's Ruby, but when the stones were reset in a nearly identical new crown, the Stuart Sapphire moved to the back of the crown, where it remains to this day.

Profoundly beautiful color, imposing size and lack of inclusions so rarely coincide that any stone in which they do is an instant classic. The Logan Sapphire, named for Mrs. John Logan, is a flawless stone of rich blue color. It is the second-largest blue sapphire known, tipping the scales at 423 carats. Its brooch setting sets it off to absolute perfection, with the remarkable sapphire bordered by 20 round brilliant-

TOP RIGHT Bulgari sapphire necklace.

CENTER Bond girl Olga Kurylenko in de GRISOGONO.

the unusual gem to a dealer who subsequently sold it to Louis XVI sometime around 1691. It was the third most prominent gem in the French Crown Jewels, a fame that turned to notoriety once the Revolution came. In 1796, the revolutionary government allowed the Museum's director, M. Daubenton, to select a few gems for the Museum's educational displays. Cleverly reclassifying the precious gem as a "sapphire crystal," Daubenton saved the extraordinary sapphire for future generations.

Despite its name, the color of the Midnight Star

Sapphire is more reminiscent of the sky just after sunset, as the twilight creeps in—a rich purple-violet. With a weight of 116.75 carats, it may be the largest star sapphire of its color in the world. The recorded history of the Midnight Star dates back to the late 19th century, when it joined the dazzling jewel collection of financier J.P. Morgan, who also owned the famous Star of India. Morgan donated the jewels to the American Museum of Natural History in 1900, and they were among the jewels stolen (and quickly recovered) in 1964's robbery.

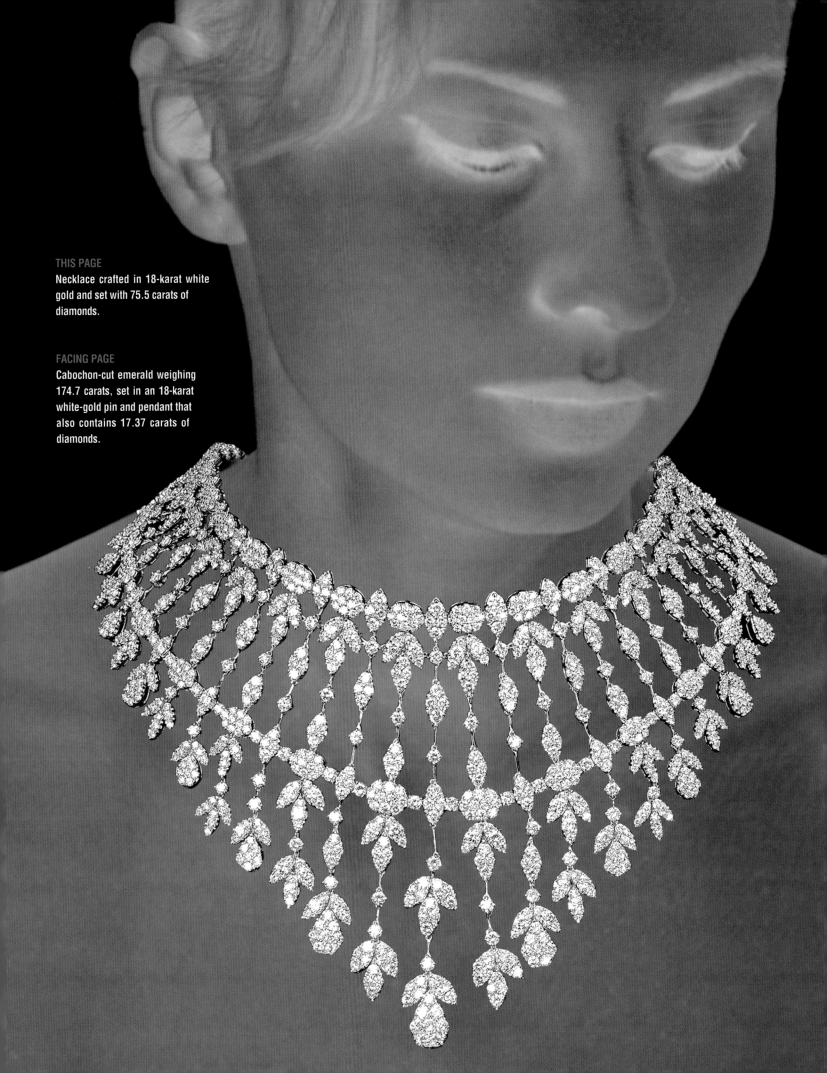

THIS PAGE
Necklace crafted in 18-karat white gold and set with 75.5 carats of diamonds.

FACING PAGE
Cabochon-cut emerald weighing 174.7 carats, set in an 18-karat white-gold pin and pendant that also contains 17.37 carats of diamonds.

Andreoli

In the early years of the twentieth century, one man began a tradition of excellence that continues to this day. Abraham Hadjibay moved to India as a young man, first trading in the sumptuous, opulent carpets of what was then Persia. Using his natural business savvy, the young Abraham soon moved into an even more luxurious field. The legendary diamond mines of India proved a fertile resource for the young Hadjibay, whose father had once sold gems to the tsars of Russia. Abraham eased out of the carpet industry to start a gem business, slowly but surely evolving into one of the world's busiest traders in precious stones. His son, Jack Hadjibay, grew up in the business, so it was a natural, even inevitable step for him to go from trading gems to designing priceless jewelry.

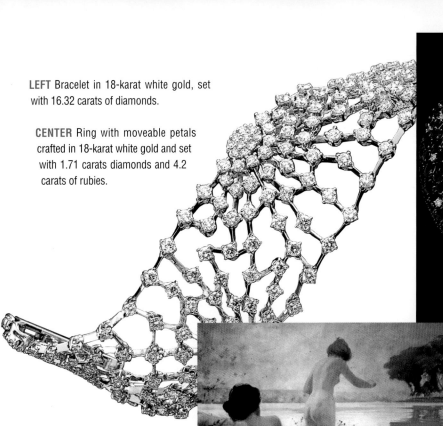

LEFT Bracelet in 18-karat white gold, set with 16.32 carats of diamonds.

CENTER Ring with moveable petals crafted in 18-karat white gold and set with 1.71 carats diamonds and 4.2 carats of rubies.

Necklace in 18-karat white gold, set with 17.41 carats of diamonds and 91.99 carats of rubies, paired with 18-karat white-gold earrings that are set with 5.54 carats of diamonds and 20.39 carats of rubies.

Andreoli

292

Though he was content in the gem business, handling the world's most exquisite stones and working alongside his father, Jack had the urge to experiment a little, to push his creative limits. He created a diamond and platinum parure—necklace, earrings and bracelet—and quietly sat back to see what the reaction would be. Within three days, every piece had been snatched up, and his customers clamored for more.

Never one to disappoint, Jack opened a jewelry factory and named it for the Andreolis, a noble Italian family that had taken his father under their wing when he first arrived in Italy. Aristocratic clients flocked to the sophisticated pieces, and Andreoli provided jewelry to royalty all over Europe and beyond, including the royal families of Greece, England, and Iran. "At first," confides Jack, "all the royalty wanted big pieces for their queens, but tastes have evolved to favor something more subtle." Dazzling or demure, Andreoli has the design to suit every preference. Later on, Andreoli expanded its

clientele. To appeal to a younger jewelry lover, Jack began to experiment with bridal jewelry and semi-precious stones, inventing a look that remained true to its classic roots while becoming more playful and youthful.

Something truly remarkable occurs in Andreoli's headquarters in Valenza: a team of the best designers from all over the world gathers together to come up with hundreds of designs, from which Jack chooses a few to produce—"the

Ruby and diamond parure including: an 18-karat white-gold necklace set with 41.6 carats of diamonds and 117.55 carats of rubies, an 18-karat white-gold bracelet set with 15.8 carats of diamonds and 79.17 carats of rubies, an 18-karat white-gold ring set with 1.72 carats of diamonds and 5.41 carats of rubies, and a pair of 18-karat white-gold earrings that are set with 3.31 carats of diamonds and 21.71 carats of rubies.

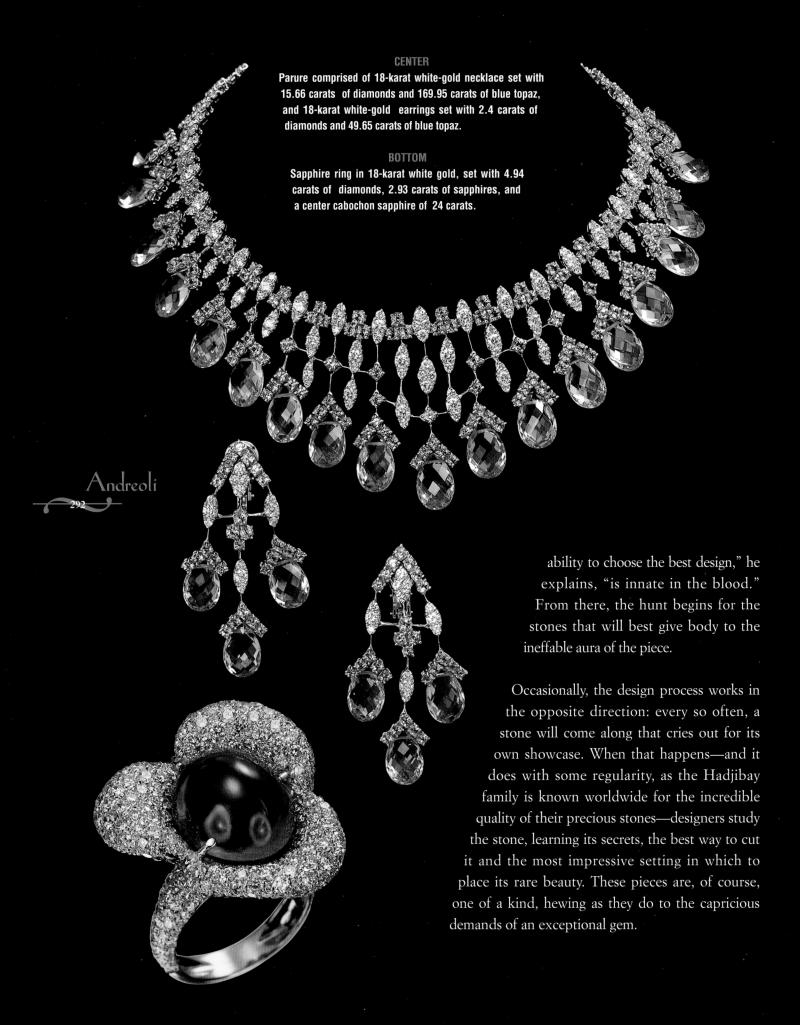

CENTER
Parure comprised of 18-karat white-gold necklace set with
15.66 carats of diamonds and 169.95 carats of blue topaz,
and 18-karat white-gold earrings set with 2.4 carats of
diamonds and 49.65 carats of blue topaz.

BOTTOM
Sapphire ring in 18-karat white gold, set with 4.94
carats of diamonds, 2.93 carats of sapphires, and
a center cabochon sapphire of 24 carats.

Andreoli
292

ability to choose the best design," he
explains, "is innate in the blood."
From there, the hunt begins for the
stones that will best give body to the
ineffable aura of the piece.

Occasionally, the design process works in
the opposite direction: every so often, a
stone will come along that cries out for its
own showcase. When that happens—and it
does with some regularity, as the Hadjibay
family is known worldwide for the incredible
quality of their precious stones—designers study
the stone, learning its secrets, the best way to cut
it and the most impressive setting in which to
place its rare beauty. These pieces are, of course,
one of a kind, hewing as they do to the capricious
demands of an exceptional gem.

Parure comprised of an 18-karat yellow-gold necklace set with citrines and 0.69 carats of diamonds, and a pair of 18-karat yellow-gold earrings that are set with citrines and 0.79 carats of diamonds.

LEFT Ring with moveable petals in 18-karat yellow gold, set with 0.45 carats of diamonds, 3.36 carats of yellow sapphires and one yellow pearl.

Parure comprised of an 18-karat white-gold necklace set with 7.55 carats of diamonds and semiprecious center stones, and a pair of 18-karat white-gold earrings set with 1.0 carat of diamonds and semiprecious center stones.

Andreoli

294

Andreoli continues to innovate and expand our notions of what jewelry can be. For the last five years, the brand has been creating pieces in titanium, an ultra-light metal—it is half the weight of gold—that is also quite difficult to work with. "We're not breaking the mold with this," jokes Jack, "because there is no mold to break. All of this is completely brand new." The advantage of titanium's weight is offset by the extreme difficulty of setting precious stones in the metal—it took

Andreoli's designers a full year of intense experimentation to achieve the desired result.

The highly original use of titanium is just one of the factors that sets Andreoli apart from the crowd. At the Haute Jewelry level, it is the tiny details, unnoticeable to anyone but the true jewelry connoisseur, that make all the difference. Micropavé diamonds coat unexpected surfaces, winking out at the wearer from the bottom or side

of a ring. Moving parts are another intriguing new development for the brand: the colorful flowers have petals that fetchingly flop about, independently of each other. Multi-hued mother-of-pearl is among the new materials being thrown into the mix, gleaming a cool violet or shocking pink. Diamonds set in unconventional materials, such as satin, may soon be added to Andreoli's palette of intriguing design ingredients.

Amid all the inventive techniques and unique designs, Jack keeps one thing in the forefront of his mind: "I want women to feel comfortable in my jewelry," he says. "I want them to love the piece, to love themselves and for everything to fit together perfectly." More than a simple adornment, Andreoli's jewelry is a living thing: the vibrant colors and lacy details in hidden places fit the style of every woman and enhance her natural beauty.

TOP Titanium and 18-karat white-gold earrings set with 5.51 carats of diamonds, 13.52 carats of pink sapphires and 9.93 carats of yellow sapphires.

LEFT Titanium and 18-karat white-gold bracelet set with 3.16 carats of diamonds, 5.61 carats of pink sapphires, 0.86 carats of yellow sapphires and 5.53 carats of tsavorite.

CENTER Ring crafted in 18-karat yellow and white gold, set with 8.52 carats of black diamonds, 1.63 carats of yellow diamonds, and a center white diamond weighing 9.64 carats.

Audemars Piguet

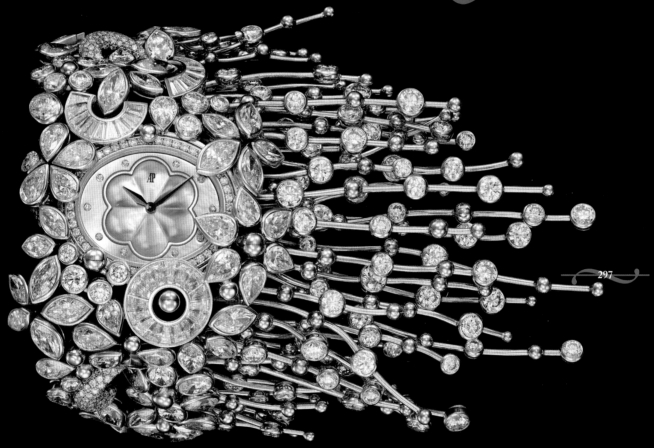

Already legendary in the
world of Haute Horology for over 130
years of peerless, innovative watchmaking, Audemars
Piguet has entered the equally imposing world of Haute
Jewelry, and a more spectacular entrance could not have
been hoped for. The same mixture of precious
materials and meticulous craftsmanship that the world has come
to expect from the makers of the Royal Oak has been translated
into the language of diamonds and white gold, with
breathtaking results.

Audemars Piguet

The twin collections at the heart of Audemars Piguet's new jewelry line spring from the fascinating world of nightlife—the Coup de Théâtre collection springs a string of theatrical surprises, and the Carnet de Bal collection fills up the dance card of women everywhere.

The Coup de Théâtre line is Haute Jewelry at its most unexpected, as well befits its name—an expression for dramatic, unforeseen turns of events. The seamless melding of innovative design and impeccable jewelry expertise weaves a theatrical plot that draws us in as eager spectators, absorbed, dying to know what happens next. The thrill of the unexpected lurks around every corner.

Paradoxically, surprises—the good kind, at least—must be carefully planned and staged. In the Coup de Théâtre collection, every step of the production is meticulously planned out, from the initial cascading design to the painstaking, extraordinarily precise execution. The necklace, which shimmers with the light of 1,673 diamonds, tumbles around the neck and down the chest like a precious waterfall with seeming

Pieces from the Royal Oak Offshore collection: pendant in 18-karat rose gold and white rubber, set with 0.32 carats of diamonds, and ring in in stainless steel and black rubber, screws set with 0.48 carats of diamonds.

nonchalance and ease, perfectly camouflaging the 800 hours of work that went into its creation. The piece flows like luminous silk around the curve of the neck and down the wearer's neckline, as sinuous and fitting as its partner piece, the cuff watch, which grips the wrist like a velvet glove. Both pieces benefit from the claw setting technique for the main elements: by pushing back tiny claws over the table of the diamond, the craftsman releases the stone from the grip of the metal and sets it off to magnificent advantage, allowing the light to pass through unimpeded. The alternating rows of larger

TOP Ring from the Millenary Précieuse collection in 18-karat white gold, set with 69 diamonds bearing a total weight of 1.6 carats.

RIGHT From the Millenary Précieuse collection: a watch housed in an 18- karat white-gold case, set (case, lugs and buckle) with 147 brilliant- cut diamonds, and necklace in 18-karat white gold, set with 79 diamonds.

CENTER Watch from the Millenary Précieuse collection housed in an 18-karat pink-gold case, set (case, lugs and buckle) with 187 brilliant-cut diamonds.

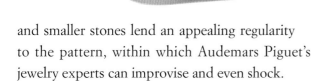

Audemars Piguet

302

and smaller stones lend an appealing regularity to the pattern, within which Audemars Piguet's jewelry experts can improvise and even shock.

This structural evenness provides an intriguing contrast to the loose, fluid, almost ecstatic *pampilles*— or tiny pendants—that provide a touch of glamour to the whole enterprise. Little clusters of pendants erupt at the edges of the designs. The cuff of the watch

bursts into diamond arabesques that also adorn the dial's right side and add flirtatious fun to a manual-winding movement that impresses on its own merits. The necklace drips with *pampilles* and manages to appear impeccably tailored and charmingly free-spirited at the same time. The thrill and intrigue of an unforgettable evening permeates every twinkle of the collection's carefree yet intricate and meticulous look.

As we know from countless novels by Jane Austen and Honoré de Balzac, the most popular form of

Anggun, wearing the Millenary Précieuse Gourmande collection. From the Millenary Précieuse Gourmande collection: 18-karat white-gold earrings set with 4.3 carats of diamonds and a red tourmaline of 19.6 carats, 18-karat white-gold ring set with 1.6 carats of diamonds and a red tourmaline of 19.9 carats.

socialization in centuries past was the ball, where the most beautiful, wealthiest people of their time gathered to forget their intrigue-filled lives, while adding still more complications to the pot. One focus of interest among the women at these points was their *carnets de bal*, dance card, in English. Over time, these *carnets* became more and more elaborate, eventually becoming *objets d'art* in their own right. The Carnet de Bal collection continues this feminine tradition, combining the elegance of the dance with the eternal grace of floral themes. Petals, leaves, stems and blossoms abound in riotous exuberance, mirroring their living inspiration. Nothing is so wonderfully diverse as nature, and the creation of the Carnet de Bal pieces reflects that, with diamonds in marquise, pear, baguette and brilliant cuts, set with closed, claw

FACING PAGE
CENTER From the Coup de Théâtre collection,
an 18-karat white-gold necklace set with 1,673
brilliant-cut diamonds of varying diameters,
including 58 certified by the Gemological Institute
of America, for a total of 204 carats.

BOTTOM Michelle Yeoh wearing the Coup de Théâtre
High Jewelry set.

or grain techniques. As the expert artisans at Audemars Piguet sift through the purest gemstones and bring their savoir-faire to bear on how exactly the stones should fit together, each piece remains miraculously balanced and harmonious as the design is fleshed out.

The ease and fluidity of the design belies the weeks of intense labor that go into its creation. Glimmering with 1,039 diamonds, the necklace alone took over 500 hours of work. The execution, however, appears effortless: tiny diamond blossoms on stems of all different lengths adorn the choker in a delicately cambered composition that sways and quivers with every motion of its wearer. The ethereal interlacing of the piece is a study in the interplay of softness and movement. The cuff-watch plays against the same expectations on our part; the fine stems creep towards the hand like lacy ferns in a lush garden.

THIS PAGE
The Coup de Théâtre watch in 18-karat white gold, set with 853 brilliant-cut diamonds, including 33 certified by the Gemological Institute of America, for a total weight of 123.8 carats.

THIS PAGE

Necklace comprised of 75 carats of oval sapphires, of which the largest stone is 66 carats, and 22 carats of diamonds set in platinum. Bracelet with 40 carats of oval sapphires and 8 carats of marquise diamonds set in platinum. 12-carat cushion pink sapphire earrings set with 6 carats of diamonds in platinum and 18-karat yellow gold. 22-carat cushion pink sapphire ring set with 2 half-moon diamonds in platinum and 18-karat yellow gold. 19-carat cushion sapphire ring flanked by two epaulette diamonds in platinum and 18-karat yellow gold.

FACING PAGE

Necklace containing 20 pear-shape and 9 oval pink sapphires weighing 45 carats and 220 diamonds weighing 45 carats set in platinum and 18-karat yellow gold. Pair of earrings with oval pink sapphires weighing 7 carats and round diamonds weighing 7 carats set in platinum and 18-karat yellow gold. 8-carat cushion pink sapphire ring bordered by two half-moon diamonds set in platinum and 18-karat yellow gold.

Bayco

"We make jewelry for kings and queens," exclaims
Giacomo Hadjibay, co-CEO of Bayco Gem, before
reconsidering and expanding Bayco's target clientele:
"... and princes and princesses." This is, of course, a
metaphorical conception of Bayco's audience; the modern
idea of royalty has grown to include everyone who
hungers luxury and who understands the intricate
labor and savoir-faire that goes into every Bayco
piece. The sophistication once enjoyed only by half
a dozen people in each country has
spread to a more generalized—
but still rarefied—luxury-
loving elite.

TOP Ruby and diamond bracelet comprised of 50 rubies weighing 52 carats and 550 diamonds weighing 53 carats set in platinum and 18-karat yellow gold.

RIGHT Necklace consisting of 122 carats of emerald-cut rubies and 42 carats of round and pear-shape diamonds set in platinum. Pair of 12-carat oval ruby earrings set in platinum and 18-karat yellow gold with 8 carats of marquise diamonds. 15-carat cushion ruby ring set with 6 diamonds in platinum and 18-karat yellow gold.

CENTER 13-carat oval ruby ring flanked by two shield-shaped diamonds set in platinum and 18-karat yellow gold.

Bayco

Though Bayco is a relatively new name in the world of precious gems, the expertise and passion it brings to the field is generations old. The family saga began with Amir Hadjibay, a young man with an entrepreneurial bent. Traveling between Iran and India, he began to develop an interest in precious gemstones, trading them for elaborately woven Persian rugs. Soon he began to visit India's regal maharajahs, leaving with bits and pieces of their legendary jewelry collections—show-stopping diamonds, carved emeralds and fiery rubies, among other gems.

After Amir moved to Italy in 1957, he used his considerable gemstone experience and contacts in jewel capitals around the world to take advantage of Italy's postwar taste for gems and position as a trade hub. A little over twenty-five years later, Amir's sons Moris and Giacomo teamed up in New York, working together as co-CEOs at Bayco Gem, which Giacomo founded in 1981. It didn't take long for the two brothers to find success; they had years of individual and collective experience, gorgeous stones in their collection, and an exceptionally jewel-centric family history.

It was a simple step to create their own designs, populating them with the cherished gems they knew so well. There would be no mass production; the Hadjibay brothers decided from the beginning that they would create only one-of-a-kind pieces, the better to devote their resources to the greater glory of the exquisite stones they wanted to showcase. The family bonds persist into the next generation; Moris's son Marco recently joined the company, bringing a youthful enthusiasm, vigor, and commitment to the future.

The Hadjibay brothers design as a team—having grown up together around the world of gems, they share a design vision and impeccable taste. Though neither has had any formal training in jewelry design, finely honed instinct and decades of experience guide their steady hands to create pinnacles of jewelry. These creations are among the most exceptional in the world— ravishing rubies that emanate aesthetic richness, dazzling emeralds that beguile the mind, celestial sapphires that capture the

Bayco

TOP Three generations of the Hadjibay family: Amir, Roberto, Moris, Giacomo, and Marco.

sublime and enrapturing diamonds that transcend all epochs and eras.

The family expertise in gems has led to astonishing opportunities rediscovered. Moris remembers asking his father about his greatest regret. Amir told his son about "the one that got away"—a stunning 60-carat pear-shaped sapphire of the deepest blue. It came from the Kashmir mines, Amir told Moris, a source of the world's most exceptionally blue sapphires, which has been closed for decades. The equal of such a gem would be

impossible to find again. Years later, Moris came across a sapphire the likes of which he had never seen—a huge, exquisitely perfect gem. He immediately recognized the stone that had eluded his father years before. Proving how near the apple falls to the tree, Moris bought the gem on the spot. The perfect sapphire, Amir confirmed, had indeed made its way back to the Hadjibays. Such a regal stone deserved nothing less than an aristocratic home, and the happy gem now resides in one of the most important royal collections in the world.

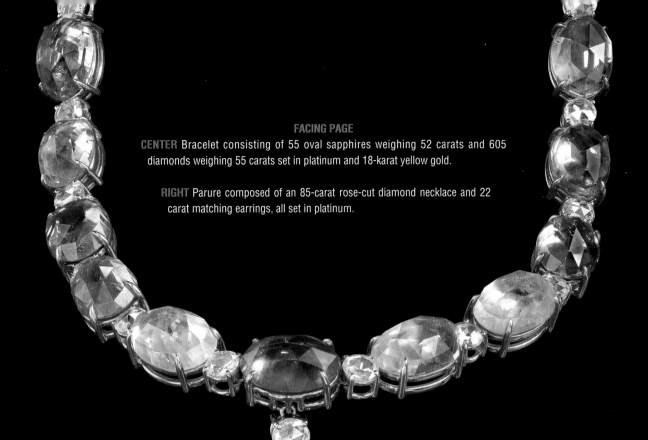

FACING PAGE
CENTER Bracelet consisting of 55 oval sapphires weighing 52 carats and 605 diamonds weighing 55 carats set in platinum and 18-karat yellow gold.

RIGHT Parure composed of an 85-carat rose-cut diamond necklace and 22 carat matching earrings, all set in platinum.

Bayco jewelry effortlessly mixes old and new trends: its pieces are often influenced by the Mogul era, jewelry of the Indian maharajahs, and classical jewelry, which makes the beauty of each stone stand out. Jewelry is eternal; its beauty never dies, so old designs and ideas live again when paired with a new neck or wrist. The story starts with the stone, but it does not end there. The larger the stone, the more likely its design will include traditional elements. "A woman who buys a large stone wants something classic," explains Giacomo. A fashion statement, no matter how original or compelling, cannot be worn every day, and it runs the risk of becoming dated.

The Hadjibays must recut every gem that passes through their hands in order to ensure that its full beauty shines through. Another aspect of their art enters into the equation when matching stones for an exquisite bracelet or necklace: Giacomo and Moris have access to an encyclopedic mental palette, instantly comparing a new stone to those waiting to shine, ready to pounce on a sapphire of the exact blue needed to complete a design. "Matching color depends on taste and

309

THIS PAGE
294-carat multi-color rose-cut sapphire and rose-cut diamond necklace and 62-carat matching earrings set in platinum and 18-karat yellow gold.

experience," explains Moris, and the Hadjibay brothers have both in spades. The designs are classic, yet youthful—and the stones within are justly renowned for being the finest in the world. Bayco's precious testimony of a passion for stones is a delineation of ultimate beauty in all of its forms. It is their devotional ode to every gem.

Bayco's pursuit of gemstone purity is its own aesthetic truth—indulging in the exquisite, coveting the finest treasures, nurturing the uniqueness of each stone, creating an emblem of the wearer's singular aura. "We are always in search of that ultimate beauty," says Giacomo, adding that the fuel for his passion lies in the awed faces of people who lay eyes on his family's creations for the first time. "We get to see things that other people don't even see in their dreams."

FACING PAGE

LEFT Emerald and diamond necklace consisting of 11 oval emeralds weighing 27 carats and 35 carats of diamonds set in platinum and 18-karat yellow gold. 12-carat pear-shape emeralds and 6 carats of diamonds set in a pair of platinum and 18-karat yellow gold earrings.

RIGHT One-of-a-kind emerald necklace set in platinum and 18-karat yellow gold with a 42-carat emerald-cut emerald, a 4-carat emerald-cut emerald, and 88 diamonds weighing 63 carats. Pair of 24-carat emerald-cut emerald earrings set with 15 carats of diamonds in platinum and 18-karat yellow gold.

THIS PAGE

RIGHT Pair of 24-carat pear-shape emerald earrings set with 26 carats of diamonds in platinum and 18-karat yellow gold.

BOTTOM Necklace made with 155 carats of briolette emeralds and 32 carats of rose-cut diamonds set in platinum. 14-carat cushion emerald ring set in platinum and 18-karat yellow gold with two half-moon diamonds.

Jessica Alba attending the launch of the 2009 Campari Calendar in Milan on December 2008. She is wearing a pair of vintage earrings with rubies and diamonds (circa 1955). Each pendant earring is designed as a scroll-shaped surmount supporting a detachable spindle-shaped drop, set throughout with cushion-shaped rubies, baguette- and brilliant-cut diamonds; the drop is detachable and the ear-clip fitting may be adapted to a dress clip.

Bulgari

A perfect balance of classical and
contemporary, along with a constant quest for new design
ideas, materials and chromatic combinations are the hallmarks of
Bulgari style. An exquisite sense of volume, a love for linear, symmetrical
forms and a discerning eye for details inspired by the history of art and architecture
make every Bulgari creation unique and unmistakable. A dynasty of jewelers that
began 125 years ago in Rome, Bulgari has become synonymous with luxury and
Italian style. In 2009, which marks the 125th anniversary of its founding, Bulgari
pays homage to this illustrious history with a retrospective exhibition entitled
*Bulgari "Between History and Eternity" 1884-2009 – 125 Years of Italian
Jewelry* and the launch of a major fund-raising initiative for the
protection of children's rights in collaboration
with Save the Children.

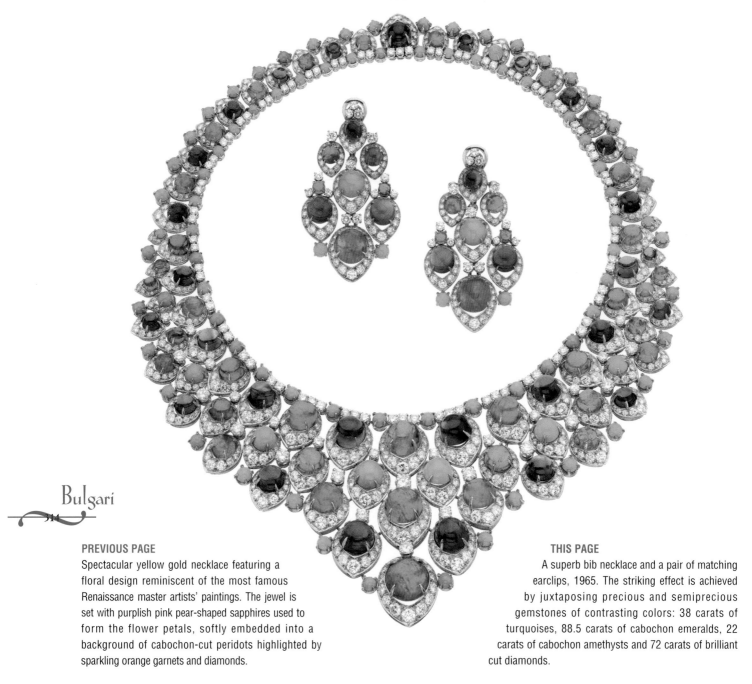

Bulgari

It was in the spring of 1884 that the first Bulgari
shop opened in Via Sistina, in the heart of Rome's
most fashionable street. The subsequent history of
the brand is narrated in a large-scale exhibition that
opens in June 2009 at the Palazzo delle Esposizioni in
Rome – a comprehensive survey of the evolution of
Bulgari style and Bulgari values as told by its most
enduring symbols: 350 one-of-a-kind pieces, including
jewelry, watches and *objets d'art* ranging from the late
nineteenth century to the 1990s, a hundred or so of
which have been selected from the treasures of the
permanent *Bulgari Vintage Collection*. From the silver

jewelry crafted by Sotirio Bulgari himself to the
Art Deco marvels of the 1920s; from the creations
of the '30s, framed by rigorous geometry or adorned
with diamond fringes, clovers and spirals to the softer
designs of the '40s, studded with gemstones while
emphasizing the subtle tones of gold; from the period
of the *dolce vita* and the company's ever closer
connection with the film industry to the inexorable
evolution of Bulgari's style over the decades that
followed. From the very beginning, every Bulgari
creation has been an expression of a truly rare
approach to jewelry making, one that is built on the

Fine vintage diamond-set necklace from the 1930s. The front was designed as a fringe of seven circular-cut diamonds, graduated in size from the center, alternating with diamond-set trefoil motifs, the chain set with baguettes and further circular-cut stones terminating at the clasp in a scroll motif. The necklace may be worn as a tiara when mounted on the appropriate frame.

TOP LEFT Actress Claudia Cardinale photographed during a Bulgari Jewelry Exhibition Gala Opening at the Italian Embassy in Paris in 1962, wearing an elegant necklace set in platinum and diamonds suspending a large diamond of approximately 66 carats.

CENTER Tubogas cuff bracelet in yellow and white gold with three ancient coins, ca 1975. The wide flexible bracelet formed of six bands of Tubogas alternate between yellow and white gold, and the center is decorated with three bronze Roman imperial coins.

twin pillars of peerless craftsmanship and unmistakably original design. Gems of extraordinary quality inspire the designers, whose ideas in turn inspire the expert artisans to transform them into unique works of art. This combination of creativity and craft brings out the best in gems, highlighting the beauty for which they were selected through meticulous workmanship and innovative design. The use of vivid colors, and the most refined, often unconventional shapes, makes Bulgari's distinctive style apparent in each of its creations, resulting in jewelry that transcends the passage of time and of shifting tastes – precisely like the timeless values upon which Bulgari is founded.

Within a year of its opening in 1894, Sotirio Bulgari's first shop moved to Via dei Condotti 28. The sign read "S. Bulgari – Argenteria, Artistica, Antiquités, Curiosités, Bijoux." In 1905, he opened the historic boutique at number 10, which remains today the symbol of the company's heritage and one of the most important Bulgari shops in the world. Over the course of the decades that followed, the new shop became the preferred destination of the American elite and an extraordinary coterie of international celebrities, immortalized in a collection of photographs at the entrance.

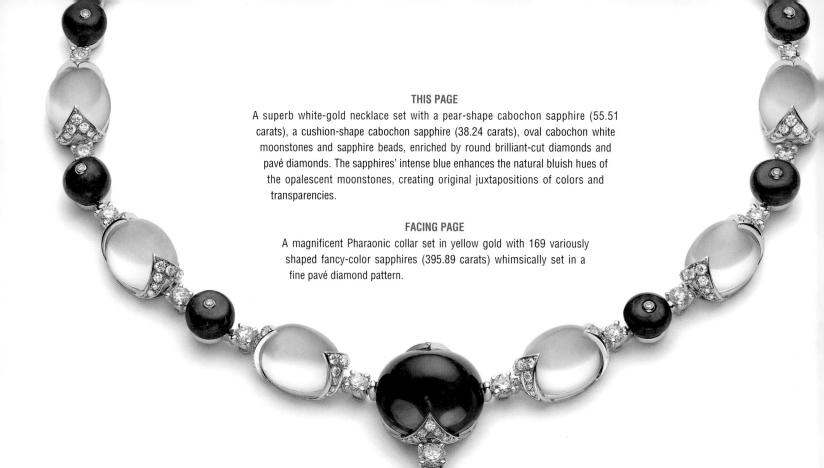

Bulgari

Immediately after World War II the company began refining its own unique language, inspired by Greco-Roman classicism, the Italian Renaissance and the 19th-century school of Roman jewelry-making. This period, the height of Modernism, saw an important stylistic shift at Bulgari: the asymmetrical floral motifs of French provenance gave way to forms that were more structured, symmetrical and compact. Bulgari's designs began to assert smoother, rounder, more linear contours and to favor the use of *cabochon*-cut colored stones placed prominently or juxtaposed in unprecedented combinations. From Audrey Hepburn to Kirk Douglas, the *paparazzi* immortalized the visits of the stars to the shop in Via Condotti. "The only word in Italian that Liz knows is Bulgari," Richard Burton used to say about Elizabeth Taylor's linguistic priorities. Assiduous frequenters of Via Condotti during the '60s, the Burtons famously fought rather often, but invariably made up with a Bulgari jewel.

Certain themes – the incorporation of ancient coins into gold jewelry; the spiraling snake motif of the *Tubogas* watch bracelet; the use of the BVLGARI logo, inspired by Roman epigraphy, as a conspicuous decorative element; the unusual combination of colors and materials – progressively became the distinguishing features of the company's creations, exemplified in the highly original production that runs from the 1970s to the '90s.

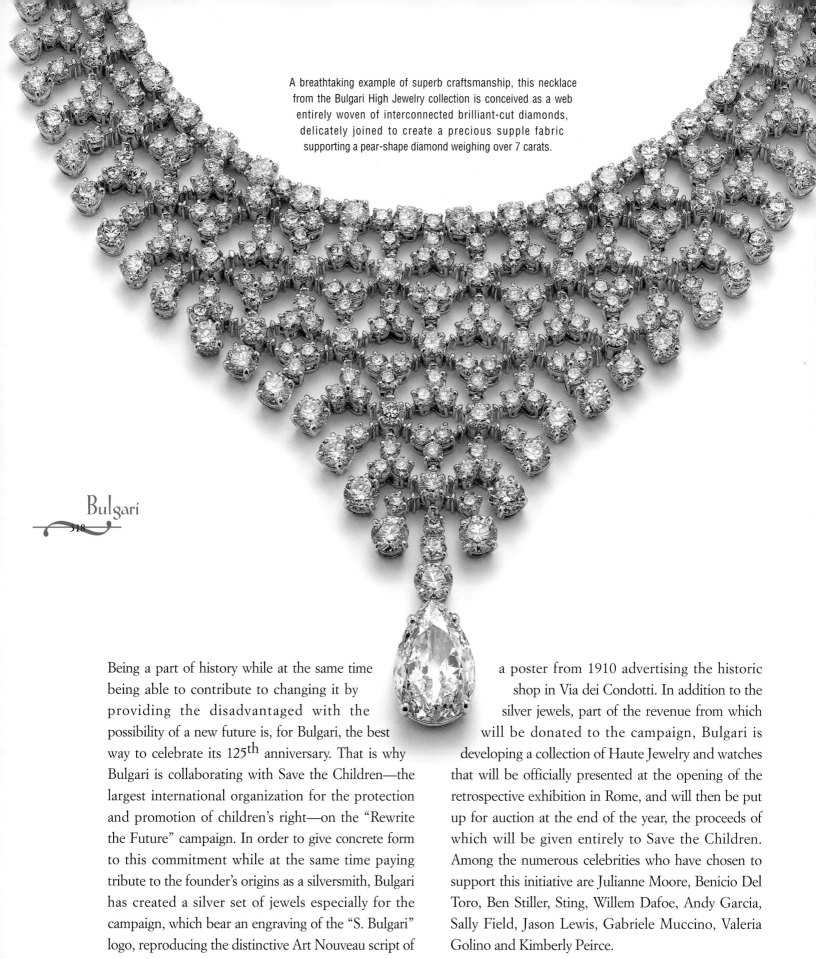

A breathtaking example of superb craftsmanship, this necklace from the Bulgari High Jewelry collection is conceived as a web entirely woven of interconnected brilliant-cut diamonds, delicately joined to create a precious supple fabric supporting a pear-shape diamond weighing over 7 carats.

Bulgari

Being a part of history while at the same time being able to contribute to changing it by providing the disadvantaged with the possibility of a new future is, for Bulgari, the best way to celebrate its 125th anniversary. That is why Bulgari is collaborating with Save the Children—the largest international organization for the protection and promotion of children's right—on the "Rewrite the Future" campaign. In order to give concrete form to this commitment while at the same time paying tribute to the founder's origins as a silversmith, Bulgari has created a silver set of jewels especially for the campaign, which bear an engraving of the "S. Bulgari" logo, reproducing the distinctive Art Nouveau script of

a poster from 1910 advertising the historic shop in Via dei Condotti. In addition to the silver jewels, part of the revenue from which will be donated to the campaign, Bulgari is developing a collection of Haute Jewelry and watches that will be officially presented at the opening of the retrospective exhibition in Rome, and will then be put up for auction at the end of the year, the proceeds of which will be given entirely to Save the Children. Among the numerous celebrities who have chosen to support this initiative are Julianne Moore, Benicio Del Toro, Ben Stiller, Sting, Willem Dafoe, Andy Garcia, Sally Field, Jason Lewis, Gabriele Muccino, Valeria Golino and Kimberly Peirce.

Valeria Golino attending the Red
Carpet of the movie Burn after Reading
in Venice on August 2008. She is wearing
a necklace set with 5 cabochon emeralds
(33.54 carats), 5 oval sapphires (7.91 carats),
5 pink tourmalines, 32 amethysts, 48 citrines and
767 diamonds (28.43 carats) from the Bulgari
Vintage Collection (ca 1989).

FACING PAGE
Necklace in platinum, with ribbed emeralds, engraved rubies, emeralds and sapphires, sapphire beads and brilliants.

THIS PAGE
Inde Mystérieuse parure in platinum, emeralds, rubies, sapphires and diamonds.

Cartier

The story of the House of Cartier
has always been inextricably entwined with the
most beautiful stones in the world. From Jacques
Cartier's epic voyage through India, to the legendary Hope
Diamond, to the iconic panther perched upon a cabochon
sapphire, to Cartier's one-of-a-kind pieces produced
today, the name of Cartier is practically
synonymous with extravagant, historic,
legendary stones.

In November of 1913, a Fifth Avenue window shone with the light of a new movement. The House of Cartier had arranged an exhibition of twenty pieces of jewelry inspired by Indian art and culture—created with, of course, the gems for which India was famous. The was accompanied by a catalog whose design owed a debt to Indian and Islamic art, illustrated as it was with Indian miniature paintings and Arabic verses.

This exhibition may have been the impetus behind a journey integral to Cartier's history. In 1919, Jacques Cartier traveled through India, cementing his relationship with the nation's maharajahs, who were fascinated by Western designs, and who had the coffers and gem collections to satisfy their curiosity. Cartier designed unprecedented adornments for these monarchs, but also gained an invaluable expanded perspective on jewelry design. The traditional Indian pieces to which Jacques Cartier was exposed had a tremendous influence on him—the appreciation for colored stones, the elemental color combinations, the engraving, ribbing and other modifications to the surface of the stone. The result of the meeting between Western jeweler and these ancient traditions was the birth of a new jewelry icon: the Tutti Frutti necklace.

The Tutti Frutti used the historical themes of flowers, fruit and leaves to modern effect, throwing carved stones into the mix for good measure. Rubies, emeralds and sapphires bloomed from every crevice. Two worlds collided in this one piece of jewelry: the Indian affection for profusions of colorful jewels, within the Western strictures of European setting and the harmonious arrangement of disparate visual elements. The result was the perfect mixture of lush sensuality and a new chapter in geometric artistry.

Later works also amply demonstrated the huge influence that India, one of the world's first and most boisterous cultural melting pots, had had on Cartier's design aesthetic. In 1925, Cartier set in a necklace an enormous emerald engraved with the likenesses of Shiva and Parvati, two Hindu deities. Five years later, the House mounted for Aga Khan an emerald that had been engraved with Koranic verses. In fact, the Eastern influence showed

through quite plainly in many of Cartier's works, through colored gems that had been ribbed or engraved, and through diamonds cut in briolettes or fashioned in a rose cut.

The colored stones that served as paints for Cartier's canvas in exotic jewelry were often works of art in their own right, and treated as such by the House. In the early years of the twentieth century, Cartier often set large stones in long diamond chains, precursors to the sautoirs that would become popular in the 1920s. One famous sapphire cabochon set in this way tipped the scales at over 300 carats.

Jewelry from the Inde Mystérieuse collection, with brilliants, brown diamonds, yellow diamonds, an engraved emerald and a blue-green sapphire.

Cartier

Cartier
328

LEFT One platinum ring set with a 17.98-carat rubelite and brilliants.

RIGHT Necklace in platinum with 1 cushion-cut 18.88-carat rubellite, chrysoberyl beads, brown diamonds and brilliants.

While Jacques Cartier was making his famous trip through India, being inspired by sapphires, a different sort of sapphire was being celebrated half a continent away. In San Sebastian, an enormous 478-carat sapphire attracted the admiration of all who glimpsed it. Queen Vicoria Eugenia of Spain tried on the jewel and remembered it fondly, but King Alfonso demurred, saying, "Only the nouveaux riches can afford such luxuries—we kings are the nouveaux pauvres of today!" Perpetually dissatisfied, the stone went through several incarnations and almost as many sets of hands before being given to Queen Marie of Romania, who wore it on an elaborate diamond necklace.

One of the most extraordinary necklaces ever made was born in the ateliers of Cartier, as a custom-made, impossible-to-replicate necklace for Mahrajah Nawanagar, owner of a superlatively enviable gem collection. Two strands of sizable round diamonds encircled the neck, linked by larger pink fancy diamonds; a sextet of exceptional diamonds in vivid pink, blue and green dropping down the center of the piece included the star of the show: the Queen of Holland, a stunning blue-white stone weighing 136.32 carats.

These legendary pieces, and others like them, have left a mark on the Cartier brand that persists even today. The House's intimate knowledge of and experience with diamonds, emeralds, rubies and sapphires, and its endless aesthetic curiosity and openness to new experiences and influences, make its art—and all of our lives—immeasurably richer.

Chopard

For many, it is the culmination
of a career, a short walk that encapsulates
all the work they've done. The famous "mounting
of the steps" at the Cannes Film Festival says, "You've
made it," both artistically and sometimes commercially.
Caroline Gruosi-Scheufele, co-president and head designer
of Chopard, is intimately familiar with the ritual of "mounting the steps," having performed it herself for 11 years now.
Every detail is of the utmost importance on such a night—
that is why the world's biggest stars turn to Caroline
and Chopard for the most elegant, show-stopping baubles that only its superlatively
talented artisans can create.

TOP LEFT Mischa Barton in the pearl necklace from the Red Carpet collection.

TOP RIGHT AND CENTER The making of the sumptuous Red Carpet pearl necklace, adorned with 18 multi-colored cultured pearls, 34 carats of diamonds and 2 brilliant-cut diamonds weighing respectively 1.2 and 1.26 carats.

BOTTOM RIGHT From the Haute-Joaillerie Collection: magnificent diamond necklace set with 170 fancy-shaped diamonds.

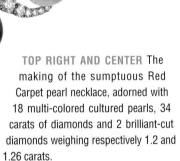

As both the heart and the face of the venerated brand Caroline is returning to her trusted favorites in Chopard's new Haute Jewelry collection. The diamond—Caroline's most beloved stone—takes center stage in the new Haute Jewelry pieces. The line shimmers with diamonds of every imaginable size and shape—emerald, heart, marquise, square, rose, brilliant, rose—set in a fantasy framework that includes rings, ear pendants, necklaces, bracelets and even hair jewelry. In her

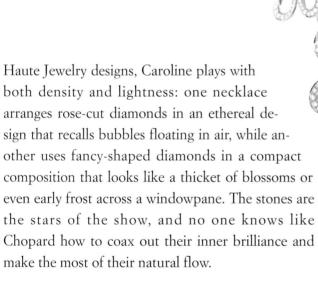

Haute Jewelry designs, Caroline plays with both density and lightness: one necklace arranges rose-cut diamonds in an ethereal design that recalls bubbles floating in air, while another uses fancy-shaped diamonds in a compact composition that looks like a thicket of blossoms or even early frost across a windowpane. The stones are the stars of the show, and no one knows like Chopard how to coax out their inner brilliance and make the most of their natural flow.

Caroline designed Chopard's Red Carpet Collection especially for the legendary Cannes Film Festival, and the partnership between the great brand and the festival extends across several arenas. In 2007, when the festival reached its 60th year, Caroline created 60 breathtaking baubles, one for each year of cinematic glory. For 2008, she completely redesigned Chopard's Haute Jewelry collection, creating 61 brand-new pieces

TOP LEFT Watch from the Haute-Joaillerie Collection in rose gold set with diamonds.

RIGHT From the Red Carpet Collection: diamond floral necklace set with 3,150 brilliant-cut diamonds.

that correspond to any and all desires a woman could have for the most important night of her life.

Lovingly pieced together with the world's most exquisite stones, the Red Carpet collection comes together in hushed ateliers, where the world's foremost jewelry-

FAR LEFT Caroline Gruosi-Scheufele, co-president and head designer of Chopard.

LEFT Laurent Cantet and the Palme d'Or he won for *The Class*.

CENTER The making and presentation of the Palme d'Or.

BOTTOM Cannes Film Festival 2008: Gwyneth Paltrow wears an elegant pair of colored diamond and white diamond earrings from the Red Carpet Collection.

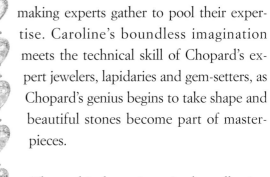

making experts gather to pool their expertise. Caroline's boundless imagination meets the technical skill of Chopard's expert jewelers, lapidaries and gem-setters, as Chopard's genius begins to take shape and beautiful stones become part of masterpieces.

The multivalent pieces in the collection reflect the incredible diversity of taste among the stars themselves. Caroline knows from the inside the impact that the intense media attention at the famous "mounting of the steps" can have, and understands through personal experience, uncanny intuition, and her friendships with many of these supernova stars exactly what these high-powered women will want to wear through the intoxicating whirlwind. Caroline puts it thusly: "My professional life enables me to take part in some extraordinary events and to meet wonderful women: movie

stars, artists, designers, business women… My creativity is nurtured by all these talents around me and the fantastic personalities I am privileged to encounter."

That famous creativity never wants for ways to express itself. A delicate white-gold necklace shimmers with the diamonds set in its lacy flowers. Pure and playful daisies, immortalized in the precious materials, link together in a way that is playful yet deliberate, youthful yet elegant. Another stunner of the Red Carpet collection is a necklace composed of multi-colored pearls, linked by undulating diamond arabesques. The exotic hues of these cultured pearls are a perfect match for a

FROM LEFT Cate Blanchett, Eva Herzegova
and Bar Refaeli all chose Chopard
for the Cannes Film Festival 2008.

star looking to indulge in the ultimate feminine luxury
that pearls represent.

"The art of cinema has always been one of my passions," Caroline has said. "There is fabulous synergy
between our two worlds: the creation of magnificent
jewelry on one hand, and unforgettable films on the
other." This incredible synergy has been amply
demonstrated ever since Pierre Viot, former President of the Cannes Film Festival, asked Caroline to
reimagine the classic, coveted Palme d'Or. The tim-
ing could not have been better, as Chopard had recently opened a boutique on La Croisette. The two

335

international icons of glamour joined forces to re-design the much-desired trophy, the perfect symbol of their fruitful partnership.

This year, Chopard's partnership with the festival has extended further than ever. Apart from the svelte Palme d'Or, Caroline has also designed (in partnership with Alberta Ferretti), the stunning Desiderio dress, which was modeled by supermodel Bar Refaeli and auctioned off in aid of amfAR. Chopard also celebrated the new Cannes tradition of the "Trophée Chopard," now in its eighth year of recognizing exceptionally talented up-and-coming young actors.

Stunning emerald Haute Jewelry set: earrings in white gold set with 4 oval-shape cabochon emeralds weighing a total of 32.01 carats, 270 smaller emeralds weighing 5.74 carats, 2 oval-shape white diamonds weighing 4.02 carats and 296 smaller diamonds weighing 4.85 carats, and necklace in white gold set with 7 cabochon emeralds weighing 64.87 carats, 725 smaller emeralds weighing 38.77 carats, 9 oval-shape diamonds weighing 21.17 carats and 815 smaller white diamonds weighing 42.82 carats.

de GRISOGONO

The world of Haute Jewelry can be an intimidating place, populated with pedigreed gemstones and storied, grand Houses. de GRISOGONO sweeps through this universe like a breath of fresh air, combining its own dedication to excellence in design and in stone quality with a wry visual wit that makes even the most precious pieces playful and accessible.

Only the most elite jewelers, artisans and antique dealers in the world are invited to display their exquisite wares at the Bienniale des Antiquaires, hosted in the magnificent Grand Palais in Paris. To celebrate the milestone of its 15th anniversary, de GRISOGONO made a stunning entrance at the 2008 Bienniale, showcasing its finest creations among the highest caliber of artistic colleagues.

As befits the de GRISOGONO standard of luxury and elegance, the brand chose to exhibit in an immaculately imagined and executed stand. Recalling Fawaz Gruosi's visionary work with black diamonds, the walls of the stand were bathed in a rich, inky black, engraved and backlit with the brand's trademark volute pattern. The lustrous black and luminescent white served as a fitting backdrop to the accents of white roses and white amaryllis that adorned the intimate space.

The spectacular diversity of precious stones was an inspiration for Fawaz Gruosi in creating pieces for the Bienniale. Sapphires, rubies and emeralds abound in witty, expressive designs. Thirty rubies adorn a pink-gold ring that boasts a stunning 21.57-carat tourmaline, on a sinuous band that is also studded with white and brown diamonds, as well as light and dark pink sapphires. The organic-looking design of the ring gives the stones on the pavé band the look of having grown there naturally—an intrinsic part of the

TOP LEFT Naomi Campbell wearing the Instrumento Grande S03 watch, crafted in 18-karat white gold, set with white diamonds and pale blue sapphires, on a blue galuchat strap.

TOP RIGHT Earrings in white gold set with 80 briolette-cut white diamonds weighing 35.74 carats, 82 briolette-cut pink sapphires weighing 41.04 carats, 43 white diamonds weighing 0.26 carats, 43 pink sapphires weighing 0.31 carats, with 2 amethyst drops weighing 62 carats.

CENTER Amethyst ring in white gold set with 320 dark and light pink sapphires weighing 13.89 carats and set with a cabochon oval amethyst weighing 77.97 carats.

Sapphire ring in white gold set with one Ceylon octagonal-cut blue sapphire weighing 17.65 carats, 257 blue sapphires weighing 2.67 carats, 32 baguette-cut white diamonds weighing 5.28 carats and 689 smaller white diamonds weighing 1.06 carats.

finished product. Rubies also appear to vivid effect in a pair of earrings in which pavé ruby drops emerge from the bottom of a cascade of briolette-cut white diamonds.

One particularly impressive ring highlights several aspects of de GRISOGONO's design philosophy at once. The center emerald-cut blue sapphire is impressive in its own right, with stunning azure clarity. On one side of the band is a geometric formation of baguette-cut diamonds, complemented on the other side by curvy emerald-pavé prongs.

CENTER Earrings in white gold, set with one pear-shape blue sapphire weighing 18.65 carats, one pear-shape Colombia emerald weighing 14.62 carats, 28 baguette-cut diamonds weighing 5.6 carats, 28 baguette-cut emeralds weighing 7.76 carats, 463 emeralds weighing 1.73 carats, 142 blue sapphires weighing 1 carat, 14 rubies weighing 0.02 carats, 311 white diamonds weighing 1.33 carats and 503 white diamonds weighing 2.22 carats.

A pair of earrings also emphasizes de GRISOGONO's trademark asymmetry. One piece begins in a sinuous cascade of emeralds and ends in a beautifully cut sapphire, while its mate is an almost perfect reflection in diamonds and emeralds. Cabochon-cut emeralds take pride of place in a spectacular necklace and pair of earrings

341

RIGHT Naomi Campbell wearing emerald earrings in white gold, set with 83 diamonds weighing 0.57 carats and 10 cabochon emeralds weighing 211 carats, and an emerald necklace in yellow gold set with 969 yellow sapphires weighing 17.87 carats, 543 emeralds weighing 7.2 carats, 16 white diamonds weighing 0.49 carats, and 241 Colombian cabochon emeralds weighing 427.43 carats.

that emphasize the brand's interest in organic forms, flair for combining stones, and access to exceptional gems.

de GRISOGONO continues to expand its design horizons with its playful Boule collection. The first pieces in the collection were light mesh cuff bracelets that bubbled with precious balls. The explosive popularity of the cuffs led to several more designs, each one using the original concept in a novel way. The attention paid to the execution of the designs proves that Fawaz Gruosi gives careful consideration to not only the look of the jewelry, but also its feel and comfort. With meticulous expertise, the spheres that constitute the bubbly effervescence of the titular "boules" have been completely hollowed out. This makes

LEFT Amethyst ring in white gold set with 651 emeralds weighing 16.14 carats and one cabochon amethyst weighing 94.08 carats.

BOTTOM Crafted in pink gold, necklace set with 125 white diamonds weighing 6.35 carats, 1,508 tsavorites weighing 96.65 carats, and 2 white pearls weighing 16.16 carats.

FACING PAGE
TOP Boule Pendant Watch S03,
crafted in 18-karat pink gold and set
with 122 brown diamonds weighing
0.8 carats and 212 white diamonds
weighing 4.33 carats.

RIGHT Naomi Campbell wearing earrings
from the Boule collection, crafted in pink
gold and set with 703 pink sapphires
weighing 76.25 carats and 6 white diamonds
weighing 1.2 carats.

CENTER Earrings from the Boule collection,
crafted in white and pink gold and set with 402
pink sapphires weighing 31.9 carats and 12 white
diamonds weighing 1.3 carats.

Pink-gold Boule necklace set
with 1,854 white diamonds
weighing 78.5 carats, set in 9 gold
balls of 30mm diameter.

the jewelry supremely light and airy, an
important consideration when creating
bold pieces for delicate ears and fingers.

The cuff watches that introduced Boule to the
world are still being reimagined in different
materials—white diamonds, pink sapphires, white
gold and rose gold all take their turn in the spotlight
for this effervescent treat. However, the basic idea
has evolved to inspire earrings, rings, necklaces and
pendants. Rings feature the playful sphere in smooth
balls of white and yellow gold, or as a glittering
specimen in white diamonds, amethysts, rubies or—
of course—black diamonds, Fawaz Gruosi's

trademark. Earrings descend the curve of the neck in
several variations—some plunge straight down on a
chain with diamond links, while others spring from
the lobe on several chains, with smaller balls
suspended on the way down. In a truly stunning
display of de GRISOGONO versatility, one pair of
earrings dangles like a bunch of ripe grapes.

Necklaces and pendants play an important part in the Boule collection, as they provide the base to string together different varieties of precious orb, or to spotlight a particular bauble on a chain. The latest addition to the pendant line combines de GRISOGONO's penchant for lighthearted jewelry and the brand's expertise in watchmaking: the jewelry pendant watch. Brainchild of de GRISOGONO artisans, the pendant watch is extremely lightweight—between 38 and 45 grams, depending on the variation selected. Inside the cheerful, ethereal bubble lies an ETA quartz movement identical to the one that powers the brand's popular Lipstick watch collection. The pendant watch is available in 11 variations, each more bewitching than the last. In pink, brown and yellow gold, adorned with a sprinkling of stones or a full pavé of white or brown diamonds, emeralds or pink sapphires, the jeweled timepiece closes at the back with a delicate diamond-set or diamond-pavé plate.

Guy Ellia

When a renowned diamond
dealer launches his own jewelry line,
expectations are high. Thus it was with
great anticipation that the world of Haute
Jewelry welcomed Guy Ellia's first jewelry
collection in 1999. He did not disappoint. In
fact, the Guy Ellia name has come to
symbolize extraordinary creativity,
exquisite beauty, perfection, and
above all else, innovation.

Guy Ellia

Ellia was among the first prestige jewelers to juxtapose priceless gems with surprising materials. His Nylon collection combines fabulous diamonds with transparent cord. The effect is ethereal—the stones seem to hover in space like tiny iridescent hummingbirds. At once youthful and classic, Ellia's Elysa brooch marries leather with whimsically provocative interchangeable diamonds. As one of the first jewelers to design creations made entirely of black diamonds, Ellia initiated a trend

that is still going strong ten years later. "Guy Ellia is brilliant," says Carla Chalouhi, owner of the famed Parisian Arije boutiques. "He isn't one to point out his own accomplishments, however, and that's why many jewelry insiders don't realize how much influence he has had on our industry." Before launching his Haute Jewelry and watch lines, Ellia spent decades combing the globe—from Southeast Asia to Eastern Europe, South America to South Africa—in quest of the world's

THIS PAGE
Bollywood At Tea Time Set.

FACING PAGE
Bollywood At Midday Set.

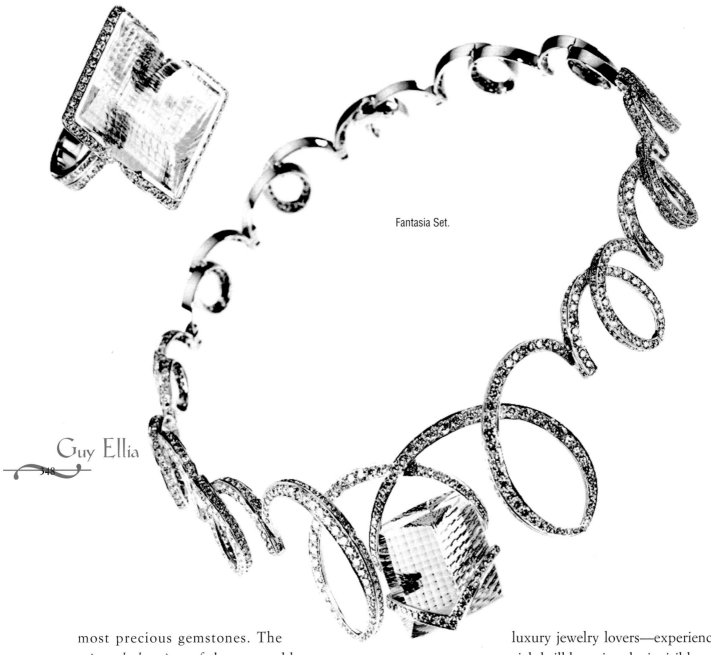

Fantasia Set.

Guy Ellia

most precious gemstones. The *crème de la crème* of these emeralds, rubies, sapphires and diamonds found their way, years later, into his own creations. While Ellia is a lover of all gems, diamonds—particularly fancy-colored diamonds—hold the dearest place in his heart and designs.

Ellia's love of diamonds inspired his indiscriminate use of them—he was among the first designers to entirely envelop his rings in dazzling diamonds, covering the inside as well as the outside. Women who wear Ellia designs—the most discerning of

luxury jewelry lovers—experience a special thrill knowing the invisible parts of their rings are precious secrets known only to them.

Jonquil-colored diamonds bloom in rings, pendants bracelets and earrings. Orange, green and coffee-colored diamonds join with 17 carats of yellow diamonds in one of Ellia's notable masterpieces, the Bollywood Party necklace, which was inspired by the colors and scents and sounds of India. Tahitian, Akoya and South Sea pearls mingle with cappuccino-colored diamonds that highlight

Diabless Rings.

the pearls' luminous tones. Yet Ellia also creates equally mesmerizing pieces in the monochrome palette of black and white.

Gleaning inspiration from virtually everywhere—movies, museums, fashion, culture—Ellia exudes an intellectualism that informs his designs. "The most important thing is for me to stay open to inspiration. When I go to a museum, I don't just look at the painting. I look at the painter himself and what's going on behind the painting. I try to understand how this painter came to make this painting. Sometimes I understand. Sometimes not. Sometimes I understand later."

This introspection is reflected in the sheer breadth of Ellia's designs. Evoking the images and romance of the Côte d'Azur, the Majestic necklace incorporates multiple ebony and ivory hearts on a turquoise backdrop the exact color of the Mediterranean Sea. Spain's steamy capital and its grand palace inspired the Puerta del Sol creation, which shows diamond raindrops sprinkled on mother-of-pearl. Paying homage to Hyde Park's

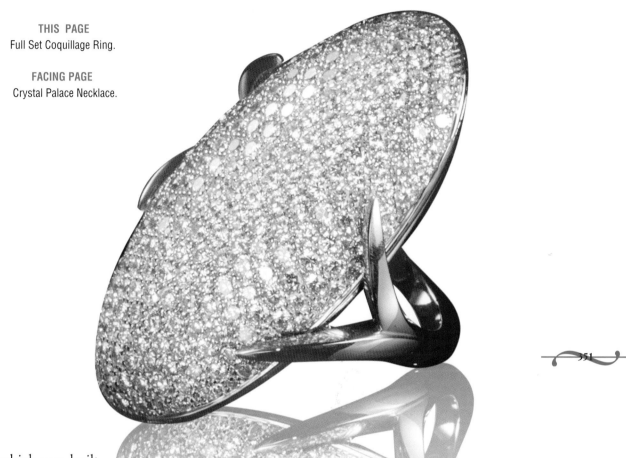

351

Crystal Palace, which was built in 1851 for the World's Fair and gutted by fire in the early twentieth century, Ellia uses round pieces of mother-of-pearl and ivory accented with diamonds. The effect is a dazzling display of refracted light.

Most of Ellia's designs are created in three or four colors of gold—yellow, white, pink and black, with an equally colorful array of gems. While jewelry design, like fine art, is wholly subjective, trends do apply. And yet the pieces must be timeless. "A new ring should be new, but at the same time it should be an investment for the next fifty years," Ellia says.

With the opening of his first boutique on Sloane Street in London, Ellia is evolving his businesses even further. As a retailer, his company will develop intimate relationships with some of its key customers, which will provide invaluable feedback for developing future lines of both Haute Jewelry and luxury watches.

As one of a handful of contemporary jewelry designers to break into the world of Haute Jewelry that is dominated by centuries-old jewelry houses, Ellia enjoys a unique position in his industry. For Guy Ellia, the best is yet to come.

"In order to be irreplaceable
one must always be different."

- *Samir Bhansali*

La Reina

Unparalleled in its vibrancy and opulence—emerald, ruby and sapphire-colored embroidered silk saris paired with equally extravagant gems, the clinking of pure gold bangles stacked from wrists to elbows mingling with the sounds of sitar music—India gave birth to the idea that jewels are de rigueur for every woman on every occasion. Jewelry designer Samir Bhansali, who was born in Mumbai, ushers this concept into contemporary life while paying homage to his rich heritage. "La Reina," an assemblage of Art Deco elements fashioned from La Reina's trademark enormous-but-light, laser-cut diamonds, mixes ancient techniques with innovation. The result is simply *sui generis.*

"I don't like to think of myself as making jewelry but as creating art."

- Samir Bhansali

La Reina's work is at once still life and sculpture, a cornucopia of colors, textures and motifs. Like Michelangelo coaxing "David" from a slab of marble, Bhansali lures life-size butterfly wings from wispy slices of diamonds that are credit card thin and nearly that large. White diamond pavé adds a dew-like quality to wildflower petals. Pink and blue sapphires are fashioned into eye-popping peacock brooches. In Bhansali's world, size matters. "I design looks that can be worn by an Indian woman in a sari or by an American in a little black dress," Bhansali says. "Elaborate fashions call for even more elaborate jewelry. Simple designs need elaborate jewelry to give the style a punch."

As an artist who studied fashion design, Bhansali faced the same challenges with which all couturiers grapple—reinterpreting high fashion into wearable pieces. Conventional jewelry materials cannot always convey his extraordinary vision and desire for a palette that captures the richness of Indian culture. In order to create his jeweled imaginings, he turned to alchemy, transforming a metal not ordinarily associated with haute jewelry—titanium—into the canvas on which he paints.

TOP Titanium and black onyx teardrop earrings pavé with white diamonds.

CENTER White and black onyx bangles set with white and black diamonds.

BOTTOM Titanium and black-gold Mask brooch set with flat diamonds and white onyx.

Attention to detail is the hallmark of La Reina's innovative, award-winning work. Pieces have no backside; they are fashioned so that they are stunning from every angle. The "Yellow Passion Flower" bracelet from the "Art du Jour" collection won Town & Country magazine's honors for Best Design in 2007. La Reina's latest collection, "Evoluzione," spotlights the "Mughal Flower" brooch—a two-carat fancy yellow diamond, surrounded by smaller pink and yellow diamonds, blooming amid deep purple petals formed from oxidized titanium. The kaleidoscope effect of the titanium casts ever-changing metallic hues—scarlet, magenta, cerulean, indigo.

In addition to the spectrum of colors Bhansali can paint with titanium, the metal is also exciting for its design possibilities. As an ultra-lightweight material that is virtually indestructible, titanium can be sculpted into enormous, elaborate pieces that otherwise would be unwearable. Imagine earrings the size of orchid blossoms that are as light as hollow gold hoops.

"Life is pretty simple: You do some stuff. Most fails.
Some works. You do more of what works. If it works big,
others quickly copy it. Then you do something else.
The trick is the doing something else.
This is what my designs represents."

- Samir Bhansali

Bhansali's transcendent use of
titanium was inspired by love. His mother, Pushpa,
who is one of his three muses (his wife and daughter
being the other two), could not tolerate wearing
earrings that pulled on her ears. So Bhansali began
researching ways to create lighter earrings. After four
years of perfecting his technique, La Reina launched
its one-of-a-kind titanium collection. In his
mother's honor, Bhansali created the
elegant "Pushpa" collection, which
features Art Deco's geometric
symmetry and
streamlined
shapes.

THIS PAGE
TOP Flat diamond Butterfly brooch
set with vivid yellow diamonds.

BOTTOM LEFT 2007 Town &
Country award winner "Yellow
Passion Flower Cuff" in black
gold, set with flat diamonds.

BOTTOM RIGHT Butterfly ring in
black gold, set with flat yellow
diamonds and pear-shaped
diamonds, accented with pavé
black diamonds.

FACING PAGE
White and black onyx bangles set
with white and black diamonds.

TOP Titanium Flower ring set with fancy color diamonds.

FAR LEFT 2008 Town & Country award winner "Mughal Brooch" with a 2-carat fancy yellow pear-shaped diamond in the center.

BOTTOM CENTER "Morning Dew" brooch-cum-pendant made in a combination of titanium, gold and silver with pear-shaped diamonds in the center.

RIGHT Titanium brooch-cum-pendant with natural fancy color diamonds and rose-cut white diamonds.

BOTTOM RIGHT Titanium Flower ring with yellow diamonds.

La Reina

358

As a third-generation diamond dealer, Samir Bhansali was destined to design jewelry. Within merely a few years of launching La Reina in 2001, he has become a rising star in the haute jewelry industry. The breath of Bhansali's creativity is as staggering as the prolific amount of work he produces. When in India, Bhansali combs antique shops for jewelry he can elevate from valuable antiquity to invaluable opus. He adds diamonds and rubies set in gold to ivory bracelets fashioned from wooly mammoth tusks; he accents a 19th-century pink gold cross pendant with diamonds and sapphires. In every design, La Reina creates a fusion of India's age-old history with cutting-edge style. Antique-cut diamonds are juxtaposed with his diaphanous diamond slices; pearl, onyx, wood, rhodium and crystal mingle with gold and diamonds. Diamonds are set within pearls. One princess-cut and two pear-shaped diamonds are convincingly arranged to look like a three-carat heart-shaped solitaire; the result is, quite literally, brilliant.

Bhansali has lived in Los Angeles, where La Reina is headquartered, for the past 27 years. Yet every piece of jewelry is made in India, where gems and metals are highly prized not only for the inherent beauty and value but for their mystical and healing properties as well. This could be why wearing a La Reina piece can feel magical.

With his newest titanium line available through Neiman Marcus, La Reina is now poised to join the ranks of other instantly identifiable designers; he will be the designer who made significant jewelry appropriate regardless of occasion. "You cannot wear big stones every day," Bhansali says. "But if you wear artistic pieces, it's different. Artistic pieces work as well during the day as they do in the evening." Day to night, east to west—La Reina bridges generations and cultures with his dazzling designs.

TOP RIGHT Dragonfly Brooch in black gold and titanium set with flat diamonds.

BOTTOM Black onyx Mask brooch set with flat yellow diamonds.

LEFT Flat yellow diamond ring in white gold set with rose-cut and black diamonds.

THIS PAGE
Fancy yellow and white diamond earrings:
16 cushion-shaped fancy yellow diamonds
totaling 14.93 carats and 6 cushion-shaped
diamonds weighing 12.32 carats mounted
with collection white pavé, hand-crafted in
18-karat yellow gold and platinum.

Fancy vivid yellow diamond ring: fancy vivid
yellow diamond weighing 10.04 carats
mounted with collection white pavé diamonds,
hand-crafted in platinum.

FACING PAGE
Fancy vivid yellow diamond ring: square
emerald-cut fancy vivid yellow diamond
weighing 10.41 carats highlighted by yellow
pavé-set diamonds weighing 1.39 carats, hand-
crafted in 18-karat yellow gold.

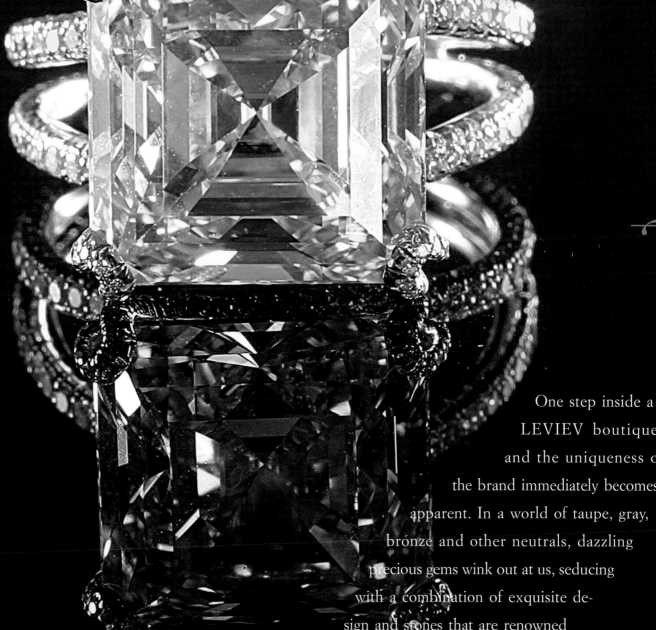

One step inside a
LEVIEV boutique,
and the uniqueness of
the brand immediately becomes
apparent. In a world of taupe, gray,
bronze and other neutrals, dazzling
precious gems wink out at us, seducing
with a combination of exquisite design and stones that are renowned
worldwide for their purity,
clarity and rarity.

TOP Emerald and diamond cufflinks, hand-crafted in platinum.

CENTER Diamond ring: cushion-shaped D internally flawless diamond weighing 26.72 carats flanked by two shield-cut diamonds weighing total of 1.06 carats, hand-crafted in platinum.

Incredibly, each of LEVIEV's retail spaces—in London, New York, Moscow and Dubai—contain more carats than all the other jewelry stores in their respective cities *combined*. This is not due to endless acres of display; rather, the modestly sized display cases sit at respectable distances from each other. It is the diamonds themselves that are immodest, flaunting their impeccable quality and astonishing size. After some time around LEVIEV pieces, what once seemed a perfectly reasonable size for a diamond now seems to fall on the small side. This is understandable—after all, points out Thierry Chaunu, President and COO of

LEVIEV, "we have dozens of 10-carat diamonds," a size that would stand out in any other environment.

Amidst the abundance of large diamonds at LEVIEV, a stunning array of stones stand out from even this elite crowd. The brand's current star is a 102.9-carat D Internally Flawless Type IIa, which has no trace elements at all to color or muddy the stone in any way. It is absolutely perfect, and unique in the world. LEVIEV also possesses the largest green diamond (eight carats) ever certified by the GIA. The very best stones often get snapped up immediately by

Hopscotch eternity band: 9 round
brilliant-cut diamonds weighing .90
carats accented by collection white
pavé diamonds weighing .90
carats, hand-crafted in platinum.

Fancy vivid yellow diamond ring: round brilliant-cut fancy vivid yellow diamond weighing 16.54 carats mounted with 2 baguette-cut diamonds totaling 1.51 carats, hand-crafted in 18-karat yellow gold and platinum.

Fancy intense yellow and white diamond necklace: 36 fancy intense yellow radiant-cut diamonds totaling 36.32 carats, mounted with 39 pear and marquis-shaped diamonds weighing 33.04 carats, suspended from diamond LL clasp, hand-crafted in platinum and 18-karat yellow gold.

eager clients. Recalling a mint-green diamond ring that was sold even before the press release announcing its arrival had been finalized, Chaunu "says It's always a bit sad to see unique stones go, but then, we are so happy for the privileged person who will wear it." Any red diamonds—the rarest of all colored diamonds—also have extremely short lives on display before an avid collector swoops in. These stones leave all too quickly, but reinforcements are always on the way. The LEVIEV spectrum encompasses startling orange and intense pink, deep violet and glacial blue, all set among perfectly clear white diamonds.

All diamonds used in LEVIEV's pieces are untreated and conflict-free—in fact, Lev Leviev was an early initiator of the UN-mandated Kimberley Process.

In addition to the characteristically exceptional diamonds in its jewelry designs, LEVIEV has added a distinctive, yet subtle, branding element to its designs. The interlocked double "L" of the logo has begun to show up as a motif, often as a clasp. "It's a modern, very discreet identification of the brand," says Chaunu. This geometric element acts as a counterpoint to the curvier Russian and Eastern influences on the jewelry.

Extraordinary diamond earrings:
2 pear-shaped D internally
flawless diamonds weighing
33.51 and 31.27 carats,
mounted with 6 marquise
and 2 round brilliant-cut
diamonds totaling 15.77
carats, hand-crafted in
platinum.

LEVIEV

Onion domes and arabesques have shown up as themes in recent collections, but "the stones demand that we remain classical," says Chaunu of the influence that remains foremost at LEVIEV.

Though LEVIEV's most devoted fans are very wealthy individuals with a taste for exceptional diamonds, the retail stores are all designed to be very welcoming to the public. The sales staff combines a keen diamond expertise with a refreshing lack of condescension. "We don't use the usual sales tactics," points out Chaunu. "We know we have the best prices, because we supply

everyone else." Lev Leviev's companies control one-third of worldwide diamond production, and LEVIEV is the largest diamond cutter and polisher in the world, supplying other luxury brands. The best stones, however, he keeps for the LEVIEV brand. The brand has always specialized in the über-luxury end of the spectrum, catering to the highly demanding connoisseur. It has, however, expanded its offerings to a price point of $75,000-$100,000—an entry price point that serves as an "exit point" for many other jewelry brands. "Other brands have one-carat engagement rings," explains Chaunu. "Our engagement rings are two to five carats, and they are all in the DEF range." In even its simplest pieces, LEVIEV outclasses the competition.

Sapphire and diamond ring: cushion-shaped sapphire weighing 39.71 carats, mounted with collection white pavé diamonds, handcrafted in platinum.

Tassel diamond and sapphire earrings: 218 sapphire beads totaling 98 carats and 25 beads and 12 briolette diamonds weighing 19.14 carats mounted on a diamond-pavé dome suspended with 8 round brilliant-cut diamonds totaling 4.61 carats, handcrafted in 18-karat white gold.

Tassel diamond and sapphire necklace: 125 sapphire beads totaling 78.77 carats, accented by 18 diamond beads and 7 briolette diamonds weighing 15.72 carats, mounted on a diamond-pavé dome suspended from 127 round brilliant-cut diamonds totaling 15.61 carats, mounted with a LL collection white diamond clasp, handcrafted in 18-karat white gold.

Another point of entry to the brand, for many clients, is LEVIEV's increasingly sophisticated line of watches, the quality of which, according to Chaunu, is "on a par with the diamonds that we sell." The cases, movements and designs of LEVIEV watches are completely exclusive to and created for the brand, by Swiss ateliers who specialize in custom-made pieces for demanding clients. Adhering to its practice of bringing its clients the best of everything, LEVIEV has joined forces with Christophe Claret, a luxury brand name in its own right. The partnerships have engendered such advanced horological works as the Double Eagle Tourbillon, which enjoys a world-first 110-hour power reserve. Of course, it wouldn't be LEVIEV without diamonds—every man's watch includes a diamond on the crown, and the Double Elle women's watch line features the interlocked "L" set in diamonds as a distinctive type of bezel. Like LEVIEV's classic jewelry, these watches are available only at the brand's own boutiques.

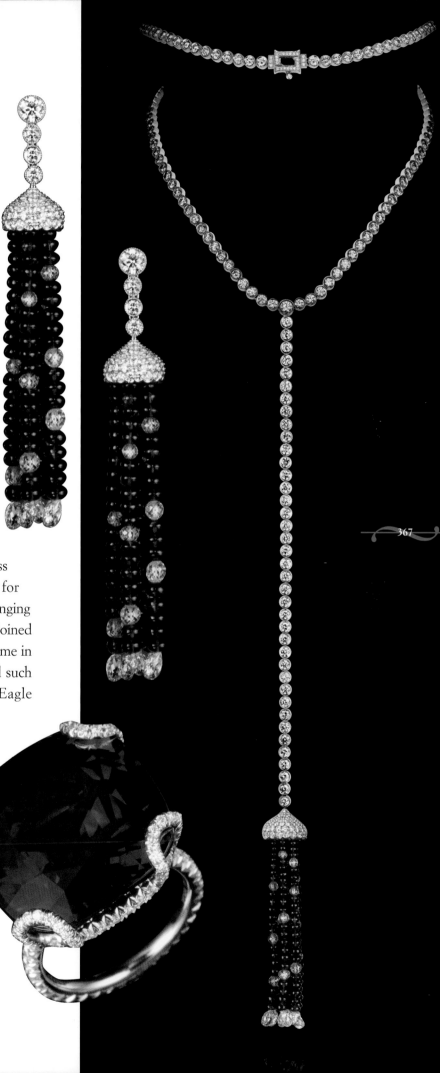

THIS PAGE

Eva Green wearing the superb Lumière necklace, which features 3,050 briolette-cut diamonds (378.74 carats). A masterpiece of stone combination and construction, it can be worn in different ways including on the front or on the back of the body. The main necklace can be detached and worn alone and the endings can also be detached and worn separately from the necklace.

FACING PAGE

Romantic and seductive, the beauty of the Bouquet necklace is enhanced by 3 blooming roses, studded with diamonds. At its heart is the exclusive Montblanc Diamond, which took 7 years to develop and was introduced in celebration of the company's 100th anniversary in 2006. Formed in the shape of the company's star-shaped symbol, the Montblanc Diamond shines in the center of the necklace, which has a total of 1,001 carefully set diamonds of 25.07 carats that come together to present a flattering rose bouquet.

MONT BLANC

Montblanc

Towering above the rest of
the Alps, Mont Blanc seems to have
been there forever, created by forces of
nature beyond human comprehension. Its
solidity, integrity and timelessness have always been
inspirations for the Montblanc brand. As
Montblanc expands its offerings to fine jewelry, the
core values of the brand find new expression in
the Montblanc Diamond, a novel cut that
encapsulates the evolving identity of
the company.

TOP Dita Von Teese wearing the Bouquet diamond necklace from the Étoile de Montblanc Haute Jewelry Collection.

CENTER Stunning bracelet in white gold with round cut VVS clarity diamonds and black spinel precious stones.

BOTTOM Bold La Dame Blanche ring in white gold with diamonds and jade set in an invisible setting. The exclusive Montblanc Diamond rotates around the surface of the ring.

The name of Montblanc, best known for its high-quality writing instruments, bears a special significance for its customers. "Montblanc is used to celebrate life," says Carlo Giordanetti, International Creative Director of the company. "It's a reward for an accomplishment, a recognition of a milestone." Inspired by the close relationship between Montblanc and its clientele, the brand sought to affirm its values—values shared by its customers—through a symbolic interpretation of the brand in a precious material. One of the most instrumental aspects influencing the decision to make fine jewelry was what Giordanetti calls "the amazing adventure" of the Montblanc Diamond. The enthusiastic response of Montblanc's aficionados to this specialized cut, and their spontaneous association between Montblanc and fine jewelry, added a new layer of significance and provided an additional boost of energy and passion to the endeavor.

The ice and snow of Mont Blanc, which have covered it for untold millennia, call to mind the diamond in its purity and

changelessness. The eternal stone corresponds wholly with iconic Montblanc values: perfection, timelessness, elegance and power. If the perfect material to represent Montblanc was never in question, nor was the form it should take. What could be more representative of Montblanc, after all, than its emblematic star? The Montblanc Star has represented the brand for nearly its entire existence. The simplicity of its design, inspired by a bird's-eye view of the perpetually snow-covered tor, has remained intact and unchanged. Though the concept was simple, the actual creation of

the Montblanc diamond cut was a bit more complicated, taking eight years to develop and perfect. "The basic shape was easy to originate," says Valentina Masu, International Marketing Manager of Jewelry for the brand. "What was problematic, was harmonizing the demands of our special cut with traditional standards of beauty for diamonds." To resolve this contradiction, Montblanc combined traditional hand-cutting methods with computer software that lined up the angles of the stone's facets to provide maximum brilliance. As in any quest for perfection, the process is never-ending.

A subtle chain supports a precious pendant of white gold and black spinel stones accompanied by a 1.64-carat Montblanc Diamond.

Montblanc

"We keep exploring opportunities to improve the cut," says Masu of the brand's constant experimentation.

There are certain values that every Montblanc product expresses. An iconic, timeless, unwavering sense of style permeates the brand; every piece is an instant classic. Crucial to this aesthetic is flawless craftsmanship: production of Montblanc pens takes place right next door to the company's offices in Hamburg, Germany. The brand's own manufacture in Switzerland plays a crucial role in its horological production, and for Montblanc's top-end line,

FACING PAGE
TOP RIGHT Claudia Schiffer wears the magnificent
Éclat necklace.

CENTER Clair de Lune earrings from the
Montblanc 4810 fine jewelry collection.

BOTTOM Magie en Blanc et Noir ring in
white gold with diamonds and black jade.

Montblanc Collection Velleret 1858,
the manufacturing of each component is
done in-house. This close relationship with
the products, from conception to delivery,
ensures the highest level of craftsmanship and
guarantees a continuation of the authenticity for
which Montblanc is known.

Man does not live by authenticity and craftsmanship
alone, however. Montblanc's experience with writing
instruments lends it expertise in an underrated
element of jewelry design: sheer sensuality. "Our
products and even points of sale are designed to

Diamonds and precious black spinel
embrace, creating the perfect frame for
the 1.66-carat Montblanc Diamond.

Montblanc master goldsmiths have captured the very special moments of luck, romance, and passion in the form of a traditional charm bracelet studded with round-cut diamonds in a pavé setting totaling 1.5 carats.

Montblanc

appeal to all five senses," says Giordanetti. The tactile pleasure of holding a round, substantial fountain pen is taken into account when designing the smooth lines of Montblanc's Haute Jewelry collection. There is also an intellectual sense of enjoyment that comes from Montblanc's immersion and embrace of culture. Never trendy or faddish, the company derives part of its timelessness from its association with cultural touchstones, including the Writers Edition collection of writing instruments, each model named for a different legendary writer. The Haute Jewelry

collection Mélodies Précieuses holds that same relationship with culture, naming the different collections after classic arias and love songs that remain the consummate expression of emotion.

The introduction of jewelry to the Montblanc universe has changed the brand in subtle yet unmistakable ways. The new emphasis on femininity and grace has permeated the design of watches and writing instruments, bringing in a softer perspective and a greater appreciation for

TOP The captivating Éclat necklace from the Montblanc Haute Jewelry Collection shines like a brilliant star and features the unique Montblanc Diamond at the center of the white-gold necklace, which contains 1,464 diamonds and a total weight of 58.75 carats.

RIGHT Draped in diamonds, Katherine Jenkins wears Lumière earrings and necklace and Joan Collins wears the mesmerizing Éclat necklace.

precious materials. For example, the Étoile de Montblanc pen features the Montblanc diamond in the tip of its cap, bringing to life the idea of jewelry that just happens to write—the purity and uniqueness of the Montblanc diamond shine in the cap's transparent dome, and pieces in the Étoile Précieuse collection also include a diamond-set clip and cap top. The brand's multi-layered expertise in writing instruments, watches and jewelry brings a cross-hybridization of sensuality, precision and beauty to every aspect of the world of Montblanc.

In a design inspired by the most memorable milestone, the platinum wedding band is set with pavé diamonds, and the Montblanc Diamond replaces the traditional stone shape found in most rings marking this very special occasion. The unique design allows the rings to be worn alone or together in three different ways.

THIS PAGE
These rings from the Flamenco collection beautifully portray Oliva's flair for the dramatic. Both crafted in 18-karat yellow gold, the top and bottom ring are set with 0.69 and 0.46 carats of diamonds, respectively.

FACING PAGE
From the Flamenco collection, this ring is as passionate and seductive as its namesake. Crafted in 18-karat yellow gold and set with 1.36 carats of diamonds.

Oliva

Five generations in the
family business add up to a lot of
genetic know-how. Is it nature or nurture?
An appropriate question for Oliva, which has
carved out a sizable niche for itself in the
competitive world of diamond jewelry. An aesthetic
descendant of the jewelers to Europe's most
sumptuous royal courts, Oliva is run with a
single-minded dedication to beauty and
an obsessive attention to quality.

TOP LEFT The ever-popular Bridal collection features these rings in 18-karat white gold. From left to right, they are set with 9.5 and 2.25 carats, respectively.

CENTER The Flamenco collection lives up to its name, undulating with grace and passion. The pendant features 0.88 carats of diamonds in 18-karat white gold, and the ring, also in 18-karat white gold, is set with 0.63 carats of diamonds.

Oliva
378

LEFT Three different rings from the Bridal collection show the versatility Oliva shows in working with different designs, all in 18-karat white gold, and set with, from top: 1.15 carats of diamonds, 1.86 carats of diamonds and 2.25 carats of diamonds.

Oliva's pieces are designed exclusively in 18-karat gold and platinum, but the brand's true claim to its extraordinary reputation stems from its diamond expertise. Located right around the corner from Israel's Diamond Exchange, Oliva's office has its pick of the finest, most exceptional diamonds in the world. Full-time expert diamond cutters and setters pour their passion and skill into every stone, often coming up with innovations that permanently change the playing field.

"It's a big, unique look," explains Nilly Gross, partner in Oliva. She isn't kidding. Several years ago, the designers at Oliva invented a new diamond cut—the Oliva cut—that changed the possibilities in the field. Taking advantage of their faceting savoir-faire and knowledge of the play of light within the stone, the designers came up with a cut that makes any diamond appear larger than its actual weight. Because diamonds are priced by weight (among other factors), a woman sporting the Oliva cut always gets more bling for her buck.

Another Oliva innovation is the use and adaptation of invisible diamond setting. This is, of course, not new—many high-end jewelers use invisible settings, often to magical effect. But the Oliva approach is uniquely inventive; differently shaped diamonds are fitted together like puzzle pieces, forming never-before-seen shapes. An octagon in the center of a pendant looks like a solid stone that sparkles, impossibly, with the scintillation of all its component facets. Other fanciful forms expand the possibilities of what a diamond can look like.

TOP LEFT This saucy set from the Flamenco collection is crafted in 18-karat rose gold; the earrings contain 1.83 carats of diamonds, and the pendant is set with 0.92 carats of diamonds.

TOP RIGHT The Shapes collection is endlessly customizable; the client can choose any number and combination of diamond shapes to fit any mood. This Oliva Shapes pendant, crafted in 18-karat white gold, is set with 1.82 carats of diamonds.

CENTER This earring from the Flamenco collection is crafted in 18-karat gold and the pair is set with 0.78 carats of diamonds.

BOTTOM These rings from the Oliva Cut collection show off the innovative Oliva cut to its best advantage. Both crafted in 18-karat white gold, the rings are set with, respectively from left, 1.14 carats and 1.44 carats of diamonds.

TOP Stunning earrings in 18-karat white gold from the Oliva Cut collection, set with 3.5 carats of diamonds.

LEFT Simple forms make a big impact in the Shapes collection; crafted in 18-karat white gold, the ring is set with 0.91 carats of diamonds, and the earrings contain 2.07 carats of diamonds.

CENTER From the versatile Shapes collection: pendant in 18-karat white gold and 0.99 carats of diamonds, and 18-karat white-gold earrings set with 1.66 carats of diamonds.

The effect can also be seen in Oliva's renowned "three-dimensional" pieces. Of course, all jewelry is three-dimensional, but Oliva uses the tricks that the eye can play on the brain to beautiful illusionary effect. The concept is this: a stone, or a cluster of invisibly set stones, hangs from a pendant, surrounded by baguettes that shoot forward and out like rays of sunlight. Because of the diamond's unique ability to capture light, we end up seeing the pendant as a particularly convincing optical illusion: the stone appears to be leaping out at us!

TOP LEFT Uniquely charming rings from the Bridal collection, in 18-karat yellow or white gold, are each set with 1.94 carats of diamonds.

TOP RIGHT Pendant from the Shapes collection in 18-karat white gold, set with 0.73 carats of diamonds.

CENTER Charming bracelet from the Shapes collection in 18-karat white gold, set with 5.59 carats of diamonds.

BOTTOM Earrings from the Oliva Cut collection, set with 1.8 carats of diamonds.

Oliva's employees are expert goldsmiths, diamond setters and Italian-trained jewelry designers, all performing their art under one roof. This centralization of design production means that Oliva's quality control is among the strictest in the world, as every step of the creation process is carried out within shouting distance of the next.

The "Four C's" of diamonds are known around the world—cut, color, clarity and carat. Oliva, however, also answers to a "Fifth C," that of customer service. With its prime location near the

Diamond Exchange and its in-house team of perfectionists, Oliva is uniquely positioned to fulfill its customers' wishes—on a tight deadline. With the entire family and team wholly committed to and passionate about their work, the customer gets top priority, even on impossible deadlines.

The core of the Oliva line is a collection of the classic motifs: designs with baguette cuts, princess cuts, three-dimensional effects, trademarked cuts and South Sea pearls. These eternal classics exert a powerful pull on Oliva's collections, which are

Oliva

TOP LEFT From the Flamenco collection, this 18-karat yellow-gold ring is set with 1.36 carats of diamonds.

BOTTOM AND RIGHT These pieces from the Flamenco collection combine a playful joie de vivre with Oliva's peerless way with diamonds. The ring is set with 0.66 carats of diamonds, and the pendant is set with 0.92 carats of diamonds. Both pieces are crafted in 18-karat yellow gold.

constantly evolving, incorporating influences from fashion, to art, to architecture, to individual people. "We are inspired by everything, consciously or not," says Gross. Ideas that are in keeping with the company's unique vision, become sketches and designs, all entered into Oliva's computer database. "A jewelry designer is like a painter," explains Gross. "We have to translate what we see in our mind's eye, into reality." The demands and aesthetic considerations of jewelry design, however, are much different than those of a painter. A designer must be practical and precise, keeping in mind the precise measurements and exigences of each individual piece of jewelry, the most pressing, of course, being "Will anyone want to wear this?"

Many times, that question is asked and answered before the production process starts, as it is often Oliva's clientele who suggests new pieces or evolutions in the design. A particularly dazzling necklace, for example, will give birth to a matching set of earrings. These pieces, the ones inspired by clients, are the ones that seem best to exemplify Oliva's mission to make dreams come true, with exceptional stones, unique designs and the highest standard of perfection in production.

RIGHT Elegantly feminine pieces from the Pearls collection, all in 18-karat white gold: earrings set with pearls and 1.71 carats of diamonds, pearl pendant set with 0.96 carats of diamonds, and rings featuring a white or black pearl, each set with 2.31 carats of diamonds.

CENTER AND BOTTOM Timeless pieces in 18-karat white gold from the Oliva Classic collection: ring set with 1.2 carats of diamonds, pendant set with 0.85 carats of diamonds and earrings set with 1.65 carats of diamonds.

THIS PAGE
From the Paris Couture collection: corset-inspired ring in 18-karat white gold, set with 324 brilliant-cut diamonds (5.14 carats) and one rubellite (56.55 carats), worn with cuff-watch in 18-karat white gold with case, dial and bracelet pavé with 1576 brilliant-cut diamonds (85.8 carats) and 83 baguette-cut diamonds (7.5 carats).

FACING PAGE
Necklace in 18-karat white gold from the Limelight Paris New York collection, Paris Architecture theme, set with Paris Architecture collection, set with 632 brilliant-cut diamonds (25.08 carats) and 43 pear-cut diamonds (7.8 carats).

Piaget

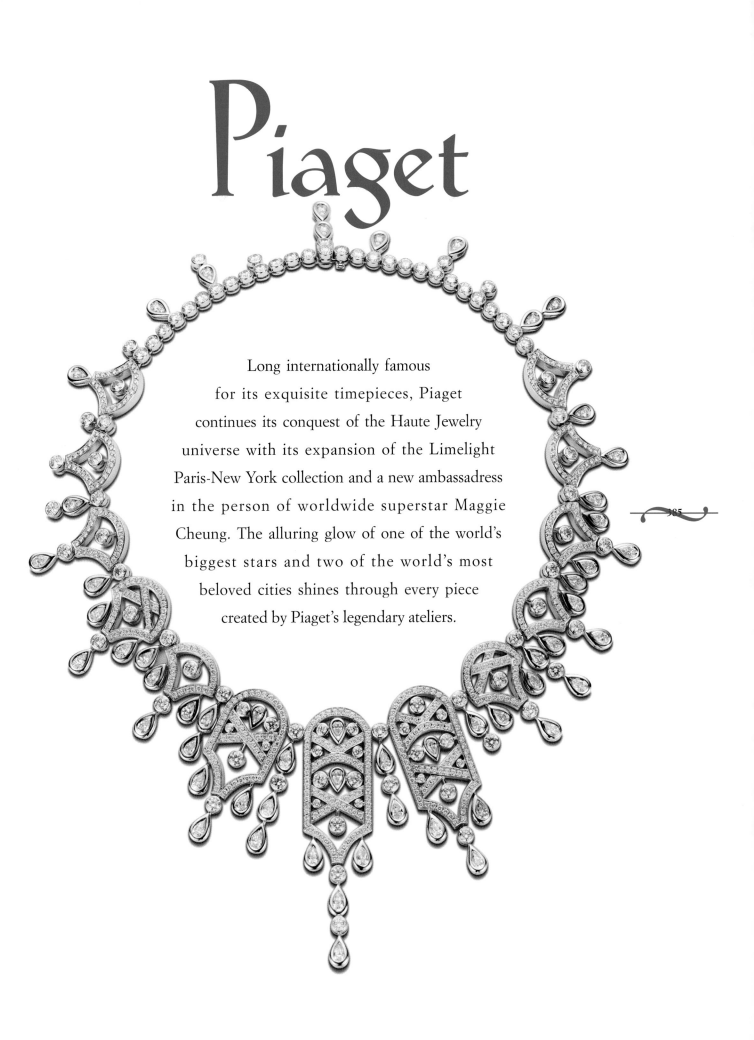

Long internationally famous
for its exquisite timepieces, Piaget
continues its conquest of the Haute Jewelry
universe with its expansion of the Limelight
Paris-New York collection and a new ambassadress
in the person of worldwide superstar Maggie
Cheung. The alluring glow of one of the world's
biggest stars and two of the world's most
beloved cities shines through every piece
created by Piaget's legendary ateliers.

FACING PAGE
A jewelry set inspired by the braces and curves of the Eiffel Tower: 18-karat white-gold earrings set with 142 brilliant-cut diamonds (6.65 carats) and with 20 pear-shape diamonds (1.92 carats), and an 18-karat white-gold necklace set with 1,095 brilliant-cut diamonds (28.15 carats), 48 pear-shape diamonds (6.72 carats) and 3 pear-shape dangling diamonds (8.6 carats).

Piaget's Limelight collection is the epitome of cosmopolitan glamour, and no two cities are more cosmopolitan—or more glamorous—than New York and Paris. Paris, the City of Lights, has inspired countless love songs, classic novels and beloved films, and now it lends its ineffable grace and beauty to Piaget's spectacular Limelight collection. For most people, the very word "Paris" immediately evokes the Eiffel Tower, the marvelously engineered temple of contradictions—light and lacy, yet steely and sturdy. The personality of this iconic structure peeks out of several diamond-studded jewelry designs. The glittering necklaces and earrings evoke the Tower's intricate supports—the ones that occasionally light up in a sudden rush of sparkling light, to the delight of visitors and locals alike. Briolette-cut diamonds dangle from the ears and neckline, referencing the long, lean lines that make the Tower a visual synonym for elegance.

The elegant Eiffel Tower is not the only landmark to quicken the pulse of Francophiles—the famous Ferris wheel ("la Grande Roue") on Place de la Concorde also serves as inspiration for Piaget's master artisans.

THIS PAGE
TOP Ring in 18-karat white gold inspired by Paris Architecture, set with 157 brilliant-cut diamonds (1.31 carats) and one blue sapphire (14.07 carats).

BOTTOM From the Paris Architecture theme, a watch housed in an 18-karat white-gold case, with bracelet and integrated clasp set with 620 brilliant-cut diamonds (11.8 carats) and 8 pear-cut diamonds (0.9 carats). The 18-karat white-gold dial is set with 64 brilliant-cut diamonds.

387

The revolving seats lend their form and whimsy to jewelry and secret watches that incorporate the magic of movement into their mechanisms. Pear-cut diamonds that hang from earrings and necklaces conjure memories of floating suspended above the most romantic city in the world.

Architecture is far from the only influence on Parisian life—the world capital is justly famous for its Haute Couture. Piaget expresses its identity as "fashion capital of the world" in a line that captures the hard-edged sensuality of the fashion world. Corset details—which imply that everything that can be laced up tight, can also be unlaced—grace cuff watches, necklaces and even rings with a pleasingly symmetrical, suggestive back-and-forth. The cuff watch, which is completely paved with diamonds, literally wraps the wrist in light, completing the picture with crisscrossing diamond "laces" that seduce the eye. A ruby and pink sapphire necklace is casually tossed around the neck with carefree insouciance, paying homage to untied ribbons and their hint of abandon.

New York also steps into the spotlight with two of its most stupendous architectural icons—the Chrysler Building and the Statue of Liberty. The legendary Art Deco skyscraper lends its spiky elegance to a set of jewelry that expresses a city's pride in an irresistible design. The chandelier arrangement sparkles in white diamonds and blue sapphires, echoing the outline of the iconic building in the great city's world-famous skyline. The seven bold points of the Statue of

RIGHT Inspired by the Statue of Liberty, from the Limelight New York Architecture theme: 18-karat white-gold pendant set with 148 brilliant-cut diamonds (2.24 carats).

BOTTOM New York Architecture theme ring in 18-karat white gold, set with 528 brilliant-cut diamonds (7.17 carats), 35 baguette-cut diamonds (3.8 carats) and 116 blue sapphires (2.64 carats).

Maggie Cheung wearing necklace and ring inspired by New York's Chrysler Building, from the New York Architecture theme. Necklace in 18-karat white gold, set with 381 brilliant-cut diamonds (15 carats), 14 baguette-cut diamonds (1.17 carats), 5 kite-cut diamonds (0.56 carat) and 368 blue sapphires (25.36 carats).

Liberty's diadem appear as a recurring theme in Piaget's pendant, earrings and watch dial, which possess an inherent international flair—the seven points of her crown represent the world's seas.

In New York City, black is always the new black. New York fashion is known for its unique attitude, reflecting New Yorkers' sartorial daring as well as their assertive personal style. Piaget puts its imprint on Haute Couture bows and ribbons, interpreting them in white diamonds and black tourmaline to highlight their inner glamour. The monochromatic creations evoke the peerless chic of a New York night, featuring inventive luxe touches like a black satin and diamond bow that helps hide the mystery of a "secret" watch whose diamond-pavé cover discreetly moves aside. The mysterious allure of black tourmaline and black spinel is showcased in necklaces with formal diamond bow-tie motifs.

This fascination with New York and Paris extends to the timepieces in this showstopping collection as well. Two Piaget Polo Tourbillon Relatif models, issued in limited editions of three, combine sophisticated design and dazzling horology. On the Paris watch, the twelve avenues that radiate from the city's Place d'Étoile are etched on the dial, and the sides of the timepiece's case feature quintessentially Parisian landmarks. The New

York watch's dial boasts engravings of the city's twelve highest skyscrapers, and two views of the city's legendary skyline grace the sides of its case.

Though it was founded in a tiny Swiss village, Piaget has effortlessly captured the magic and enchantment of a wild night in the world's biggest cities. Small wonder, then, that the brand decided to join forces with Maggie Cheung, one of the world's biggest stars. The actress and the company both combine beauty with grace, intelligence and a wicked audacity that leaves fans of both wanting more. The artistic ambition that both possess in abundance leads to ever more aesthetic risks—which always pay off, in such skillful hands.

THIS PAGE
Diamond Chain necklace in
platinum and 10 carats of
diamonds.

FACING PAGE
Flamme ring in 18-karat yellow
gold, set with diamond pavé
and multicolored sapphires.

Waskoll

There is a place between dreams and
waking, and it is here that Waskoll's designs take shape,
coalescing and giving body to ideas and forms straight out of our
collective unconscious. Diamonds and colored stones mix and mingle in
a cascade of glamour that is nonetheless meticulously planned and carefully
controlled. "I found my stones in Ali Baba's cave," jokes Cyril Waskoll, the
jovial co-founder and head designer of the brand. All kidding aside, Waskoll's
jewels occasionally have the otherworldly look of a half-forgotten fairy tale,
where princesses dance the night away and pumpkins become coaches
with the wave of a wand. In a unique twist, however, Waskoll's
jewelry is also infinitely adaptable, wearable not only with
enchanted gowns, but jeans and a sweater.

393

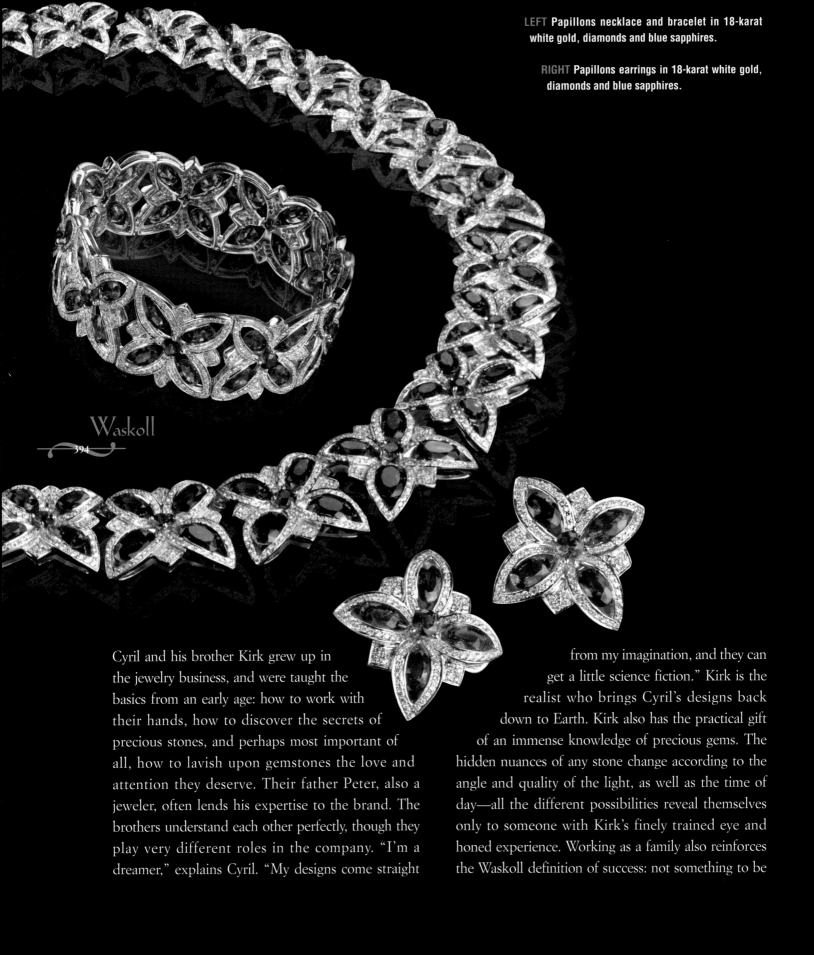

Waskoll
394

Cyril and his brother Kirk grew up in the jewelry business, and were taught the basics from an early age: how to work with their hands, how to discover the secrets of precious stones, and perhaps most important of all, how to lavish upon gemstones the love and attention they deserve. Their father Peter, also a jeweler, often lends his expertise to the brand. The brothers understand each other perfectly, though they play very different roles in the company. "I'm a dreamer," explains Cyril. "My designs come straight from my imagination, and they can get a little science fiction." Kirk is the realist who brings Cyril's designs back down to Earth. Kirk also has the practical gift of an immense knowledge of precious gems. The hidden nuances of any stone change according to the angle and quality of the light, as well as the time of day—all the different possibilities reveal themselves only to someone with Kirk's finely trained eye and honed experience. Working as a family also reinforces the Waskoll definition of success: not something to be

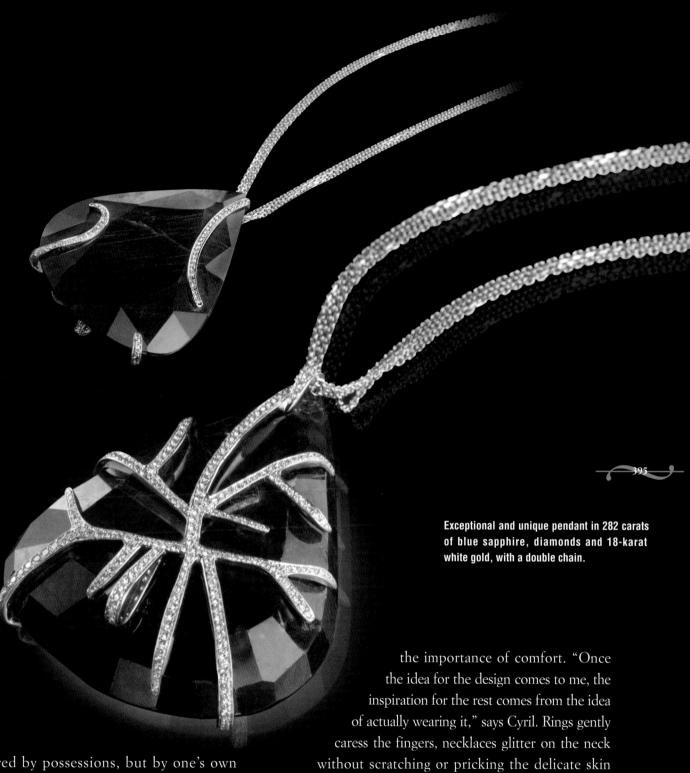

Exceptional and unique pendant in 282 carats of blue sapphire, diamonds and 18-karat white gold, with a double chain.

measured by possessions, but by one's own happiness and the joy one brings to others. "I'm a happy man," says Cyril, "and a loyal one." The combination guarantees success for Waskoll, no matter how it is defined.

One of the most vital themes in Waskoll's designs is the importance of comfort. "Once the idea for the design comes to me, the inspiration for the rest comes from the idea of actually wearing it," says Cyril. Rings gently caress the fingers, necklaces glitter on the neck without scratching or pricking the delicate skin beneath. "Women have a very strong emotional connection to their jewelry—it shouldn't hurt them! Jewelry isn't just to look at, but to touch and to wear."

This attention to the life of jewels is reflected in the women who love Waskoll. They are an elite set who

Romance earrings in 18-karat white gold, diamonds and blue sapphires.

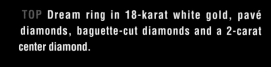

397

TOP **Dream ring in 18-karat white gold, pavé diamonds, baguette-cut diamonds and a 2-carat center diamond.**

CENTER **Papillons bracelet in 18-karat white gold and diamonds.**

BOTTOM **Solitaires rings in 18-karat white gold, pavé diamonds and blue sapphires.**

express a certain freedom and originality in their tastes—independent, spontaneous, feminine women who make their own choices and buy their own jewelry (as well as receiving it from the men in their lives). Waskoll caters to these women with a nearly infinite selection of pieces in stones of all colors of the rainbow. The immense variety of color in these creations makes them suited to any mood, outfit or situation. This adaptability is the key to the longevity of Waskoll's designs—they always fit in perfectly, whether at a moonlight gala or a casual coffee with friends.

TOP Parfums du Monde pendant in 18-karat white gold, diamonds and multicolored sapphires.

LEFT Parfums du Monde pendant in 18-karat white gold, diamonds and pink sapphires.

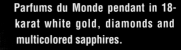

Parfums du Monde pendant in 18-karat white gold, diamonds and multicolored sapphires.

Waskoll

The uniqueness of Waskoll's collections owes much not only to Cyril's fertile imagination, but also the brand's production methods. All its jewelry is entirely hand made in Europe—"Our pieces cannot be mass produced," says Cyril—and the irreplaceable human touch means that every piece, even those produced from the same design, is an individual.

The Waskoll design philosophy might be compared to a crystal vase full of exquisite, freshly cut flowers. Flowers, like new trends in jewelry, start out with a big splash, and gradually fade away. There are certain pieces in Waskoll's garden that come and go with the seasons, bringing vibrant, though ephemeral, notes to the line. Then, there is the vase: the signature collections, the pieces that attract generations of women, the lines that emphasize Waskoll's virtuosic use of precious gems and reputation for wearability, such as the Wave or the Flamme Collections. These timeless pieces form the foundation of the brand, but the ever-changing variety of new collections plays an important role as well. "It's like adding new flowers," is how Cyril describes the process of designing new pieces, adding that the process "regenerates our creative juices." To succeed,

Golden Gate ring in 18-karat white gold, set with diamond pavé and 2-carat center diamond.

Waskoll relies on both fresh new ideas, and the longstanding aesthetic into which they fit.

One new piece that seems destined for longevity is Waskoll's Diamond Chain, the lightest diamond necklace in the world. Waskoll also prides itself on its one-of-a-kind pieces, designed around the most exceptional stones that pass through Kirk's and Cyril's hands. These pieces are momentous, in the way that all great jewelry is. "Behind every piece of jewelry is a story," says Cyril. We buy jewelry to mark an occasion, to express affection, to mark our status or our taste—every piece a woman wears, expresses something about her. Waskoll jewelry always carries a sentimental charge that goes far beyond monetary value. The House invites us to dream, to dare, to approach the mysterious cave and say, "Open Sesame!"

Yvel

Sophisticated jewelry with a splash of sexiness is the hallmark of Yvel, a
company whose focus remains squarely on the mysterious, miraculous
pearl. The brand's name is the mirror image of the name of its founders,
Isaac and Orna Levy, and their aesthetics and values permeate every
last inch of Yvel's exquisite collections. Pearls are the most
ultra-feminine of all precious materials, and Yvel's creations
are as sensual as the gems they use, while incorporating
their natural, unique personalities.

Yvel

402

It might have seemed like an unlikely partnership: though Orna's family had been in the jewelry industry for decades, she had never imagined that that is where her future would lie. In 1986, as the story goes, Isaac asked Orna what she knew, and she replied that she knew pearls. He gave her $2,000 to purchase pearls, and the rest is Yvel history. The couple began making jewelry in their bedroom, shopping around their creations to local retailers. After a few years, the Levys began to realize that there was a real unmet need in the market—clients were requesting unique, very high-end pieces, and the Levys were quick to oblige with limited edition collections.

Finding the right pearls is only the beginning of the design process, and in some ways, it is the easiest. Yvel is one of the few companies to be invited to the most elite worldwide pearl auctions, in a system similar to the one of sightholders in the diamond world. The next step in the process is charming in its playful simplicity: Isaac and Orna sit down with their

precious materials and stick them into a lump of Play-Doh, letting the shape and hue of each pearl determine its relationship to its neighbor. The freeform designs that result are organic looking and completely sui generis, dependent on the natural contours and shades of each pearl. Diamonds and gold play a supporting role in this "wearable art."

Yvel is famous for its use of pearls that go beyond the typical round, white gem. The aesthetic philosophy of the brand treats pearls as material for art, not

commodities. This creative, artistic approach shines through all Yvel's collections, which treat the pearl as not just a gem, but an inspiration. Every piece of Yvel jewelry expresses far more creativity than a single strand of round white pearls could ever do.

The Golden Brown collection takes its cues from the South Sea pearls in brown, gold, copper, champagne and even light green that populate its designs. In an exploration of the warmest hues available in the pearl world the

TOP Necklaces, bracelets and a ring from the Pavé collection, all pavé-set with diamonds and sapphires.

LEFT Pieces from the Biwa collection: an 18-karat yellow-gold necklace with 15- to 17-millimeter freshwater coin pearls, a handmade 18-karat yellow-gold bracelet with 13- to 14-millimeter freshwater coin pearls, and handmade 18-karat yellow-gold earrings with 13-millimeter freshwater coin pearls.

collection binds its themes together with 18-karat yellow gold and cognac-colored diamonds.

Yvel's One of a Kind collection takes full advantage of the company's vast resource of extraordinary pearls. The rare gems—pearls and diamonds—in Yvel's archives get the chance to take the spotlight in these pieces, which are designed to showcase their attributes. One piece in particular took three years of intensive labor to create. Combining impeccable artistry with stunningly unique gems and pearls, it sold in just three days.

From the Rainbow collection: 18-karat yellow-gold necklaces with 109.5 carats of multi-colored tourmaline, set with 2.4 carats of natural cognac diamonds.

From the One of
a Kind collection:
2006 Town & Country
award-winning cuff bracelet
with 10- to 15-millimeter golden
green natural Indonesian Keshi pearls
and set with 11.4 carats of natural multi-
colored diamonds in different shapes and
sizes, all set in 18-karat yellow gold, and an
18-karat yellow-gold ring with 8- by 11-
millimeter multi-colored free shape
Keshi pearls set with 0.57
carats of diamonds.

407

LEFT Necklaces from the One of a Kind collection created in white baroque Australian South Sea pearls, clasp set with 5.07 carats of diamonds.

RIGHT Orna (second from left) and Isaac Levy posing with models in Yvel creations. The model between Isaac and Orna is wearing the 2007 winner of the Town & Country Couture Design award.

Luxurious contrasting textures take the stage in Yvel's Pavé Collection, which mixes structure and elasticity to dazzling effect. Thousands of gems nestle together in a handmade golden mesh chain, creating the effect of a diamond rope, which is then punctuated by the occasional pearl. Several color combinations add a winsome variety to the collection—gold and brown South Sea pearls, pink sapphires with pink and lavender freshwater pearls, and even rubies mixed with gray and black Tahitian pearls. The satiny, smooth textures of the pearls provide a refreshing contrast to the glitter and sparkle of the gems on the chain.

The Biwa collection utilizes the underrated coin pearl for a sexy, youthful take on pearl jewelry. The line's namesake, Lake Biwa in Japan, was known for its incredibly lustrous coin-shaped pearls until it had to shut down in 1985 due to pollution. When Isaac learned the a company in Japan was going out of business—and auctioning off its entire inventory of Biwa pearls—he immediately flew from Israel to

Japan to snap up the lot. He returned having bought over 1,400 pounds of pearls for $2.2 million. Though the market for these new gems was slow at first, once pearl aficionados learned more about Biwa pearls, demand skyrocketed, and hasn't slowed since. Yvel now has contacts with two pearl farms for fresh coin pearls, which the company blends with original Biwa pearls for a consistent luxury.

Yvel's accomplishments have not gone unnoticed. The brand has won the Town & Country Couture Design award (the Oscar of the jewelry world) for pearl jewelry three years in a row (2005, 2006 and 2007), an unprecedented honor. The winning piece in 2007 was an exuberant pearl flower whose 21 petals are made of baroque pearls. "We respect all things that come from nature," Isaac has said. "I wanted to create something that would show the natural beauty of the pearls."

Listing

ANDREOLI
PAGE 288
Diamond necklace.

ANDREOLI
PAGE 289
Cabochon-cut emerald pendant.

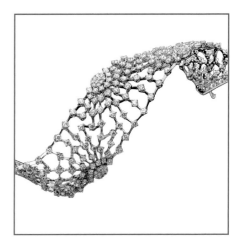

ANDREOLI
PAGE 290
Diamond bracelet.

Listing
408

ANDREOLI
PAGE 290
Diamond and ruby necklace,
with earrings.

ANDREOLI
PAGE 290
Diamond and ruby ring.

ANDREOLI
PAGE 291
Diamond and ruby necklace.

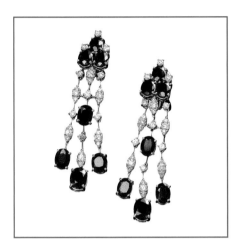

ANDREOLI
PAGE 291
Diamond and ruby earrings.

ANDREOLI
PAGE 292
Diamond and blue topaz necklace.
Matching earrings also available.

ANDREOLI
PAGE 292
Sapphire and diamond ring.

ANDREOLI
PAGE 293
Yellow-gold necklace set with citrines
and diamonds. Matching earrings also
available.

ANDREOLI
PAGE 293
Yellow sapphire ring with white
diamonds and a pearl.

ANDREOLI
PAGE 294
Necklace with diamonds and semiprecious stones. Matching earrings also
available.

ANDREOLI
PAGE 295
Titanium and white-gold earrings.

ANDREOLI
PAGE 295
Titanium and white-gold bracelet.

ANDREOLI
PAGE 295
Ring set with yellow and black diamonds, with white center diamond.

Listing
410

AUDEMARS PIGUET
PAGE 296
Carnet de bal collection.

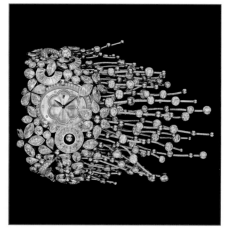

AUDEMARS PIGUET
PAGE 297
Carnet de bal collection.

AUDEMARS PIGUET
PAGE 298
Private collection.

AUDEMARS PIGUET
PAGE 298
Private collection.

AUDEMARS PIGUET
PAGE 299
Royal Oak Offshore collection.

AUDEMARS PIGUET
PAGE 299
Royal Oak Offshore collection.

AUDEMARS PIGUET
PAGE 300
Millenary Précieuse collection.

AUDEMARS PIGUET
PAGE 300
Millenary Précieuse collection.

AUDEMARS PIGUET
PAGE 300
Millenary Précieuse collection.

AUDEMARS PIGUET
PAGE 301
Millenary Précieuse Gourmande
collection.

AUDEMARS PIGUET
PAGE 301
Millenary Précieuse Gourmande
collection.

AUDEMARS PIGUET
PAGE 302
Coup de Théâtre collection.

Listing
412

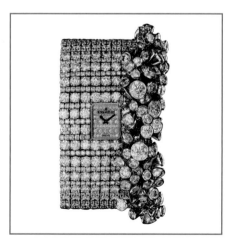

AUDEMARS PIGUET
PAGE 303
Coup de Théâtre collection.

BAYCO
PAGE 22
Carved emerald and diamond ring.

BAYCO
PAGE 23
Carved emerald and diamond necklace.

BAYCO
PAGE 24
Pink sapphire and diamond suite.

BAYCO
PAGE 24
Pink sapphire and diamond ring.

BAYCO
PAGE 25
Pink sapphire and diamond ring.

BAYCO
PAGE 25
Multi-color sapphire and diamond necklace.

BAYCO
PAGE 26
Ruby and diamond suite.

BAYCO
PAGE 26
Emerald-cut ruby and diamond ring.

BAYCO
PAGE 27
Oval-cut ruby and diamond ring.

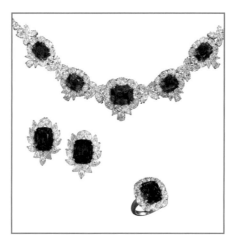

BAYCO
PAGE 28
Sapphire and diamond suite.

BAYCO
PAGE 29
Cushion-cut sapphire and diamond ring.

Listing
414

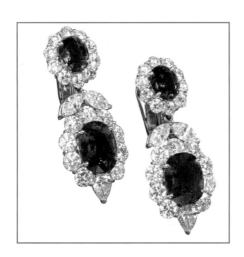

BAYCO
PAGE 29
Sapphire and diamond earrings.

BAYCO
PAGE 29
Sapphire and diamond necklace.

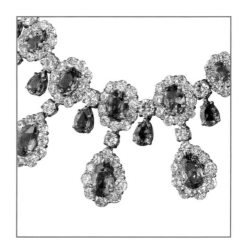

BAYCO
PAGE 305
Pink sapphire and diamond
necklace. Matching earrings
and ring also available.

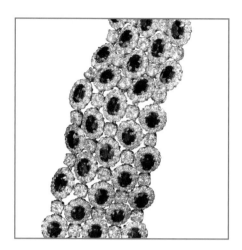

BAYCO
PAGE 306
Ruby and diamond necklace.

BAYCO
PAGE 306
Ruby and diamond necklace. Matching
earrings and ring also available.

BAYCO
PAGE 307
Cushion-cut sapphire and diamond ring.

BAYCO
PAGE 307
Pink sapphire and diamond
necklace. Matching earrings
and ring also available.

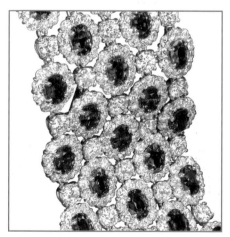

BAYCO
PAGE 308
Oval-cut sapphire and diamond
bracelet.

BAYCO
PAGE 308
Rose-cut diamond necklace.

BAYCO
PAGE 309
Multi-color sapphire and diamond earrings. Matching necklace also available.

BAYCO
PAGE 310
Emerald and diamond necklace.

BAYCO
PAGE 310
Emerald and diamond necklace.

Listing
416

BAYCO
PAGE 311
Emerald and diamond ring.

BAYCO
PAGE 311
Emerald and rose-cut diamond necklace. Matching earrings also available.

BULGARI
PAGE 312
Vintage ruby and diamond earrings. Private collection.

BULGARI
PAGE 313
Yellow gold necklace with pink sapphires, peridots, garnets and diamonds.

BULGARI
PAGE 314
Necklace set with turquoise, emeralds, amethysts and diamonds.

BULGARI
PAGE 315
Diamond necklace.

BULGARI
PAGE 315
Private collection.

BULGARI
PAGE 315
Private collection.

BULGARI
PAGE 316
White-gold necklace with sapphires, white moonstones and sapphire beads.

BULGARI
PAGE 317
Multi-color sapphire and diamond necklace.

BULGARI
PAGE 318
Bulgari High Jewelry collection.

BULGARI
PAGE 319
Private collection.

Listing
418

CARTIER
PAGE 321
Inde Mystérieuse collection.

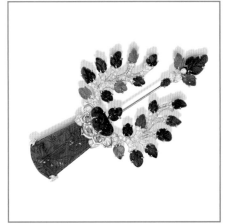

CARTIER
PAGE 322
Inde Mystérieuse collection.

CARTIER
PAGE 323
Inde Mystérieuse collection.

CARTIER
PAGE 323
Inde Mystérieuse collection.

CARTIER
PAGE 327
Inde Mystérieuse collection.

CARTIER
PAGE 327
Inde Mystérieuse collection.

CHOPARD
PAGE 328
Trillion-cut diamond necklace.

CHOPARD
PAGE 329
Haute-Joaillerie Collection.

CHOPARD
PAGE 330
Red Carpet collection.

CHOPARD
PAGE 330
Haute-Joaillerie Collection.

CHOPARD
PAGE 331
Haute-Joaillerie Collection.

CHOPARD
PAGE 331
Red Carpet collection.

Listing
420

CHOPARD
PAGE 332
Red Carpet collection.

CHOPARD
PAGE 333
Diamond ring.

CHOPARD
PAGE 333
Haute-Joaillerie Collection.

CHOPARD
PAGE 333
Red Carpet collection.

CHOPARD
PAGE 334
Red Carpet collection.

CHOPARD
PAGE 334
Red Carpet collection.

CHOPARD
PAGE 334
Red Carpet collection.

CHOPARD
PAGE 335
Red Carpet collection.

CHOPARD
PAGE 335
Red Carpet collection.

CHOPARD
PAGE 335
Red Carpet collection.

deGRISOGONO
PAGE 336
Emerald and diamond necklace.

deGRISOGONO
PAGE 337
Emerald and diamond earrings.

Listing
422

deGRISOGONO
PAGE 338
Heart necklace.

deGRISOGONO
PAGE 339
Emerald and diamond necklace.

deGRISOGONO
PAGE 339
Amethyst earrings with briolette-cut
white diamonds.

DE**GRISOGONO**
PAGE 339
Amethyst ring.

DE**GRISOGONO**
PAGE 340
Sapphire ring.

DE**GRISOGONO**
PAGE 340
Sapphire, emerald and diamond earrings.

DE**GRISOGONO**
PAGE 341
Amethyst and emerald ring.

DE**GRISOGONO**
PAGE 341
Emerald earrings and necklace in
white gold.

DE**GRISOGONO**
PAGE 341
Necklace set with pearls, diamonds
and tsavorites.

DEGRISOGONO
PAGE 342
Boule collection.

DEGRISOGONO
PAGE 343
Boule collection.

DEGRISOGONO
PAGE 343
Boule collection.

Listing
424

DEGRISOGONO
PAGE 343
Boule collection.

GUY ELLIA
PAGE 344
Future fancy diamond ring.

GUY ELLIA
PAGE 345
Peau d'Ane Set.

GUY ELLIA
PAGE 346
Bollywood At Midday Set.

GUY ELLIA
PAGE 347
Bollywood At Tea Time Set.

GUY ELLIA
PAGE 348
Fantasia Set.

GUY ELLIA
PAGE 349
Diabless Rings.

GUY ELLIA
PAGE 350
Crystal Palace Necklace.

GUY ELLIA
PAGE 351
Full Set Coquillage Ring.

LA REINA
PAGE 352
Titanium pavé bangles.

LA REINA
PAGE 354
Butterfly cuff.

LA REINA
PAGE 355
White diamond and black onyx
teardrop earrings.

Listing
426

LA REINA
PAGE 355
White and black onyx bangles.

LA REINA
PAGE 355
Titanium and black Mask brooch.

LA REINA
PAGE 356
Flat diamond Butterfly brooch.

LA REINA
PAGE 356
Yellow Passion Flower Cuff.

LA REINA
PAGE 356
Butterfly ring in black gold.

LA REINA
PAGE 358
Titanium flower ring.

LA REINA
PAGE 358
Mughal Brooch.

LA REINA
PAGE 358
Morning Dew brooch-cum-pendant.

LA REINA
PAGE 358
Titanium brooch-cum-pendant.

LA REINA
PAGE 358
Titanium Flower ring with yellow diamonds.

LA REINA
PAGE 359
Flat yellow diamond ring.

LA REINA
PAGE 359
Dragonfly Brooch.

Listing

LA REINA
PAGE 359
Titanium flower ring.

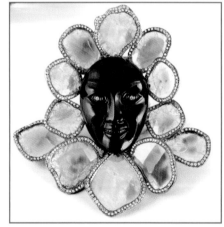

LA REINA
PAGE 359
Black onyx mask brooch.

LEVIEV
PAGE 32
Diamond ring.

LEVIEV
PAGE 37
Diamond ring.

LEVIEV
PAGE 38
Diamond necklace.

LEVIEV
PAGE 38
Diamond flower ring.

LEVIEV
PAGE 39
Diamond ring with pink and green
diamonds.

LEVIEV
PAGE 39
Ring with colored diamonds.

LEVIEV
PAGE 361
Yellow diamond ring.

LEVIEV
PAGE 362
Diamond ring.

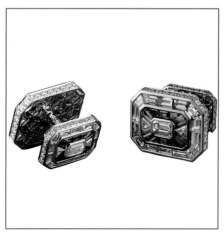

LEVIEV
PAGE 362
Diamond and emerald cuff links.

LEVIEV
PAGE 363
Diamond Hopscotch ring.

Listing
430

LEVIEV
PAGE 365
Yellow and white diamond necklace.

LEVIEV
PAGE 365
Yellow diamond ring.

LEVIEV
PAGE 366
Diamond earrings.

LEVIEV
PAGE 367
Sapphire and diamond Tassel earrings.

LEVIEV
PAGE 367
Sapphire ring.

LEVIEV
PAGE 367
Sapphire and diamond Tassel necklace.

MONTBLANC
PAGE 368
Lumière collection.

MONTBLANC
PAGE 369
Bouquet collection.

MONTBLANC
PAGE 370
Diamond and black spinel necklace.

MONTBLANC

PAGE 370

La Dame Blanche collection.

MONTBLANC

PAGE 371

Coeur à Coeur collection.

MONTBLANC

PAGE 372

Clair de Lune collection.

Listing

432

MONTBLANC

PAGE 372

Clair de Lune collection.

MONTBLANC

PAGE 372

Diamond ring.

MONTBLANC

PAGE 373

Magie en Blanc et Noir collection.

MONTBLANC
PAGE 374
Gold charm bracelet with diamonds.

MONTBLANC
PAGE 375
Éclat collection.

MONTBLANC
PAGE 375
Diamond ring.

OLIVA
PAGE 376
Flamenco collection.

OLIVA
PAGE 377
Flamenco collection.

OLIVA
PAGE 378
Bridal collection.

OLIVA
PAGE 378
Bridal collection.

OLIVA
PAGE 378
Bridal collection.

OLIVA
PAGE 378
Bridal collection.

Listing
434

OLIVA
PAGE 378
Flamenco collection.

OLIVA
PAGE 378
Flamenco collection.

OLIVA
PAGE 379
Shapes collection.

OLIVA
PAGE 379
Flamenco collection.

OLIVA
PAGE 379
Oliva Cut collection.

OLIVA
PAGE 379
Oliva Cut collection.

435

OLIVA
PAGE 379
Flamenco collection.

OLIVA
PAGE 380
Oliva Cut collection.

OLIVA
PAGE 380
Shapes collection.

OLIVA
PAGE 380
Shapes collection.

OLIVA
PAGE 380
Shapes collection.

OLIVA
PAGE 381
Shapes collection.

Listing
436

OLIVA
PAGE 381
Bridal collection.

OLIVA
PAGE 381
Oliva Cut collection.

OLIVA
PAGE 381
Shapes collection.

OLIVA
PAGE 382
Flamenco collection.

OLIVA
PAGE 382
Flamenco collection.

OLIVA
PAGE 383
Oliva Classic collection.

OLIVA
PAGE 383
Pearls collection.

OLIVA
PAGE 383
Oliva Classic collection.

OLIVA
PAGE 383
Oliva Classic collection.

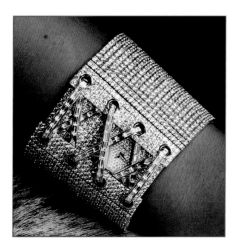

PIAGET
PAGE 384
Paris Couture collection.

PIAGET
PAGE 384
Paris Couture collection.

PIAGET
PAGE 385
Paris Architecture collection.

Listing
438

PIAGET
PAGE 386
Paris Architecture collection.

PIAGET
PAGE 387
Paris Architecture collection.

PIAGET
PAGE 387
Paris Architecture collection.

PIAGET
PAGE 388
New York Architecture collection.

PIAGET
PAGE 388
New York Architecture collection.

PIAGET
PAGE 389
New York Architecture collection.

PIAGET
PAGE 390
New York Couture collection.

PIAGET
PAGE 391
New York Couture collection.

WASKOLL
PAGE 392
Diamond Chain necklace.

WASKOLL
PAGE 393
Flamme collection.

WASKOLL
PAGE 394
Papillons collection.

WASKOLL
PAGE 394
Papillons collection.

Listing
442

WASKOLL
PAGE 395
Blue sapphire pendant.

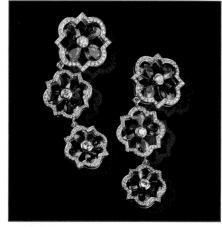

WASKOLL
PAGE 396
Romance collection.

WASKOLL
PAGE 397
Dream collection.

WASKOLL
PAGE 397
Papillons collection.

WASKOLL
PAGE 397
Solitaires collection.

WASKOLL
PAGE 398
Parfums du Monde collection.

WASKOLL
PAGE 398
Parfums du Monde collection.

WASKOLL
PAGE 398
Parfums du Monde collection.

WASKOLL
PAGE 399
Golden Gate collection.

YVEL
PAGE 400
Biwa collection.

YVEL
PAGE 401
One of a Kind collection.

YVEL
PAGE 402
South Sea collection.

Listing
442

YVEL
PAGE 402
Golden Brown collection.

YVEL
PAGE 402
One of a Kind collection.

YVEL
PAGE 403
Golden Brown collection.

YVEL
PAGE 403
One of a Kind collection.

YVEL
PAGE 404
Pavé collection.

YVEL
PAGE 404
Biwa collection.

445

YVEL
PAGE 405
Rainbow collection.

YVEL
PAGE 406
One of a Kind collection.

YVEL
PAGE 407
One of a Kind collection.

PHOTO CREDITS

BIBLIOGRAPHY

"A Hoard of Gold That Afghanistan Quietly Saved; 2,000-Year-Old Heritage Narrowly Escaped the Taliban," Carlotta Gall, *The New York Times*, June 24, 2004.

"An Honest Man and His Gold Dollar," Jed Stevenson, *The New York Times*, September 12, 1993.

Bachmann, Hans-Gert. *The Lure of Gold: An Artistic and Cultural History.* New York, London: Abbeville Press Publishers, 2006.

Balfour, Ian. *Famous Diamonds.* London: Art Books International, 1992.

Bologna, Giulia, with Marcel Garrigou and Alessandro Vezzosi. *Bijoux et Reliures: Artistes du XXe Siècle.* Paris: La Bibliothèque des Arts, 1992.

Borel, France. *Orfèvres Lointains: Bijoux d'Afrique, d'Asie, d'Océanie et d'Amérique.* Vanves: Éditions Hazan, 1995.

Durando, Furio. *Greece: Splendours of an Ancient Civilization.* London: Thames & Hudson, 1997.

Eluère, Christiane. *L'Or des celtes.* Fribourg: Office du Livre, SA, 1987.

Finlay, Victoria. *Jewels: A Secret History.* New York: Random House Trade Paperbacks, 2007.

"From a Burial Pit in Southern Peru, a Golden Oldie," Henry Fountain, *The New York Times*, April 1, 2008.

Guadalupi, Gianni, ed. *The World's Greatest Treasures: Masterworks in Gold and Gems from Ancient Egypt to Cartier.* London: Thames & Hudson, 1998.

"In Glitter and Glory, the Rock of All Ages," Roberta Smith, *The New York Times*, November 18, 2006.

Legrand, Jacques. *Diamonds: Myth, Magic and Reality.* New York: Crown Publishers, Inc., 1980.

Liberati, Anna Maria, with Fabio Bourbon. *Splendours of the Roman World.* London: Thames & Hudson, 1996.

Mascetti, Daniela, with Amanda Friossi. *The Necklace: From Antiquity to the Present.* New York: Harry N. Abrams, Inc.,1997.

Phillips, Clare. *Jewels & Jewellery.* London: V&A Publishing, 2000.

"Rare Gold Baubles: Small, Ancient and Radiant," Rita Reif, *The New York Times*, April 4, 1993.

Raulet, Sylvie. *Van Cleef & Arpels.* New York: Rizzoli, 1987.

Reeves, Nicholas. *The Complete Tutankhamen: The King, The Tomb, The Royal Treasure.* London: Thames & Hudson, 1997.

Scarisbrick, Diana. *Rings: Symbols of wealth, power and affection.* New York: Harry N. Abrams, Inc., 1993.

"Scythian Gold From Siberia Said to Predate the Greeks," John Varoli, *The New York Times*, January 9, 2002.

"Secrets of the Deep," John Colapinto, *The New Yorker*, April 7, 2008.

Singer, Jane Casey. *Bijoux en or du Tibet et du Népal.* Geneva: Éditions Olizane, 1996

Stierlin, Henri. *The Gold of the Pharaohs.* Paris: Éditions Pierre Terrail, 2003.

"The Heist at Harry's," Doreen Carvajal, *The New York Times*, December 12, 2008.

Walters Art Museum, The. *Bedazzled: 5,000 Years of Jewelry.* Baltimore, 2005.

Ward, Fred. *Emeralds.* Bethesda: Gem Book Publishers, 2001.

Ward, Fred. *Rubies & Sapphires.* Bethesda: Gem Book Publishers, 2003.

"Where El Dorado Has Become a Golden Reality," Rita Reif, *The New York Times*, May 9, 1993.

Zucker, Benjamin. *Gems and Jewels: A Connoisseur's Guide.* New York: The Overlook Press, Peter Mayer Publishers, Inc., 2003.

WASKOLL
PARIS

*Joaillier de la lumière
et des couleurs*

www.waskoll.com

BRAND DIRECTORY

ANDREOLI
Vicolo dei Sarmati, 1/A
15048 Valenza (Al) Italy
Tel: 39 01 31 94 66 65

One Rockefeller Plaza
Suite 323
New York, NY 10020
Tel: 212 582 2050
www.andreoli-gioielli.com

AUDEMARS PIGUET
Route de France 16
1348 Le Brassus
Switzerland
Tel: 41 21 845 14 00

40 East 57th Street
New York, NY 10022
Tel: 646 375 0810
www.audemarspiguet.com

BAYCO
580 Fifth Avenue
Suite 1221
New York, NY 10032
Tel: 212 382 3390
www.bayco.com

BULGARI
Via dei Condotti 10
00187 Rome, Italy
Tel: 39 06 688 101

730 Fifth Avenue
New York, NY 10019
Tel: 212 315 9000
www.bulgari.com

CARTIER
13, rue de la Paix
75001 Paris, France
Tel: 33 1 44 55 32 20

653 Fifth Avenue
New York, NY 10022
Tel: 212 753 0111
www.cartier.com

CHOPARD
1 Place Vendôme
75001 Paris, France
Tel: 33 1 55 35 20 10

709 Madison Avenue
New York, NY 10065
Tel: 212 223 2304
www.chopard.com

de GRISOGONO
824 Madison Avenue
New York, NY 10021
Tel: 212 439 4240

358 bis rue St-Honoré
75001 Paris, France
Tel: 33 1 44 55 04 40
www.degrisogono.com

GUY ELLIA
21 rue de la Paix
75002 Paris, France
Tel: 33 1 5330 2525
USA: 212 751 9824
www.guyellia.com

LA REINA
606 South Olive Street
Suite 1950
Los Angeles, CA 90014
Tel: 213 623 8482
www.lareinacollection.com

LEVIEV
700 Madison Avenue
New York NY 10065
Tel: 212 763 533

31 Old Bond Street
London W1S 4QH
Tel: 44 20 7493 3333
www.leviev.com

OLIVA
50 Bezalel Street
Ramat-Gan 12521
Israel
Tel: 972 3 7510 211
www.olivacom.com

PIAGET
16 Place Vendôme
75001 Paris, France
Tel: 33 1 58 18 14 15

645 Fifth Avenue
New York,NY 10022
Tel: 212 355 6444
www.piaget.com

WASKOLL
48, rue Lafayette
75009 Paris, France
Tel: 33 1 47 70 45 74
www.waskoll.com

YVEL
15 Yad Harutzim Street
Jerusalem 91101 Israel
Tel: 972 2 673 5811

645 Madison Avenue
Suite 701
New York, NY 10021
Tel: 646 519 3518
www.yvel.com

For more locations, please see company websites.